THE DECISION
OF DESIRE

A Univocal Book
Drew Burk, Consulting Editor

Univocal Publishing was founded by Jason Wagner and Drew Burk as an independent publishing house specializing in artisanal editions and translations of texts spanning the areas of cultural theory, media archeology, continental philosophy, aesthetics, anthropology, and more. In May 2017, Univocal ceased operations as an independent publishing house and became a series with its publishing partner the University of Minnesota Press.

Univocal authors include:

Miguel Abensour
Judith Balso
Jean Baudrillard
Philippe Beck
Simon Critchley
Fernand Deligny
Jacques Derrida
Vinciane Despret
Georges Didi-Huberman
Jean Epstein
Vilém Flusser
Barbara Glowczewski
Évelyne Grossman
Félix Guattari
David Lapoujade
François Laruelle
David Link
Silvia Lippi

Sylvère Lotringer
Jean Malaurie
Michael Marder
Serge Margel
Quentin Meillassoux
Friedrich Nietzsche
Peter Pál Pelbart
Jacques Rancière
Lionel Ruffel
Felwine Sarr
Michel Serres
Gilbert Simondon
Étienne Souriau
Isabelle Stengers
Eugene Thacker
Elisabeth von Samsonow
Siegfried Zielinski

The Decision
of Desire
SILVIA LIPPI
Translated by Peter Skafish

A Univocal Book

 University of Minnesota Press
Minneapolis | London

Originally published in French as *La décision du désir,* copyright 2013 by
Éditions Érès

Copyright 2020 by the Regents of the University of Minnesota

Published by the University of Minnesota Press
111 Third Avenue South, Suite 290
Minneapolis, MN 55401-2520
http://www.upress.umn.edu

Printed in the United States of America on acid-free paper

The University of Minnesota is an equal-opportunity educator and employer.

26 25 24 23 22 21 20   10 9 8 7 6 5 4 3 2 1

Library of Congress Cataloging-in-Publication Data
Names: Lippi, Silvia, author.
Title: The decision of desire / Silvia Lippi ; translated by Peter Skafish.
Other titles: Décision du désir. English
Description: Minneapolis : University of Minnesota Press, 2020. | Series:
    A Univocal Book | Includes bibliographical references.
Identifiers: LCCN 2019023551 (print) | ISBN 978-1-5179-0529-3 (pb)
Subjects: LCSH: Lacan, Jacques, 1901-1981. | Desire.
Classification: LCC BF575.D4 L56 2020 (print) | DDC 150.19/5092—dc23
LC record available at https://lccn.loc.gov/2019023551

To the memory of my father

Love, this I know, has its stampings.

—André Breton

Contents

Preface to the American Edition

This book is about what Lacan calls the "history of desire." That history engenders the structure out of which the subject's desire emerges. "History of desire" means "choice," since we know from Freud that it is choice that determines one's history.

The choice in question is between neurosis and "the decision of desire," that is, between the jouissance of repetition and the *joy* provoked by the detachment from the power of the phallus and the errancy of desire. This is a paradoxical choice, since it is unconscious, but the subject is indeed involved. The decision of desire entails a fundamental and contradictory leap, as psychoanalytic practice endlessly demonstrates.

The notion of such a decision didn't occur to me when I initially inquired into the question of desire. In fact, this book was only developed over several years, across several hiatuses—in different moments, which had different aims. This is why its writing style changes with the different chapters, topics and purposes. The book, today, is a *mélange* between older layers of writing, certainly useful from a didactic point of view, since they seek to clarify Lacan's structuralist doctrine of desire, and new ideas, aspiring to develop the hypothesis that unconscious desire involves a decision, ideas oriented by Lacan's late teaching and the philosophy of Spinoza. Some sections of the book express, perhaps naively, my enthusiastic encounter with Lacanian psychoanalysis and French theory, while others are rigorous close readings of texts, or free interpretations opening to unexpected hypotheses.

In fact, at the beginning the text that became this book was a postsecondary academic work, undertaken in 2005 in the Sorbonne Department of Philosophy. A year later I enriched it with some properly psychoanalytic studies and used it as a thesis for a master's of research in the Department of Psychoanalysis at the University of Paris–Vincennes. At the time I had no intention to make a book of the resultant manuscript, and it remained in my drawer for many years.

My academic and analytic training being finished, I started my own practice, both as a clinical psychologist in a public mental health center and as an independent psychoanalyst. It was at that moment that I decided to come back to the topic of desire and to transform this previously academic writing into a book. It was essentially a clinical question that led me back to this project: the problem of the symptom, in its connection to desire.

Indeed, a symptom is a unique way both to express and to avoid desire at the same time. If the unconscious *acts* through symptoms (but also through slips, dreams, witticisms, and puns)—that is, *decides* to express desire—what is the role of the subject in this process? Can the subject resist the unconscious, or is it condemned to move in accord with its structure? Yet moving in accord with one's structure need not entail being passive or submissive: during analysis, the subject acknowledges, undertakes, becomes responsible for its specific desire, as led by the unconscious and articulated in a singular montage. Getting to this *ethical necessity* is one of the main stakes of treatment.

A large amount of the Lacanian studies today focus on the concept of the real, topology, and the clinic of Borromean knots, while others use Lacan's work to attempt to analyze the catastrophic consequences of the era of postliberalism. *The Decision of Desire* takes a very different tack. The challenge of this book is to attempt to think "structure" and "jouissance" together, through the concept of desire. In other words, my aim here is to reconcile Lacan's structuralism with a Deleuzian framework: thinking the unconscious as a structure—that is, as "structured like a language," in Lacan's words—does not entail imprisoning subjectivity, events, bodies, and indeed desire, within supposedly transcendental structures that prevent them from changing.

For this reading of Lacan, the main philosophical influence is best located in Spinoza rather than Hegel: the line between neurosis and psychosis is blurred, and clinical insight is open to creative, even transgressive, approaches to life, rather than those standing in conformity with sexual norms and bourgeois order.

The psychoanalytic ethics of desire affirms the choice to live: we are far from Socrates's maxim that "To study philosophy is to learn to die." Psychoanalysis can be practiced in the affirmative rather than the negative, and can create joy out of the tribulations of the patient.

Silvia Lippi

Preface

The supreme force is desire.

—Guillaume Apollinaire, "The Hills"

The mind of man . . . is nothing else but *desire*.

—André Breton, *Mad Love*

Eros, who is desire in Greek myth, has inherited opposite traits from his parents, who are Poros and Penia.[1] In Greek, Poros signifies the opening of a passage through a chaotic expanse, a path around certain obstacles that brings many possible directions into view. Poros is the way out, resource, and strategy[2] that allows for an exit from an impasse, or aporia—from anxiety.

In Plato's *Symposium*, Diotima recounts how Poros, who is the son of Metis (or "invention," by Sarah Kofman's translation),[3] becomes drunk, and how Penia exploits this and seduces him, which is how Poros ends up becoming the father of Eros, desire. The particularity of each parent can help us to understand the atopic and demonic nature of the intermediary that is desire. Eros brings neither wealth nor knowledge, in the sense of a well-founded and complete understanding. Rather, he arouses an aporetic emptiness, which constitutes an unlimited desire. Desire is infinite.

Eros is the son of Penia: literally, "poverty" or "misery." Penia is aporia, that is, lacking in resources. She has nothing to give, except for her lack. Aporia is at the origin of desire. It is from lack that desire is built—from a lack of structure, not a lack of something, of an object. But aporia neither blocks nor paralyzes Eros, who is always moving, searching, and inventing. Desire fixates on the aporia of lack, on an origin-point of non-knowledge, that is, its ignorance of its own cause. The cause of desire is this fixed, frozen, and unvarying point. Desire is finite.

Desire is aporia and fixedness and, at the same time, mobility and the exceeding of this same aporia. The aporia, however, is not thereby erased; the infinite movement of desire does not cover over its unvarying, finite, and unknown cause. Desire is movement and constant action, sustained by its immutable and aporetic cause.

The double character of desire is thus apparent. Because he comes from his mother, Penia, Eros is neither beautiful nor delicate, as Agathon and Phaedrus believe: "He is in fact hard and rough, without shoes for his feet or a roof over his head. He is always sleeping on the bare ground, . . . want is his constant companion."[4] But because he comes from his father, he "schemes to get what is beautiful and good, being bold [virile] and keen and ready for action, a cunning hunter, always contriving some trick or other, an eager searcher after knowledge."[5]

In reality, Eros's virility comes not from Poros but from Penia, who turned out to be active, having taken aggressive initiative. All the characteristics the myth attributes to Poros belong, in fact, to Penia, and vice versa. Penia is not the opposite of Poros, and neither, of course, is the aporia—veritable aporia is always fecund. In Penia, all opposites are blurred: she is neither masculine nor feminine, neither rich nor poor, neither a passage nor the absence of one, neither a resource nor its exhaustion. Aporia breaks with the logic of identity and rises to that of the intermediate [intermédiaire].

Penia is not a passive receptacle, a matter that receives its form, its wealth, from an active, virile father. It is really she who devises the plot. What the myth distributes into three characters, however, ends up undone and recomposed, to the benefit of just one of them: Eros, the intermediate. In him, the "active" and "passive" characteristics are confused. The two opposed forces persist, creating in Eros a certain tension, which is also characteristic of every desire.

The sole poros of Man is neither Poros nor Penia-aporia but their child, Eros—desire—who is neither man nor god, neither knowledgeable nor ignorant, but characterized only by a desire for knowledge.

At the beginning, desire is the desire to know more about desire, particularly about what sets in motion, and sustains, each person's desire. Desire is poros, opening, in the sense of an opening onto being: desire opens the questions asked about what is specific to every subject, about the singularity of each and all of us.

Until the sign again face to face
though separated

Desiring eyes seal an absolute pact

the spasm of delirium can shake the earth
tears flow over the desert's cheeks

the tree fed on absence embodies unheard-of strength
from root to hollowed log
in a desire so great that it cannot be sated
and if sated, the desire is dreamt
even greater

until forgotten

—Martine Broda, *Grand jour* (Paris: Belin, 1994), 14.

Acknowledgments

I would like to thank Renaud Barbaras, Orsola Barberis, Patrick De Neuter, Marcel Drach, Thierry van Eyll, Patrice Maniglier, and Bernard Toboul for their valuable suggestions, and Drew Burk for welcoming this book into Univocal's library of titles.

Special thanks to Peter Skafish: without him, this American adventure wouldn't have been possible.

Introduction
Desire—Between Alterity and Decision

From an ontological point of view, man desires because he lacks.[1] He tries to allay a lack in the structure of his subjectivity. This is something that Sartre reveals in *Being and Nothingness*: desire is the desire for a flawless ontological plenitude, and corresponds to the desire to be God.[2]

This form of realizing desire is impossible. Desire is necessarily expressed by a consciousness characterized by nihilation and distance from self. It is impossible to overcome this distance, for it is caused by the other *[autrui]*. The other is neither an object nor a double of myself but a "freedom in act" that limits my freedom and calls it into question. The existence of the other is logically deduced but registered empirically. "The Other *[Autrui]* is encountered;" Sartre affirms, "we do not constitute him."[3]

It is on account of the other that my subjectivity escapes itself and can never gather back together, is always dispossessed of itself. I am therefore for Sartre a "detotalized or indefinite totality":[4] the other thingifies me, alienates me from my freedom, and positions the sense of my being outside myself (nihilation).

This thingification is ontological degradation; the other reduces me on account of its gaze, bringing me to realize "that I am vulnerable, . . . that I am seen," Sartre writes.[5] The omnipresent and ungraspable presence of the other proves to be a threat, as its gaze deprives me of my power. Again, Sartre: "for me the Other is first of all the being for whom I am an object; . . . is always there out of reach. . . . I experience the Other's infinite freedom. . . . I am thrown, abandoned at the heart of the Other's freedom."[6] I can only desire this freedom from the other, in order to be to myself my own foundation.

The for-itself is defined by Sartre as non-identity with self: a perpetual escape from itself and from its other/opposite, the in-itself. The ego,[7] experiencing itself as nihilation of and difference from itself, is thus dedicated to searching for the being—the "sameness"—that it lacks. Desire is therefore the desire to fill nothingness, a nothingness that defines man in his essence. "Man is fundamentally," Sartre writes, "the desire for being,"[8] being for which the in-itself is the model. This project, emanating from consciousness, cannot aim to nihilate the latter in its realization of the in-itself, the reason being, as Sartre specifies, "the fundamental value of this project is the in-itself-for-itself";[9] in other words, the possibility for consciousness of engendering its other and forming a synthetic totality with it.

The in-itself-for-itself is the motor of desire, a desire that allows man a glimpse of the absolute, which it is in a position to envisage but not attain.[10] An ideal of omnipotence, at once impossible and sought after, the synthesis between the in-itself and the for-itself is for Sartre the horizon toward which human reality is irresistibly drawn. This horizon is neither given nor is it ever accessible: I cannot be, except in death, identical to myself.

The title of one of Levinas's major works, *Totality and Infinity*, evokes the co-presence of ontology and metaphysics: the latter is, in effect, turned toward "the elsewhere and the otherwise and the other."[11] That which is presented gives way to the desire for something else or other: the desire for alterity, alterity "of the Most-High,"[12] as Levinas writes, which gives us an idea of that for which there is idea, and that exceeds the framework of thought (as with the experience of the infinite God of Descartes).

If desire is for Sartre the desire for being and oriented to the notion of *totality*, for Levinas, on the contrary, it is desire for the other, and polarized by the *infinite*. Desire for the other as pure transcendence,[13] an infinity that shatters the sphere of immanence of totality and causes the ego to leave the order of being qua absolute. This transcendence is that of alterity, and not of freedom, as it is in Sartre: "Alterity makes for all the other's power."[14] He continues: "I do not initially posit the Other as freedom, a characteristic in which the failure of communication is inscribed in advance. For with a freedom there can be no other relationship than that of submission of enslavement. In both cases, one of the two freedoms is annihilated."[15] The intersubjective relations between the subject and the other are modified with Levinas: alterity, no longer a threatening freedom, becomes the object of a nonappropriating desire. Alterity is radical and the other is beyond phenomenal manifestation, not given as such. In other words, its presence refers back to its absence, its exteriority overflows every grasp of it that I might obtain.[16]

For Levinas, the infinite "overflows the thought that thinks it."[17] Yet I cannot be in relation with that which exceeds me, and can be only with its trace, which is the face.[18] Inasmuch as it is expressed, the face of the other undoes every relation of power: "the absolutely other— the Other—does not limit the freedom of the Same; calling it to responsibility, it founds it and justifies it. The relation with the other as face heals allergy. It is desire, teaching received, and the pacific opposition of discourse."[19] The freedom of the care for oneself is revealed, in Levinas's view, to be secondary in relation to the freedom of the care for the other.

Where for Sartre, alterity qua freedom is my alter ego, for Levinas there is a fundamental dissymmetry between ego and other. The ancestral character of the other, the presentation of the infinite, cannot be reabsorbed by the ego: the infinite is not assimilable, and steals away from the framework of identity. And this irreducible difference of the other prevents its appropriation by the same.

The subject, then, is oriented toward a relation that is not ontological but ethical: the order of the human replaces—dethrones—the order of being; the ego discovers its ends in the relation to the other, and not in the affirmation of its essence.

This conception is, for Levinas, more powerful than being and totality, and precedes them. The ego, impelled by its desire for the infinite, is thus capable of giving up its will to assimilate (knowledge, goods, etc.), by opening of itself: "Subjectivity is welcoming of the other, hospitality."[20] The transcendence of the other, far from freezing the ego, opens it to the desire and care for the other. Only desire, according to Levinas, measures up to apprehending this infinity, for, he writes, "it is desire that measures the infinity of the infinite."[21] Desire is characterized as metaphysical desire for the infinite, an infinite that is not totality but that, on the contrary, wrecks all possibility of ontological plenitude. In aiming for the absolutely other, "desire does not fulfill it, but deepens it":[22] desire is the desire for what I cannot possess, in that this absolutely transcends me.

In the case of *eros,* Sartre considers erotic desire to be the desire for possession and foundation (through mastering the freedom of the other), while Levinas sees it as neither struggle nor fusion. *Eros* is not a relation of appropriation, for what I desire is neither an object (a body) nor a subject (a freedom), nor their synthesis. What I desire is not there, is not a question of presence, but rather is alterity as such: infinite transcendence of the other, which always remains imminent without ever being given.[23]

Sartre and Levinas show in different ways that it is impossible to possess the self and the other. Sartre insists on the failure of the in-itself-for-itself (the fusion, again, of ego and other), while Levinas stresses the ethical value of this impossibility, which allows the other to emerge as *Other [Autre]*.

The presence of the other is a sort of absence in Sartre; the absence of the other is a presence in Levinas. For the one philosopher as much as the other, alterity is irreducible. Sartre inscribes it in the quest of a self (an in-itself-for-itself) that wants to reduce it, while Levinas situates it in an opening to the other, an opening rendered possible by the insurmountable distance between subject and Other.

This comparison allows us to see that by defining desire as desire for an absolute plentitude of being, Sartre lacks, through excess, what Levinas, in treating desire as desire for a beyond of Being, lacks by deficit. Now the problematic of desire in Lacan—which is inseparable, obviously, from those of the Other,[24] the law, and enjoyment *[jouissance]*[25]—enables us to get out of this impasse. For him, desire is neither, as with Sartre, the ordeal of pursuing an impossible possession, nor a humble inclination toward alterity, as in Levinas: in Lacan, desire is the experience of the *dispossession* of Being and of the *reduction* of the Other. Lacan went so far as to affirm that "the Other does not exist,"[26] in the sense of the all-powerful Other of completeness, ontological plentitude, and absolute transcendence, not the Other of difference, alienness *[étrangeté]*, separation, distance from self, and non-sense that Lacan sometimes called "the big barred Other" (Ⱥ).[27]

It should be noted that both Sartre's and Levinas's respective developments of the question of desire were inspired by the Husserlian conception of consciousness as intentionality. Husserl opened the way to the characterization of consciousness as desire, consciousness that does not have a transcendental aim: incarnate consciousness is originally desiring consciousness in Husserl.[28]

In contrast, desire is, in Lacan, articulated in unconscious discourse: the desire in question is that of the barred subject ($), a subject cut into conscious and unconscious, split between its being as subject and its egoic image. A subject divided by a desire that is bound, on one side, to the Other, and that aims, on the other, for its own freedom. Now that subject is analyzable with respect to its different senses—the divided subject, the existential subject, the subject of consciousness, the humanist subject, the self-mastering subject, the historical subject, the grammatical subject, the subject of science, and so forth—and these senses will each be contended with as we proceed. For psychoanalysis, however, the subject is first and foremost the speaking being. This hypothesis is necessary for conducting an analysis, particularly in an institutional context, where its existence is often in doubt.

The desire that Lacan speaks of is what Freud calls *Wunsch,* which satisfies itself through the formations of the unconscious (dreams,[29] lapsi, puns, symptoms), which always have, Freud says, an infantile provenance.

The conception of desire in Lacan varies as his teaching unfolds. At the very beginning, desire is essentially defined by its imaginary fixations *[captations],*[30] but by 1958 it has become a metonymy of the signifying chain.[31] The infinite referral from signifier to signifier in desire jams desire into place in the symbolic. But by the very next year, Lacan begins inquiring, especially in 1963, into the relation between desire and law, and even goes so far as to affirm, in that year's "Kant with Sade," that they are one and the same thing. Or better, that they are, on account of prohibition, heads and tails of the same coin. Desire is at once, according to one of Lacan's formulations in that text, "defense" and "transgression." He shows, through consideration of its different aspects, that desire is caught in a movement that cuts across all three dimensions (or *"di-mentions" [dit-mensions]* as he calls them)[32] of experience: the imaginary, the symbolic, and the real.[33]

In being divided between the desire of the Other and that which blocks it, desire represents for the subject the barrier to enjoyment at the same as it does the way to access the latter. It is its paradoxical character that causes desire to escape all control, and overturning it in the category of the impossible, which exposes the flaws of logic. Gödel's theorem exposes the incompleteness of every symbolic system, each of which contains a zone in which both a thing and its opposite can be affirmed—a zone of paradox in which there is a point at which things becomes reversed, or a proposition can be simultaneously true and false.

The contradiction of desire is that it is simultaneously infinite and finite. It is *infinite* because lack will never be fulfilled, and desire will continue to insist. Desire is the permanent dissatisfaction of language as system: the displacement of each intention, the disaccord [*décalage*] between demands and their satisfaction, entails that what we obtain is never what we desire. It is this disparity [*écart*] that Lacan calls desire. But at the same time, desire is also *finite*: it can be satisfied, what remains of it is ever the same, and it always resists the same point of attachment—against its cause.

Lacan's formula, "desire is the desire of the Other,"[34] condenses the entire problematic of the linkage between desire, law, the Other, repetition, the drives, and enjoyment. Inspired by Kojève's reading of Hegel,[35] Lacan underscores the fact that in reality, one must account for the relation between consciousnesses in such a way that desire is not necessarily "for an object" but "of/for [*de*] desire." The subject not only seeks an object but also aims to *capture* the desire of the Other; in other words, the subject desires the Other's desire. That does not, of course, prevent it from wanting this or that object in reality, even if such empirical objects do not cause desire.

Lacan also stresses, in revisiting certain theses of Freud, the importance of the relationship between desire and repetition: the subject repeats, through unconscious formations—fantasies, dreams, lapsi, bungled actions, symptoms, and so on, which are indices of its desire—the first, "failed," enjoyment. For repetition always "fails": the subject encounters, in Freud's terms, castration; or in Lacan's, lack. Nevertheless this missed encounter is a necessary condition for the reactivation of the desire of the subject.

Repetition aims at the unassimilable kernel of the real and has as its model trauma. In other words, repetition is the *avoidance* of this kernel of the real, is the long-postponed meeting with a psychic reality that is always there awaiting.

Another aspect of repetition is that the subject seeks to relive, actively, that which it had undergone passively. A new psychic birth, repetition carries one to the unanticipated.[36] When at work in the transferential relation, desire shows this very well.[37] In the regressive aspect of transference, in which it is a figure derived from suggestion and hypnosis, the subject repeats its dependence on familial matrixes. In its other aspect, transference is an opening to a novel encounter, is a new and unexpected love that is capable of increasing the subject's power to act[38]—through a desire that is, thanks to that love (of the transference), forever relaunched.

It should be specified that Lacan, in *The Four Fundamental Concepts of Psychoanalysis*, took care to distinguish transference from repetition. But which repetition? At the time of the 1964 seminar, he underscores that behind *automaton*—the automatism of the signifying chain (the symbolic)—lies that which is always repeated in repetition, the *tuché*, the missed encounter, with the real as lacking.[39] *Tuché* determines the signifying chain and is then repeated *(automaton)*, unbeknownst to the subject. The subject is completely passive in this process, piloted by the real, and transported by the symbolic. The temporality of repetition is always that of a first instance, as it does not accumulate units that repeat. This form of repetition annuls time.

Yet by 1972, in the seminar . . . *ou pire*, repetition has become for Lacan "repetition that opens to the new." In an original analysis of necessity and contingency, he shows repetition to be a return that is always modified by the traumatic real.[40] The novelty in repetition is not, of course, something extraordinary or portentous but only, as he says in 1969, in *The Other Side of Psychoanalysis*, "a very minor variation in the sense of enjoyment."[41]

The traumatic retroaction *[après-coup]* of the real that is endured in repetition is not a tautology, even if it is inscribed in the series of traumas peculiar to the subject. In other words, the necessary, the real that always returns to the same place, is already in repetition contingent—the improbable, the unforeseeable, and even what is beyond the latter—and repetition is already difference, distance, and novelty. Or take, again, the example of transference: transference is not only a return to the past but also an acting on the future, owing to the connection of the real and contingency: the contingency of transference, of the symptom, of the knowledge that can be "accumulated" in the time of analysis. If the other form of repetition annuls time, this one creates it and transforms it into the knowledge of the subject.

Desire—which is repetition—is caught in the dialectic of *tuché* and *automaton,* and is at once necessary and contingent. Desire is instituted through an encounter with the real, but the enjoyment that causes it will not be of the same order as the enjoyment that the subject rediscovers through the movements of its desire.

It is this notion of an articulation between desire and enjoyment that marks Lacan's truly novel contribution to psychoanalysis. His theory of the *objet a* shows that the cause of desire exits from the field of speech and language: *a* separates, or falls, from the signifying chain. It also exits from the field of perception: *a* is neither an object of experience nor, of course, a signifier (the object that causes desire cannot say itself).[42]

Lacan never interrupts his line of questioning about the ambiguous structure of the object-cause of desire: what is this object that is not an object? And what is the relation between the object as cause of desire and as unattainable? In other words, of what sort is the link between desire and castration? Both the finitude and infinitude of desire are at issue in Lacan's inquiry.

This is paradoxical: desire has no object and nevertheless maintains, via the drive *[la pulsion]*, a relationship with the object. The drive is always "objectal," and its object "conditions" desire. What Freud called the drive is an urge *(Trieb)* that is never destroyed, a force that persists. In "Instincts and Their Vicissitudes," he calls the drive a constant force: it "never operates as a force giving a momentary impact but always as a constant one."[43] In *The Four Fundamental Concepts of Psychoanalysis*, Lacan conceives the drive as a force that is at once constant—it insists, in a regular way, in the psychism of the subject—and subject to variation. But this is not a contradiction: its nature as a pressing force remains the same, but not its intensity.

From an energetic point of view, then, the drive is a permanent force but can vary in intensity; above all, it is not canceled when the object of satisfaction is attained: the drive infinitely "resists" through being fixated on the object around which it turns but that offers no hope of alleviating it.

While we desire prior to knowing what we desire, the drive knows just what it is after, and finds it! Desire cannot find what it wants, as it does not know what this is. In contrast with desire, the drive is satisfied, albeit weirdly: lack of success, deception, and nonsatisfaction being it fulfillment. And relief is always put on hold, as the goal of the drive is failure, which restarts its pressing movement to the infinite.

Indefatigable, the drive follows its trajectory, and insists: the process of repetition is set running.

The story [histoire] of the subject is the sum of its unceasing missed tries at the objects of the drive, and of its equally perpetual attempts to recommence their pursuit. The satisfaction (of the failure!) of the drive is not the enjoyment that was coveted after: the object is necessarily lacking, since it is what has been *lost* from structure—the effect, for Freud, of castration, and of the nonexistence, for Lacan, of the sexual relation.

The drive, again in contrast with desire, is a demand that we cannot interpret; the drive is always certain of itself. We speak of desire when a defense is found in the drive, a defense against that very drive: desire follows the course of the drive while at the same time going against it. (Think of desire caught in transference: it is, on the one hand, fixated on the past, and, on the other, renewed in a way that is always different.)

In its pursuit of dissatisfaction—through the pressing of the drive—desire encounters enjoyment. The circuit of the drive, of the libidinal *automaton,* aims for autistic closure, for the enjoyment of the One and non-relation. So then how can desire break from the eternal return of the same of enjoyment? How can it exceed—evade—the deadening horizon of the enjoyment of the One?

Desire demolishes this orientation because of its *singular* character. This singularity exists in desire's openness to the other/Other and in difference: a desire that does not yield Oneness, that divides the subject and separates it from both itself and the Other. The singularity of any desire is expressed through its *aporias*: in its tuggings [*tiraillement*], instability, and contradictory movements. For desire is bound to the Other, but it aims at the same time to become free of it; it is articulated in language, even if it is inarticulable; it is submitted to the law of castration while also being the element that leaps away from it.

It is within paradox that the subject *decides* on his desire, from within the gap between the position of the subject as such and the contingency of its decision. In effect, it is desire that *decides*—desire that lays down the law—and the subject that follows it to the end, in his division ($).

Wo es war, sol Ich werden: There where it was, as Freud said, so shall I come to be. The subject of the unconscious designates, here, the Freudian it: the nave of repressed drives, the authority [instance] of unconscious desire—the subject, after Lacan, in "its ineffable and stupid existence."[44] It is from there that "it speaks" ("the unconscious, it speaks," says Lacan);[45] it speaks in the truth of the desire of the subject. The subject of the enunciation does not coincide with the subject of the statement [énoncé]: "the saying" ex-ists in "the said," for Lacan, as the statement occludes the truth of desire. In 1972, in "L'étourdit," Lacan affirms that "Freud's saying was inferred from the logic that had its source in the said of the unconscious. It is inasmuch as Freud discovered this said that he ex-isted."[46]

The concept of ex-sistence in Lacan should not be confused with that of ek-sistence in Heidegger, who proposes this way of rendering the term with a dash. In the seminar RSI, given 1974–75, Lacan regards the unconscious as ex-isting in the knot that links the three dimensions of the real, the symbolic, and the imaginary (aka the Borromean knot). In other words, the unconscious ex-ists in a position of ex-centricity,[47] as "an outside which is not a non-inside,"[48] according to an expression of Lacan. It is a space that engenders an interval that is conducive to the irruption of the subject of the unconscious, to "embarrassment, failure [défaillance], crack."[49] "In a pronounced, written phrase, something spreads outs," he declares.[50] The unconscious as interval, pause, interruption; it is in the interstices of language that it ex-ists. This is the pulsating function of the unconscious, its opening and closing and mark of discontinuity, where something manifests as wavering.

"One does not speak to the subject," writes Lacan in "Position of the Unconscious." "It speaks of him, and this is how he apprehends himself."[51] It should be specified that the subject of desire opposes the ego, which seeks a fictive unity and only ever attains, in this attempt to evade the real, the imaginary.

It is *unconscious desire that decides,* at the same time as *the subject decides to desire [le sujet se décide à desirer]* through the unbeknownst that animates it. The subject apprehends itself, as Lacan says, through the manifestations of its unconscious desire (the unconscious is its formations), and the subject assumes thereby the consequences of that desire in its speech and its acts. It activates, authorizes, supports, and becomes responsible for its desire. There is in this ethical responsibility—an ethical imperative that, for Lacan, ensues from the law of desire—conjoined to a decision; the decision of desire.

This decision has nothing to do with conscious choice, mastery, self-possession, and will. The decision of desire is not governed by the subject of intentionality, not directed by any consciousness.

There is an aporia in desire that results from the conjuncture of the ethical responsibility of the subject and its loss. For it is only by way of dispossession—of the self, of the Other—through the absence of self-determination, that the subject decides on its desire. As Spinoza said, I am not free to dispose of my existence *causa sui*; I can only do something on the basis of all the determinations that instituted it. But how might we *decide* on that which exceeds us? or assume that which directs us without our knowledge? And how might one move from a desire mired in the symptom and repetition compulsion to *the decision of desire*?

The subject, upon discovering that it should respond to its desire, feels itself divided by that operation. The subject intervenes in desire, without being its origin. Decided desire is anchored in unconscious determinations and decides by virtue of an impossibility, and the risk of this is that it will not be able to account for itself as desire. The subject does not decide when the cause of desire becomes the symptomatic kernel. When that occurs, the subject acts, is driven *[agit— pulsionellement]*, by the return of the repressed: if desire is implicated in the symptom, that is not its decision.

When this impossibility is once more accounted for by desire, necessity (that of unconscious desire) becomes *free* (Spinoza provides inspiration here when he says "that thing is called *free* which exists solely by necessity of its own nature").[52] What is free is the desiring being. The subject, free to live its desire, abandons itself to the necessity of the latter—to *free necessity.* There is a confluence of necessity and contingency in desire.

The decision of desire concerns unconscious desire, which is unconscious thought. It should be recalled that, according to Freud, the unconscious is constituted by "chains of thought,"[53] and that these correspond to Lacan's "unconscious structured like a language."[54] Nevertheless, these unconscious thoughts do not, like conscious thoughts, come out as meaningful discourse, but as breaks, gaps *[béances],* orifices, hollows . . . voids, that is, which open to the question of the body.[55] The unconscious presents itself, through these formations, as a knotting of body and language. There is, in the decision of desire, an *accord* between the unconscious, the body, and language. We will see, now, how their joining occurs.

For Lacan, man thinks with his body, and not, *pace* Aristotle,[56] with his soul; he thinks with a body patterned and cut by the structure of language. Thought participates in the fragmented and confused image that the subject has made of his body, and, like the body, seeks to unite and perfect itself. It is difficult to establish a radical separation, as Descartes did, between thought (mind) and body (extension), as thought is also body. "Cogitation," as Lacan stressed in 1975, "remains stuck in an imaginary that is rooted in the body."[57] We might also think of the concept of an "identity of thought" that Freud elaborates in "Outline of a Scientific Psychology."[58] The drive "transits" through thought itself, particularly analogical thought, seeking to establishing an identity between thoughts in order to obtain satisfaction; and it should be recalled that, for Freud, the first satisfaction is that of the body.

For Spinoza, thought, with the same going for the body, exceeds whatever knowledge one has of it. In the parallelism of body and thought,[59] *decision,* in thought, goes hand in hand with *determination,* of the body. "The decision of the mind," Spinoza writes, "and the appetite and determination of the body, are simultaneous in nature, or rather are one and the same thing which, when it is considered under the attribute of thought and is explained through it, we call a decision, and when it is considered under the attribute of extension and is deduced from the laws of motion and rest, we call a determination."[60] There is, for Spinoza, structural synchronization of thought and body: thought is coexistent, or coextensive, with the body, and decision (that of desire) is its determination in the body. Spinoza again: "The first thing that constitutes the essence of mind is simply the idea of a body that actually exists."[61]

There is no domination of the mind by the body. It is rather *consciousness* that is devalued in favor of a *thinking* that is rooted in *the unconscious*: *the unconscious* of thought goes hand in hand with the *unknown* of the body.[62]

Conatus is the effort—of the body and the mind—to persevere in being.[63] This effort, of both thought and body, is called desire,[64] which Spinoza defines as "the essence of man."[65] (Lacan will likewise say in 1963 that desire is "the subject's truth.")[66] Desire is effort, *conatus*, and effort is essence. There is a *dynamic* conception of human nature in Spinoza: *conatus,* recall, is the past participle of the Latin verb *conor,*[67] which means, literally, to begin, to endeavor, to attempt, or still, "to be disposed to," "to prepare," and "to enable."[68] The essence of man, which is expressed in desire, thus maintains a mobile, unstable, and precarious character that no self-mastery could ever limit.

In decided desire, there is enjoyment that cedes, and an act that cuts.[69] The Latin etymology of "to decide" *[décider]* shows this. The Latin *decidere* carries two meanings, each of which stems from a different etymology: *decido* signifies "to fall," or "to drop" (*de-cado*: to drop, to fall) as well as "to cut" *[trancher]* (*de-caedo*: to cut down, to strike).[70]

The question of lack—of lacking-being *[manque-à-être],* as Lacan, inspired by Heidegger and Marx, calls it—is articulated to that of loss: the bleeding off of enjoyment, of "surplus enjoyment" *[plus-de-jouir],* as Lacan dubs it, taking his inspiration in this case from Marx. The joint between language and body formed by this articulation proves to be a movement from the absolute—the fixity—of enjoyment to the indefinite temporality[71]—the inconstancy—of desire.

Part I
FINITE DESIRE, INFINITE DESIRE

1

Desire, Squeezed between Signifiers

In the first phase of his teaching, Lacan conceives of desire like a moralist philosopher: it has no limits, and every object is deceiving. Socrates gives, in Plato's *Gorgias,* an entirely convincing image of it: "that part of the soul where appetites are located" is a "leaky thing, a sieve . . . whose untrustworthiness and forgetfulness makes it unable to retain anything."[1] Something continually pours out, guaranteeing that the movement of desire will not be interrupted.

When Epicurus and the empiricist tradition speak of desire, they are really referring to needs. These needs are determined by different instincts and are more or less difficult to satisfy; they are "natural" desires, like hunger and thirst, for example. Such needs are to be distinguished from "vain" desires, which are mere illusions sparked by language and which cannot be fulfilled. In *Letter to Menoeceus,* Epicurus affirms that "of desires, some are natural, some groundless; and of the natural desires, some are necessary and some merely natural, and of the necessary, some are necessary for happiness and some for freeing the body from troubles and some for life itself."[2]

But could there be an original situation in which needs are only "necessary" and "natural"? In Lacan's view, "from the outset, need is motivated at the level of desire, that is, at the level of something that is destined in man to have a certain relation to the signifier."[3] This does not mean that desire must be conceived as a complication of need, as desire is given a priori in language.

The infant immediately encounters language, which is expressed not only by the speech of its mother but also by its own, as present in its cries. And he desires because the mother, what Lacan calls "the primordial or prehistoric Other," desires.[4] It is impossible to establish whether the subject's or the Other's desire comes first, as each is formed through the other, in an increasingly closed loop. What is certain is that the Other is there from the start as the "locus of speech,"[5] that is, the signifiers that come from the Other and its desire. In this sense, desire and language are circularly linked: one desires since one speaks, and one speaks, for one desires.

When Freud and Lacan speak of desire, they understand by this unconscious desire, where, as Lacan puts it, "the unconscious is the discourse of the Other," for all speech comes from the Other and determines (unbeknownst to it) the subject.[6]

But desire is also desire for recognition. In their imaginary relation (a-a'), the subject and the other are in a relation of perfect equivalence, as in Hegel's master-slave dialectic, in which there is no relation of alterity between the two terms, the master depending on the slave and the slave on the master, in an entirely symmetrical relationship.[7] Yet even if the two terms are equivalent in the specular relation, they are not from the point of view of the symbolic. As Lacan's Schema L shows, the Other is always in a position of alterity, not symmetry, in relation to the subject.[8] If we take note of the arrow that runs from A to S, in the relation between the subject and the Other (S ◊ A), A exercises causal action on S.

The body of the human being is not initially a biological body that is afterward affected by a collision with language and the desire of the Other; the forms of need follow from desire and not its inverse, from the fact that every need is the effect of a saying.[9] "Desire always manifests at the joint of speech," Lacan states, "where it makes its appearance, its sudden appearance, its surge forward. Desire emerges just as it becomes embodied in speech, it emerges with symbolism."[10] Desires and language are formed simultaneously: needs only reach us in a refracted, broken, and cut-up state, and they are structured by mechanisms that depend on the laws of language.

The child demands that its mother furnish the object of its need. Demand is thereby placed on the plane of a supposed community of registers between the subject and the Other.[11] In the signifying articulation, the metaphoric chain is installed, and the translation of the message difficult, as it is never clear who—the subject or the Other?—desires what: the meaning of every demand necessarily remains vague.

Lacan formalizes the cut between the subject and the Other—the cut of the subject from itself—with the S/s "algorithm" (which means: signifier, bar, signified).[12] In every signifying articulation, the signified

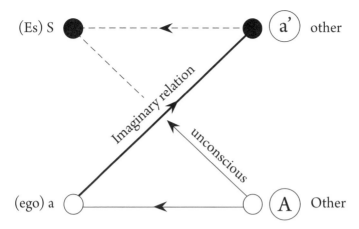

FIGURE 1. Schema L

beneath the bar is imprecise. Neither the desire of the subject not that of the Other can ever be deciphered or made to correspond, as that which puts them into relation, language, across which circulates desire, is always Other, something foreign, that "lacks." We should recall that, for Lacan, the Other too is barred ($\bar{A}$), just like the subject ($\bar{S}$).

Language is always "the language of the Other," in a *mise en abyme* (it is always in this sense that Lacan is able to say that "there is no Other of the Other").[13] The first Other of language that we encounter is different from the person who supports it: it is a pure exteriority, a place formed by particular *signs* that are *sounds,* and that are enchained together such that they refer *[réclamer]* to something beyond themselves.

The alienation of the subject is not the consequence of being biologically dependent on the Other, but of its subjection to language. Following Lacan, "the effects of this presence [of the signifier] include, first, a deviation of man's needs due to the fact that he speaks: insofar as his needs are subjected to demand, they come back to him in an alienated form. This is not the effect of his real dependence (one should not expect to find here the parasitic conception that is the notion of dependency in the theory of neurosis), but rather of their being put into signifying form as such."[14]

This demand, formulated through signifiers, is addressed to the Other and its world. The sounds of the newborn are not truly words [paroles] but can have the same value, as they also depend on the system of language [langage] that conditions the infant from birth.[15] What is certain is that these sounds are not signs. A sign always refers to an object, while the signifier is always defined in relation to other signifiers: the signifier, though structurally tied to other signifiers, is always at a distance from and opposed to them. The open ensemble of an infinite succession [suite] of signifiers that are all defined in relation to the other, can be totalized at the level of the signification of a single signifier, which Lacan writes as "S(A)." The response given to the infant remains impenetrable because it signifies this whole, the plenitude of terms that name each other. It is this signification, not the thing named, that remains confused, circular, and enclosed.

The intended recipient of the demand is seen as he or she who may be able to satisfy one's need: in this sense, he or she becomes omnipotent. But this power is established only by the demander, who also becomes omnipotent through this power to demand. We are within a specular relation, of perfect equivalence, between the subject and its other/Other. This illusion is inscribed in every demand: if I can demand, then I am omnipotent,[16] but at the same time I must concede that I lack in spite of my great omnipotence. Demand, however modest, turns the other into a means for the demander, even as it submits the latter to the behavior of the other/Other. This is a vicious circle, as it is by demand that I both affirm and deny omnipotence, as much in myself as in the other/Other.

It should be obvious, then, that what is at work on this plane is not merely the satisfaction of a need. Every demand is always the demand for something in excess of the satisfaction that is explicitly demanded: it is a question of asking [demander] the other/Other to fill the emptiness experienced by the self with recognition.[17]

The needs of the speaking being are contaminated by the desire for recognition, by a satisfaction that language alone can provide. "The desire of the Other," as Lacan says, "which is man's desire, enters into the mediation of language. It is in the other, by the other, that desire is named. It enters into the symbolic relation of 'I' and 'you,' in a relation of mutual recognition and transcendence, into the order of a law which is already quite ready to encompass the history of each individual."[18] This reciprocity between the subject and the other/Other, the circularity of desire that passes through demand, inscribes the subject in a seemingly insurmountable determinism.

The intrusion of the signifier overturns the mode of satisfaction peculiar to need. In Lacan's view, that which is "to the side of demand cannot be confused with the satisfaction of need, for the very exercise of every signifier transforms the way this need manifests itself. With the addition of the signifier, it undergoes a minimum of transformation—of metaphor, in a word—and this makes it the case that what is signified is something beyond raw need, is remodeled by the use of the signifier. Henceforth, from this beginning, that which enters the creation of the signified isn't the pure and simple translation of need, but the recapture, reassumption, and remodeling of need, the creation of desire other than need. It is need plus the signifier."[19] This "beyond [of] raw need" concerns the repression of a certain signifying articulation—"chains of thought" is Freud's expression[20]—that relates to desire.

Dreams, jokes, and slips of the tongue reveal the order of this repressed desire. Desire does not bespeak itself openly; though articulated logically in discourse, it is not itself articulable. Put in algorithmic terms, desire is situated beneath the bar, in the same way as the signified: D/d (D = demand, d = desire); S/s (S = signifier, s = signified). The signifiers of demand can surface to consciousness, which is not the case with those of unconscious desire, which chooses circuitous routes by which to manifest. Lacan showed this, in 1960, in his "Brussels Lecture on the Ethics of Psychoanalysis": "dreams, slips of the tongue, and jokes: you will never see desire articulating itself in them clearly. Unconscious desire is what is meant by the one who or the thing that proffers unconscious discourse. This is why the latter speaks. Which means that he is not obliged, as unconscious as he may be, to speak the truth. Moreover, the very fact that he speaks makes it possible for him to lie."[21]

Desire is that which, subtracted from every demand, does not demand. Yet demand, nevertheless, is the framework in which it finds its place: it guarantees the structural lack that accounts for the fact that one demands, and that demand as such can only dissimulate. The lack intrinsic to desire is not definable, unlike the difference of lack in need. Then what is this lack called desire, about which one does not know what it lacks?

Desire is a *residue,* a residue beyond every fulfillment of need and every response to demand: desire persists beyond its satisfaction[22] and is opposed to need, which is fulfilled by the object and ceases with satisfaction. To put it in Heideggerian terms, the being *[l'étant]* supposed to fulfill desire opens a *negative* remainder intrinsic to desire. For what should satisfy desire in reality does not. On the contrary, need is a lack that can always be filled, and does not yield any negativity.

Rilke's "The Open" *(das Offene),* the negative par excellence, can be envisaged as the infinity of desire. From a phenomenological point of view, desire is the original, essential opening to the world as such, and desire alone makes possible our various modes of relation to the world: will, knowing, judgment, memory, and so on.

The open is for Rilke the spontaneous and unconscious capacity to be in the world, the predisposition of animals rather than of men. Man has been wrested from the natural flux of life and cannot be in the open, for, Rilke says, he "has eyes only for death."[23] It is death, from which man can never become decoupled—because he thinks—that prevents him from entering the involuntary existence of the open. In this sense, the *logos* is death; as Rilke writes:

> With all its eyes the animal world
> beholds the Open. Only ours
> are as if inverted and set all around it
> like traps at the door to freedom.
> What's outside we know only from the animal's
> countenance; for almost from the first we take a child
> and turn him around and force him to gaze
> backward and take in structure, not the Open
> that lies so deep in an animal's face. Free from death.
> Only we see death[24]

Heidegger's conception of the open is quite different. While affirming that the open does not confine *[borner]*—for it is itself free of all confines *[bornes]*—he maintains that there is always a limit in the open: "Wherever there is an encounter, there a barrier arises," he writes in "Why Poets?" "The barring within the unbarried is constructed by human representation. The athwartness of objects that oppose him does not permit man to be directly in the open."[25] And fortunately: if there were no enclosure, the encounter with the other would be annihilating. The whole, enjoyment, life . . . would be impossible to bear.[26]

There must be a limit to the open for it to be able *to open up*. The infinite can be found only if there is the finite—something, in other words, that limits, so that one can dare to go elsewhere. For the Greeks, a limit is not the end of something, but the place from where it begins.[27] *Logos* is limiting. In poetry, for example, the word *[la parole]* draws a limit at the same time as it opens. The word demarcates, circumscribes a lexical place, and yet even as it opens this semantic space, it does not provide meaning. Poetic language always leaves us hanging, in suspense . . . It is the same with finite and infinite desire.

Objects of need, being useful, "signify" fully, and thus can only limit, while desire cannot be limited by the encounter with the object; desire insists, it endures its *open* meaning.

Desire is welcoming, aspiration. It is forever renewed, as though its cause were in itself, and it were attracted to its center and not to its object—as if it could "retrieve something, to get hold of something from somewhere, to have it come."[28] It is this "retrieval" that Heidegger calls "attraction" *(beziehen)*. This retrieving, as desiring, is a call that is distinct and specific and yet at the same time also to an Other that can only be infinite, that belongs to what he calls "unrestricted drawing-on." Heidegger says that "the traction, which as . . . risk concerns and affects all beings with traction, and retains them in traction toward itself, is attraction *[Bezug]* absolutely."[29] And in another passage, he cites Rilke:

As nature gives the creatures over
to the risk of dull desire[30]

The obscure is, according to Heidegger, "not breaking away from the attraction of an unrestricted drawing-onward."[31]

It is difficult to conceive of attraction and desire as both being, on the one hand, a pull toward something specific and limited, a fixation—and thus *finite*—and at the same time, on the other, as being open, without limits, caught in contradiction and multiple meanings: that is, *infinite*.

The notion of the infinite in the finite can be understood as that precious moment when, through the gaze cast on a thing, existence is opened, is decomposed, into a multitude of unforeseeable directions. There is a double dimensionality to desire, in that it is at once finite and infinite: there is the enigma of desire's signified, and the intrigue, the adventure, of its signification.

Desire is an *interminable* remainder that is organized in a precise virtual space, *limited* between need and demand. Demand is always double: beyond the demand for the satisfaction of a need looms the demand for something *more,* which is foremost the demand for love. The demand for love aims for the being of the Other; it is thought that the Other should give what is beyond all possible satisfaction, its very being or life. But the Other as well is lacking (Ⱥ)—it also desires!—being marked, like the subject, by the signifier.[32] The subject, through the intermediary of the barred Other that leaves its desire unsatisfied, is only able to recognize that it, too, is marked by the signifier: there will always be something left over, beyond what can be satisfied by the intermediary of the signifier, that is, by demand.

Although demand bears on the object of need, it is fundamentally *inessential.* For example, the infant desires to be the object of the desire of the mother. This desire for the desire of the Other is incarnated, according to Freud, in the "re-discovery" of an original satisfaction in which the infant was fulfilled by an object, given by the maternal Other, but without having asked for it. This first satisfaction is distinguished from subsequent satisfactions, which can occur following the demands it makes. Mediation through demand confronts the subject with loss—the object that causes desire is lost in desire's signifiers—and this loss becomes a fundamental element of the structure of desire.

Freud's and Lacan's positions on the status of desire's object are not antithetical, even if they may seem divergent. It should be noted that for Freud, desire is set in motion by "major somatic needs," and those needs are to be understood as involving a necessity—and hence as of the order the real—arising from the body. "It is first in the form of major somatic needs," Freud explains, "that the necessity of life [*die Not des Lebens*] confronts it."[33]

The object capable of satisfying these bodily needs *exists,* and is present either in reality or a hallucinatory form. Desire thus takes the nostalgic form of a search (which is infinite) for the object of the original satisfaction, whether it was real or hallucinatory. For Lacan, this object never existed, as it is equivalent to its lack.[34] The subject can invent objects to substitute for its lack, but they can never fill that hollow.

The infant must demand in order for its desire be heard, and it is thus led to signify this lack (of object). In this nomination, there is a lack of adequation between that which is unconsciously desired—which is not an object—and that which is made to be understood by the demand for an object to substitute for lack. This inadequation indexes the impossibility of re-finding the satisfaction of desire supposedly obtained by the Other's intervention.[35]

We will see that the status of this initial satisfaction remains problematic for Freud, as does its rediscovery. But we will continue in order.

In *Project for a Scientific Psychology,* Freud constructs his model of the psychical apparatus on the basis of an experience of primary satisfaction resulting from an inaugural meeting of an internal drive excitation with an external object, which makes possible, in conformity with the pleasure principle, the discharge of this excitation, providing the infant with adequate satisfaction.[36] This experience leaves in the psychic apparatus mnemonic traces of the object, which are associated with the memory of the primary satisfaction and which will thereafter orient all psychic activity to a devoted search to refind the coordinates of this first experience of *pleasure*—one cannot speak of enjoyment here—and to the realization of the identity of perception between the first object and those which return to its place.[37]

In the seventh chapter of *The Interpretation of Dreams,* Freud enunciates his theses about the satisfaction of desire, a satisfaction that presents itself, whether through dreams or the other formations of the unconscious, in a deformed form *(Entstellung)*. A good example is the hallucination of the object of desire: the absence of that object in reality entails that its perception will be sought after, but now in a hallucinatory mode. The satisfaction of desire coincides with the hallucinatory satisfaction tied to the mnemonic inscription enabled by the initial inscription. "Next time the need arises," Freud writes, "a psychical impulse will at once emerge which will seek to re-cathect the mnemic image of the perception and to re-evoke the perception itself, that is to say, to re-establish the situation of the original satisfaction. An impulse of this kind is what we call a wish; the reappearance of the perception is the fulfillment of the wish; and the shortest path to the fulfillment of the wish is a path leading direct from the excitation produced by the need to a complete cathexis of the perception. Nothing prevent us from assuming that there was a primitive state of the psychical apparatus in which this path was actually traversed, that is, in which wishing ended in hallucinating."[38]

In 1915, Freud states, in "Metapsychological Supplement to the Theory of Dreams," that all hallucination is a form of regression that leads back to the mnemic traces of the object and the character of a perception, an "imaginary" perception that is taken for "real" (it cannot be said, inversely, that every regression produces hallucination). It is in this text that Freud explicitly discusses his system of the identity of perception, and stresses the importance of distinguishing between "perceptions" and "unconscious representations," which have been intensely remembered.[39]

In the psychic process that brings about the hallucinatory satisfaction of desire, Freud writes in *The Interpretation of Dreams,* "satisfaction does not follow; need persists."[40] It is not merely the lack of an object in reality that leaves the subject unsatisfied, as non-satisfaction results from the lag, the disparity [*décalage*], between the internal stimulation of the subject and the mollifying power of the external object. To follow Freud, "the excitation arising from an internal need is not due to a force producing a momentary impact but to one which is in continuous operation."[41] The external intervention (real or hallucinatory) does not suppress the internal stimulus: for the internal and external investments to be equivalent, it would be necessary that the latter be constantly maintained.

This is what occurs in hallucinatory psychoses, in which the object subsists in a way continuous with the psychic life of the subject.[42] Melancholia is a hallucinatory psychosis in this sense: the object persists,[43] and fulfills the internal—continuous—stimulation of the subject on account of the permanence of its force. From an economic perspective, this is a perfect correspondence of subject and object, in which both their continuity and their temporal persistence match. The establishment of discontinuity (following, for example, an erotic separation) is therefore catastrophic. In hallucinatory psychosis, then, desire is not inscribed through the *continuous* force of the internal stimulus and the *intermittent* force of the investment in the external object, and it is in this sense that hallucinatory psychosis involves an impasse in desire.

This dissymmetry between the continuous character of stimulation and the intermittence of the object is, for Freud, "the bitter experience of life."[44] For although it is impossible to obtain complete satisfaction, it is because of this dissymmetry that desire exists: the process that leads to satisfaction never ends, as each satisfaction is a carrier of lack. This is why desire insists: each satisfaction engenders dissatisfaction, and each dissatisfaction spurs the subject to look for further satisfactions, along other routes. It is this paradoxical form of satisfaction/dissatisfaction[45] that restarts, infinitely, desire, and not any nostalgia for the first satisfaction.

Internal excitation—desire—cannot be quelled by the object. If the object had been capable of providing (continuous) satisfaction to the subject, the latter would not have needed to hallucinate it to find it again. Lacan explains this in *The Ego in Freud's Theory and in the Technique of Psychoanalysis*: "What is desire, as soon as it is the source of hallucination, of illusion, hence of a satisfaction which is the opposite of satisfaction? If we give the term desire a functional definition, if for us it is the tension put into play by the cycle of behavioral fulfillment, whatever that may be, if we include it within a biological cycle, the desire achieves real satisfaction. If it achieves hallucinatory satisfaction, then there is another register here. Desire is satisfied in another satisfaction than effective satisfaction."[46] In effect, it is satisfied in unconscious formations in a deformed fashion *(Entstellung)*.[47]

For Lacan, the inaugural experience of the subject takes a traumatic form. The first encounter with the Other is induced by chance, occurs in an unexpected place, and cannot be felt as a satisfaction conforming to the pleasure principle. It is, instead, the forced entry of enjoyment, a "missed or unhappy encounter," as Lacan describes it, and entirely traumatic. This first encounter belongs to the order of the *tuché*, and the pursuit of its repetitions to *automaton*.

We see that Freud's and Lacan's positions on this aboriginal experience, which is the subject's encounter with the Other, are different. What is it that the subject seeks when he desires? Is it the repetition, per Freud, of the first satisfaction of a corporeal need tied to the experience of pleasure, or, following Lacan, the traumatic repetition of the unhappy encounter at the level of enjoyment?

When Aristotle speaks of *automaton*, he does not mean repetition in Lacan's sense but the spontaneity that can be distinguished from the chance of *tuché*. Aristotle's remarks on spontaneity constitute a meditation on nature's different ways of deviating: certain events or human actions that have their own ends can produce unanticipated effects.

This is effectively the case for "the desire of the Other," an Other that desires and puts the subject in a fixed loop, a *désir/amour à deux* both oppressive and impossible. The desire *of the Other* can deviate from its determined path and toward a desire *for the other* (thing). For example, the subject can extract itself from the suffocating desire of its parents and desire *elsewhere,* for someone or something completely *other,* with characteristics the opposite of those of its first objects. As Gérard Pommier observes: "the desire of the parents initially represents the desire of the Other, 'who' is nobody. The relation with this objective Other, along with its desire itself, is objectifying. It throws the subject into distress. The infant's distress *(Hilflosigkeit)* often passes for physical distress, but it is primarily a question of psychic distress about only being an object."[48]

It is the love of the parents for the child—oblative love—that gives the child the impulse to desire and love outside the familial circle. Love becomes the prospect of an exit, the fracture in the vicious circle. It is "expansive," the possibility of a third that provides liberation from a relation that would have otherwise remained only endogamous.

Circularity of desire and subject, circularity of demand and desire . . . we have circled back to the alienation of desire caught in language, which passes through demand to become lost in chains of signification in discourse. As it goes from each object to the other, desire is sent through an infinite succession of substitutes, and hence a succession of signifiers symbolizing those substitute objects, which designate, unbeknownst to the subject, its desire. Desire is thus infinitely reborn, but *elsewhere*—outside of both the object sought after and the signifiers representing it.

Desire is forced along metonymy's way. What Lacan means by *metonymy* is "the function that a signifier, S, adopts when it relates to another signifier along the length of the signifying chain. The function that a sail has in relation to a ship exists along the signifying chain, and not in reference to the real—along the length of the chain and not in substitution; it's thus a question of the clearest way of transferring signification along this chain."[49] These contiguous signifiers, sail and boat, lying on the same syntagmatic axis (sailboat), do not for the most part emit a signification in order to evoke yet another: it is not a meaning that they name but a succession of words. "The possibility of displacement," Lacan declares, "is where the fragile equilibrium of desire can be maintained."[50]

Desire caught in the metonymic chain is a desire pinched between signifiers, that cannot halt at any object and that never refers back to any signification. Desire deprived of sense is destined to slide endlessly along the signifying chain. For it is not there, *in* the chain, that desire replaces.

In the repetition of demand that returns to itself, the circled object is missed. In other words, demand is always inadequate to signifying the object of the desire that causes it.

Insistent demand is just the inscription of repetition's automatic character: unconscious desire is what installs the metonymic movement of a series of demands.[51] These concern not only the part the subject itself plays in them—the way in which its demand can contain a desire to which it is oblivious—but just as much the Other. Demand harbors an *x* about which both subject and Other are ignorant, and that becomes a source of anxiety for the subject. "Desire is foremost constituted," Lacan states, "from its nature as that which is hidden in the Other by structure: it is impossible for the Other to become the desire of the subject. Desire is constituted as the part of demand that is hidden in the Other. This Other guarantees precisely nothing as Other, qua the locus of speech, and it is from there that it obtains its edifying effect."[52]

The neurotic indeed seeks to make its desire conform to the demand of the Other. Is it possible to disentangle this embrace? Perhaps it is, through some "turbulence"[53] capable of interrupting the circuit, rather than making it repeat infinitely. It takes something unanticipated, a surprise, shift, or leap, to extricate the subject from its tight embrace with the Other. This unforeseen element can be love,[54] despite the risk it entails of falling back into the specular hold.

It is within this double loop, infinite on the side of demand (which is not repetition) and finite on the side of desire (which is fixated on the empty point around which demand turns), that the subject exists. Muddled by the signifying chain and alienated in the desire of the Other, the subject, while existing through its desire, is absent to itself. The subject is structurally a lacking-being [*manque-à-être*]: what it lacks, that on which it is fixed, remains foreign to it.[55]

2

Perverse and
Perverted Desire

Desire is articulated with speech. According to Lacan, Freud was the very first to draw this conjuncture between desire and language: "the ancient philosophical filiation, which, from Platonism up to the Stoic and Epicurean sects, and passing through Christianity, has had the profound tendency to forget the organic relationship between desire and the signifier, to exclude desire from the signifier, to reduce it, to account for it in a particular economy of pleasure, to evade what is absolutely problematic, irreducible, and strictly speaking *perverse* within it, and to avoid what is the essential, living characteristic of the manifestations of human desire, at the forefront of which we must place its not only unadapted and unadaptable, but fundamentally marked and *perverted*, character."[1]

For the Stoics, "desire is an irrational wish,"[2] as the pleasure that might procure satisfaction is only ephemeral, if not totally unrealizable. In his *Letters on Ethics to Lucilius,* Seneca compares, after Attalus, the man who desires to a dog waiting to be fed by its master: "Have you ever seen a dog snapping at morsels of bread or meat tossed by its master? Every time he catches one, he immediately gulps it down whole, his jaws always open, intent on the next one coming."[3] The same thing, Seneca states, applies to man: everything before him he swallows without pleasure, and then he moves on to the next thing. The search for pleasure thus leads to its negation, for to consume pleasure is to annul it. The passions are like illnesses that must be treated, and the only possible cure is *askesis,* ascesis, an exercise that aims at *atharaxia,* wisdom—liberation from every passion. For the Stoics, once the soul has been healed, it remains so forever: a man content with himself knows that all the goods he demands or obtains count for nothing toward a truly fortunate life. The sage does not depend on others, as his bliss only arises from himself.

The Epicurean conception of pleasure and the happy life is quite different. For Epicurus, pleasure is a repose that comes from equilibrium in one's being. The absence of distress is equivalent to pleasure, and there are no intermediate states between pleasure and pain. By extinguishing every kind of pain, whether physical or psychic, the Epicurean sage attains blessedness. "Pleasure," in Epicurus's view, "is the principle and end of the blessed life."[4] As his disciple Lucretius writes in *De Rerum Natura*

> Do you not see that Nature cries for this,
> And only this, that pain from out the body
> Shall be removed away, and mind enjoy
> Sweet sense of pleasure, freed from care and fear?
>   Therefore we see that human nature's needs
> Are small indeed: things that take pain away,
> And such as simply pleasures supply.[5]

In sum, for the Stoics, pleasure is to be avoided, because it vanishes upon attainment. For the Epicureans, it is to be pursued, as the absence of pain. But for the one school as much as the other, it is a question of finding a state of beatitude, a lasting joy of body and soul that annuls desire. As Epicurus states, "For we do everything for the sake of being neither in pain nor in terror. As soon as we achieve this state, every storm in the soul is dispelled, since the animal is not in a passion to go after some need nor to seek something else to complete the good of the body and the soul."[6]

Hedonism as conceived by the Epicureans is not far from what Freud understood by the pleasure principle *(Lustprinzip).* The pleasure principle regulates psychic life, and its goal is to avoid unpleasure, to prevent the heightening of excitation. This principle leads to psychic homeostasis, which is obtained by relieving a need or satisfying a drive when this engenders, paradoxically, an irritating tension. "The facts," Freud states, "which have caused us to believe in the dominance of the pleasure principle in mental life also find expression in the hypothesis that the mental apparatus endeavors to keep the quantity of excitation in it as low as possible or at least to keep it constant."[7] The pleasure principle is a mechanism of self-regulation, not any goal of man. In this sense, it can be distinguished from the above hedonistic doctrines that conceive of pleasure as an end. But if man does not desire pleasure, what is it he seeks?

Freud raised the possibility, of course, of something beyond the pleasure principle, and thereby also the question of what causes desire in man. In *Beyond the Pleasure Principle,* he notes the tendency evinced by his both patients and family to repeat unpleasant experiences from the past. This compulsion to repeat the negative, which Freud calls the death drive, stands in contrast with the pleasure principle, and announces the presence of a deadening force in the principle of human desire.

Desire is thus composed of two forces that act in contradiction and toward opposite ends: even as the desiring subject seeks pleasure by limiting it, he at the same time tends, with no less constancy, to surpass the limits of this very pleasure principle. What is sought beyond these limits is enjoyment, which is, in Lacan's view, nothing but "the path toward death."[8] This does not mean that the subject wants to die, but that he unconsciously chooses his own way of doing himself harm, by desiring that which is supposed to bring him good. Certain kinds of amorous experience convey well the character of this alliance between Eros and Thanatos, and literature is replete, of course, with examples. William Faulkner's *If I Forget Thee, Jerusalem* and Dino Buzzati's *A Love Affair* will well serve our purposes.

Faulkner's novel (whose title is taken from Psalm 138, which memorializes the captivity of the Jews in Babylon) comprises two interwoven stories, "Wild Palms" and "Old Man." The first recounts the painful tragedy of two lovers, Harry Wilbourne and Charlotte Rittenmeyer. Charlotte is devoted to an exigent religion of love: she refuses to carry Harry's child, and forces him, a doctor, to abort it. In the words of the protagonist, the pair are condemned to a passion in which "love and suffering are the same thing and that the value of love is the sum of what you have to pay for it and anytime you get it cheap you have cheated yourself."[9] The novel's closing words, *"between grief and nothing, I take grief,"* are uttered by Harry when he is forced to choose between suicide and a life pervaded by the painful memory of his lost love.

Buzzati's *A Love Affair* describes the consuming passion of a fifty-something man for a young, sometimes-prostitute ballerina, along with his skillful torment of her and their acquaintances.[10] Following a veritable Calvary, the brutal end of their relation nevertheless gives way for him to an even greater anxiety, which he attempts, unconsciously, to flee through his passion for her: the anxiety of his ineluctable, approaching death.

Death qua the end of life and the death drive should be distinguished: of the former, we know nothing, while the latter, in contrast, insists at every moment in tandem with desire.

Desire, which is structurally the desire for enjoyment,[11] is necessarily perverse, for enjoyment is not the Good of man. Neither Epicurean pleasure nor Stoic blessedness, enjoyment is distinct from the sage's state of satisfaction or beatitude, as these are ruled by the pleasure principle.[12] The sage has renounced both desire and everything else that aims after enjoyment, and enjoyment always accompanies the death drive.[13] This other form of satisfaction, whether it manifests sexually or not, is tightly bound to pain. Its paradoxical character should be stressed: how can satisfaction simultaneously be suffering? Enjoyment is at once sought after and avoided: attraction and repugnance are felt in tandem about that which works against the existence of the subject—the death drive.

The attraction/repulsion pair is also at work in our relation to love. In surrendering to an intense love, we abandon ourselves to a dominating, destructive force that unleashes all its power on us. The game of love consists in resisting this force while at the same time allowing oneself to be invaded by it, and amorous enjoyment is located between these responses.

Desire aims, whether directly or circuitously, at unpleasure, and sometimes self-destruction, and it is in this sense that is related to perversion. For this reason, the state of agitated desire in need of gratification is never exhausted: jouissance is not peace, but tension—think of the most intense moment of sexual enjoyment—and a tension that the death drive guides, by pointing the way toward its satisfaction.

In another respect, enjoyment cannot be conceived as the satisfaction of a need by an object that would fulfill it. Enjoyment becomes prohibited, not in the obvious sense of being barred by censors but rather through *inter-diction [inter-dire]*, by being made the very stuff of language, where desire's impact and rules are to be found. This "locus of language" is the big Other: the whole difficulty with signifying enjoyment arises from the relationship with this big, nonfigurable Other, the locus of the signifying chain that is neither matter nor speech nor the letter.

Desire again is "marked and perverted,"[14] says Lacan, by language's introduction of a deviating route. Or better, desire is perverted *and* perverse. In psychoanalysis, perversion is a very precise clinical structure that is distinct from neurosis and psychosis while also being a sort of transfer point between them by virtue of its peculiar relation with desire.[15] Every desire maintains a rapport with perversion because of its dependence, which sometimes verges on submission, to the Other's desire. Desire is not free and autonomous but always determined, *perverted,* by what the Other desires. The latter desire feels to us like an unconditioned, strange, and universal will—like a law.

In perversion proper, this relation to the Other's desire is taken to extreme conclusions. The pervert is he who lets himself be subjected to the lawfulness of that desire. The subject becomes frozen in the position of the object, the instrument of the Other's enjoyment, like an ascetic who self-flagellates for the pleasure of a third term, God. This approach is particularly evident in sadomasochistic practices.

For the pervert, it is the Other who should enjoy [*jouir*], and the Other is not his partner but the giver of Law, whose enjoyment comes through forcing enjoyment upon the pervert. The pervert enjoys through his apathy: by becoming insensitive to the practices that he himself imposes or to which he submits, he enjoys, paradoxically, through that insensitivity. In other words, it is by making enjoyment extraneous that he enjoys.

In "Kant with Sade," Lacan conceives of Sade as a tool of the Other's will, an Other defined according to the philosophy, morality, and ideology of his time. One of the decrees of the French Revolution dictated the abolition of private property, and for Sade the bodies of others should be in the same fashion considered the property of the collective, and subject to its will. Dominated by the philosophy of that moment, Sade affirmed that the subject does not have the right to deprive his neighbor of the enjoyment of his body. The Sadean maxim by which Lacan expressed this principle in his essay is, "'I have the right to enjoy your body,' anyone can say to me, 'and I will exercise this right without any limit to the capriciousness of the exactions I may wish to satiate with your body.'"[16]

Rather than entering into a commentary on Sade's claim that there is an unconditional right to the property of the body of the other, we can simply note Sade's dependence on the Other as incarnate in the libertine thinking that intermingled with that of the revolution. It should also be noted that his unconditional submission to the will of the Other (at least as he believed it to be) is what led him to live out the large part of his life in prison.

In Lacan's view, Sade's position is not very different from Kant's: "So act that the maxim of your will could always hold at the same time as a principle in a giving of universal law."[17] Kant's imperative is not hypothetical but categorical—apodictic and a priori. The categorical imperative corresponds to what should be done unconditionally. Only those actions whose maxims conform to this principle will be moral. There can be no consideration of instrumental ends, as the categorical imperative imposes itself without additional justification.[18]

In its practical use, pure reason excludes every sensible ("aesthetic," for Kant) consideration, and can only be related to itself. This is why the will of reason, transformed into absolute morality, is autonomous rather than heteronomous, which is the case with will subject to the order of desire, which is bound for Kant to the subject's empirical interests and concerned with its well-being *(Wohl)*.

The universal legislation promised by Kant is the legislation of the Other. The categorical imperative is a Law-of-the-Law that takes nothing from the human, for the human, in its singularity—above all in the singularity of its desire—is excluded from it. As Lacan writes, "the moral imperative latently does no less, since it is from the Other that its commandment requisitions us."[19]

It was through a similar juxtaposition of the writings of Sade and Kant that Theodor Adorno and Max Horkheimer elaborated their thesis that the formalization of reason, its soldering to apathy, led to the instrumentalization of all empirical objects: others are treated as simple things submitted to a pure, absolute, and universal Law.[20]

In *Seminar V,* Lacan speaks of "the eccentricity *[ex-centricité]* of desire in relation to all forms of satisfaction," in the sense not only that it deviates from them but also that it is external and foreign to the subject.[21] Desire's persistence leaves the subject in a state of dissatisfaction, in want of something undefined—infinite—that cannot be fulfilled. Eccentric desire cannot be contained, recentered, or exhausted by its gratification.

For Lacan, there is a bond, a tension, between desire and pain, pain coming from the point where desire is fixed, about its fixation.[22] For the movement of desire is inevitably confronted with unpleasure that arises from unsatisfied excitations of the drives,[23] and desire seeks enjoyments that are suffered. Symptoms are good examples, as they are sources of pain from which the subject nevertheless draws a paradoxical enjoyment. Apparent *Unlust,* such as displeasure or suffering, is in fact *Lust.*

The experience, insistence, and search for unpleasure indicates the heterogeneity of psychic life, imposing on the subject another economy than that of pleasure, which figures of unpleasure like repetition, masochism, and enjoyment express.

In his pursuit of suffering, the masochist recognizes the truth of the human condition—of its being divided and mortal, of its "pain from existing."[24]

Desire is bound up with pain because it represents what can bring man back to his *essence,*[25] which in other words is his division, a division that stems from the fact that he speaks, and that his desire is the Other's desire.

The subject is lost in the realization of his desire because the Other's desire can never be its own, hence its separation from both that desire and itself. This separation is lived as a painful ordeal, such as a distress *(Hilflosigkeit)* or profound lack. But desire, in turn, is possible only because of this "internal" separation of the subject from itself. A vector going toward the Other runs counter another leading away from it, and this contrary movement makes desire livable, despite its being shot through with pain. Desire is situated in the same spot where distress originates and is experienced, and it is in desire that the being of the subject is expressed, to the point of its loss. And that loss is double: of the self both as a fabled being—the phallus—and of being the object of the Other's desire.

But might there be desire that is autonomous and independent, that belongs to the subject? Desire is the Other's desire, and there is no other kind. Once any desire has been followed to its conclusion, it realizes the Other's desire. That dreams are gratifications of desire is, according to Freud's theory in the *Traumdeutung,* why they easily become nightmares: it is always the Other's desire that they gratify! Every dream is, for that reason, the realization of desire and at the same time its repression. Dreams dissimulate, seeking to not understand that point at which, should desire be realized, the subject would disappear.

The perverse relation with the Other, then, dissolves the being of the subject, which remains marked by the pain of being able to desire only from within the circle of the Other's desire.

In order to better understand this, we should pause over explicitly sexual desire. It has the characteristic of rapidly exhausting itself, and of quickly abandoning the subject: the latter is left without desire, whether after its gratification or even before it.[26]

Pain follows a longer cycle than does pleasure. It is in this way that the pervert, in his dependence on the big Other that forces him to enjoy, seeks to fine-tune a desiring machine that will not snuff out desire with satisfaction but that instead perpetually, untiringly feeds it. The pervert is fixated on the suffering of the other (that, for instance, of his sexual or romantic partner) and on becoming the agent of it. Through the pervert's guidance, the other feels her division, which becomes her desubjectification; she experiences, that is, the pain of existing. This prolongs the suffering/enjoyment of the pervert and thereby prevents his desire from diminishing too quickly.

The hysteric resorts to a different tactic, taking desire itself as his or her object. He or she does not wish to satisfy their desire, or better, is satisfied by being unsatisfied. The hysteric delays enjoyment, pushing it as far away as possible so as to be able to continue, at whatever cost, to desire and enjoy (unsatisfied) desire. Such is the case with frigidity, which is not the privation of enjoyment but, rather, the enjoyment of desire—or, better, a symptom.[27]

The respective strategies of the pervert and the hysteric demonstrate, then, that desire does not directly seek gratification but instead seeks to sustain itself, by procuring a specific kind of enjoyment.

To desire one's own desire is therefore perversion, and enjoyment. In *Formations of the Unconscious,* Lacan speaks of the "character inherent in desire qua perverse desire, which is desire at the second degree, an enjoyment of desire qua desire."[28] Desire, as "desire of/for desire *[désir du désir]*," is already enjoyment and thus in rapport with the unlimited and the infinite. When a human being desires, he can find himself in a moment of existence so intense that it feels like being at the edge of annihilation: in this sense, desire is enjoyment. But when

Lacan states in "Kant with Sade" that desire is "desire for enjoyment"[29] he is maintaining the contrary: that desire distances itself from enjoyment, as the latter does not occur within it. Desire and enjoyment would in that case be opposed, with desire being what limits enjoyment, the barrier to and *prohibition* on it.

These two, discrepant theories of desire—as the limit of enjoyment, versus as already enjoyment—should be conceived as simultaneously true if we want to understand the logical paradox of desire. How can desire, as limit, be at the same time unlimited, what is outside limits? How can it be both short of and beyond the pleasure principle? If desire opens and closes the door to enjoyment, how is it that we can be at once on both of its sides?

The aporia of desire as limit and desire as outside limits is something we all live when we desire. We are unaware of just where we are, as we flip between the inside and outside. This is where another problem, anxiety, comes in: desire is brought together with enjoyment, is confounded with it. Desire's limit should be not be taken for the negation of the unlimited, for the unlimited comprises everything, including even its negation. We are imbued with the active force of our desires, which are "thrustings toward," and the concrete experience of our vital power. As Spinoza might say, desire augments our power of life. At the same time, this same power of existence is depleted from being subject to the power of desire. We face the question of how to conceive this moment that is at once a plenitude of existence and its abolition.

Desire's dynamism makes us forget the gap *[béance]* that constitutes our being while at the same time causing us to discover and enact it.

Lack is structure in human being, and desire's "deceptive" character is evident in this. That is, we both desire to fill lack and desire because we think ourselves capable of this. Our impression is that lack is canceled when we are swept along in some movement of desire. We enjoy desire and the possibility—or better, fantasy and the infinite possibilities it offers—of erasing lack and attaining plentitude.[30]

When it is supported by fantasy, desire is relieving. But desire also means to be wanting, and the subject indeed enjoys its lack in desiring not to be. It is fantasy that arranges everything: we grasp ourselves as desiring/lacking, and desire becomes, in itself, a tolerable enjoyment.[31]

The enjoyment of desire is also that of fantasy; in other words, the possibility (in the sense of the non-enactment) that is its remaining unaccomplished. This is an enjoyment of lack, of unattained fullness.

But why seek plenitude so as to enjoy its privation? Why desire enjoyment in order to enjoy its lack? In what way do speaking beings enjoy if, as Lacan reminds us, there is no enjoyment that is not castration?[32]

The enjoyment of desire is the enjoyment of expectation. When desire is enjoyed, the premises are preferred to the conclusion (to the enjoyment). Expectation is something that can only be enjoyed, as desire does not and cannot possess its object; what is expected and might fulfill us does not exist (being of the order of the impossible), and is not even thinkable—like the mother's breast, which the child creates through its love for her.[33] The other, the object, comes to the place at which I await it, from where I created it, because of my fantasy. And if the object should fail to come, I hallucinate it. Expectation is just delirium! It is desire that creates the object, so that I can desire it.

In love, desire is often more important than enjoyment. Desire preserves the illusion. There is jouissance in desire because satisfaction is often deceptive, that which is expected never being of the same order as that which is coveted. The enjoyment obtained never reaches the heights of that of fantasy, or better, that of the *two enjoyments* of fantasy: that dreamed of in fantasy, and another specific to its impossibility.

Nothing is more satisfying than dissatisfaction—that is, than desire. In *A Lover's Discourse,* Roland Barthes furnishes a perfect example of it with the short story of a mandarin who fell in love with a courtesan, but who preferred enjoying his desire to satisfying it. "I shall be yours," she told him, "only when you have spent a hundred nights waiting for me, sitting on a stool, in my garden, beneath my window."[34] But on the ninety-ninth night, the mandarin gets up, puts his stool under his arm, and leaves. The enjoyment of desire turns desire into a loop: it becomes confused with its cause, the object of its enjoyment.

Desiring desire in order to enjoy it provides protection from deception, but also from potentially destructive enjoyment: "Desire is a defense," as Lacan says, "a defense against going beyond a limit in enjoyment."[35] Inasmuch as we desire, we do not truly court risk (to desire danger does not mean to expose oneself to it). Fantasy, the support of desire, enables us to cross the barrier of the pleasure principle in an imaginary way while at the same time hemming us safe within it. This enjoyment of desire—finite and infinite, within and at the same time beyond—is contradictory but nonetheless possible. But what, in that case, would an enjoyment beyond desire be? Could it be endured? And is it indeed possible?

The enjoyment of desire differs from enjoyment beyond desire. "Past the boundary markers, there is no more limit," said Sapeur Camember, whom Lacan cites: enjoyment beyond desire is unbearable, being the realization of the deadening force of the principle of every human desire.

Giacomo Leopardi's poem "A Silvia" shows that the beyond of desire interrupts desire's living circle. Definitively: that beyond corresponds to death, as it is death that comes at the point of satisfaction. The culmination of desire coincides with death. In Renaud Barabas's words, "the achievement of perfection referred to by imperfection signifies for the living being his disappearance, by dissolution, in totality."[36] Realized desire is mortal. Lacan is explicit about this: "the way toward death is nothing other than what is called enjoyment."[37]

The satisfaction of desire is effectively death: end and accomplishment, annihilation and deliverance, there is a perfect equivalence between death and enjoyment.

Silvia died very young; her death represented the terminus of all her desires as well the poet's. We need read only the last verse:

When the truth dawned
you fell away, poor thing, and from afar
pointed out cold death
and a naked grave[38]

3
Gap, Distance, and Lack in Desire

> All is distance—, and nowhere does the circle close.
>
> —Rainer Maria Rilke, *Sonnets to Orpheus*

In 1958, Lacan spoke explicitly of being,[1] affirming in the seminar *Desire and Its Interpretation* that "desire is the metonymy of being in the subject."[2] But in 1970, during an interview for Belgian radio, and then again in 1972 and 1973, the time of the delivery of his seminar *Encore,* he radically criticized ontological discourse as such.[3]

Lacan had already broached the question of being and the unconscious in 1964, during his seminar *The Four Fundamental Concepts of Psychoanalysis,* when he defended the non-ontological status— "preontological" is what he said—of the unconscious.[4] His critique of ontology, however, remained ambiguous, as it was unclear to whose ontology (Plato's, Spinoza's, Hegel's, Nietzsche's, Heidegger's, Sartre's, Foucault's . . . ?) he was referring.

It should nonetheless be specified that being is not only the "Being" of metaphysicians, in the sense of an idea, or substance, or monad, or objectivity, or plentitude. For Nietzsche, for example, being is life: "being—we have no other conception of it than 'life.'"[5] Being can also mean "that which is in reality,"[6] and in this sense, desire relates to that which really is—we might think of Spinoza's statement, in chapter 3 of the *Ethics,* that "desire is the essence of man." Yet can this essence be disclosed?

Heidegger criticized, of course, those philosophers who expressed themselves on the ontological question, who confused being with beings or the transcendent. His conception of being envisages it as closely related to existence:[7] it is thus only through *Dasein* that being discloses itself. We can take *Dasein* as a synonym for the subject:[8] as a particular modality of being, *Dasein* is speaking being, the sole modality for Heidegger in the position to allow for the discovery, through the *logos*—in its sense as language rather than as reason—of being.

Heidegger would appear on this point to have inspired Lacan's invention, which parallels his critique of ontology, of the term *parlêtre* [or "speaking being"].[9] This neologism enabled him to stress not only that language is the locus of being—that the being of the subject is in speech—but also, more importantly, that it is through language that the very idea of being is produced.

It should be noted that Lacan's characterization of the unconscious as preontological echoes Heidegger's statement, in *Being and Time,* that the being of *Dasein* should be named in the same way. The unconscious and being, of *Dasein,* might therefore be viewed as sharing a common preontological status. But calling the unconscious preontological, Lacan states, is a way of marking its "non-realized" character, that is, that the unconscious is neither being nor nonbeing. In contrast, the preontological status of *Dasein* should be viewed, following Heidegger, as "being in the mode of an understanding of being."[10]

In criticizing ontology, Lacan sought to show that the unconscious is a locus that is neither material, nor physical, nor "existentiel," and no more ontological than ontic.[11] The tenets of ego psychology, for example, ignored the clinical difficulties raised by treating the *Spaltung*—the division of the subject of the unconscious into language and the enjoyment of the body[12]—and thereby effectively reified the unconscious, casting it as the reservoir of psychic contents whose meanings conformed to the standard interpretations.[13] The real at work between enjoyment and language is not a quantifiable physical object, as it is not at all attributable to neurological dysfunction. Lacan definitively broke with this imaginary representation of the psychic apparatus as an interior opposed to an exterior, which is based on a naive intuition still in use by some scientists.

The question of the relation between being and desire in Lacan nevertheless remains open, owing to the relations language holds both to being and, of course, to desire.[14]

Desire is metonymic not only because a multiplicity of drives determine and divide it, but also because it is caught in a signifying chain that ends nowhere, is lost and alienated in the parading of the signifier. When the subject desires, it is in relationship—albeit *partially—*

with its being. Desire represents a part, a *remainder*. Being as plenitude is lacking in the subject and, as Sartre showed us, can never be realized. But being that lacks has an index: desire, or as Lacan says, fantasy. This index shows that the unattainable being that Sartre locates on the side of the subject is instead to be found on the side of the object: "the object," Lacan states in *Le désir et son interprétation*, "is found in the position of condensing onto itself the virtues of the dimensions of being, of becoming the veritable lure of being."[15]

In fantasy, the object takes the place of what the subject has been shorn of, namely, the phallus. But the being of the object is still lacking, by virtue of the *cut* that goes through the signifying chain and thus also, with it, the object of desire. Lacan will eventually specify that this cut is the point of passage for the real in the symbolic, the moment of separation and exchange between subject and object in fantasy.

Again, desire is fleeting, never stopping at any object, with each one merely a new point of departure from which it will be displaced elsewhere. From object to object, the whole desired by the subject fragments into parts, or metonyms. It is in this roaming movement—Lacan calls it "the errancy of desire"[16]—that the being of the subject, in the form of a lure, manifests.

Lacan artfully made the thesis that being is fundamentally symbolic (in the sense that it is fundamentally related to language) coexist with the idea that being is a lure, and therefore imaginary—so as in the end to define being as "the real's irruption into the symbolic," by way of affects.[17]

But can we say that the subject encounters being, in the sense of this "irruption of the real," in desire? This would be an impossible encounter, as desire brings the subject and being into rapport while also creating an irreducible distance—a gap *[béance]*—between them.[18] The subject, therefore, is never able to rejoin being in its desire: the latter remains a stopping point that only manifests through its occlusion.

We can hazard a comparison between desire and perception as conceived by phenomenology. In *Désir et distance*, Renaud Barabas maintains that perception, by Husserl's notion of it, enunciates being, since "to perceive is to be entered into the presence of that which is, and the sole way of reaching this in person is by perceiving."[19] In the sixth of the *Logical Investigations*, Husserl affirms that "the object is not given effectively, that is, it is not given fully and integrally such as it is":[20] what is given in perception can only be incomplete, on account of the infinite multiplication of indications of other possible givings. The very same moment of a thing is manifested through a multiplicity of appearances—what Husserl calls "outlines" (Abschattungen). In Ideas I, Husserl writes that "the spatial thing is nothing other than an intentional unity which of essential necessity can be given only as the unity of such multiple modes of appearance."[21] A thing is not distinct from its appearances but instead given as its appearances, and each appearance is always the thing that it presents. Perception as a giving through outlines is characterized by ambiguity, or rather the co-belonging of the one and the multiple.

In an analogous way, how can being be given in desire, which is multiple? If desire is taken by a plurality of drives, slipping between signifiers and assuming always different and even contradictory objectal forms, then how can it be? Being can only exist as the multiplicity, instability, indefinite and infinite flight, and ungraspable character . . . of desire. In other words, being is nonbeing.

Literature provides an example of this liaison between being and multiplicity. In the brief text Giacomo Joyce, an autobiographical fragment narrating an amorous episode, James Joyce succeeds at giving things and feelings a contradictory and poignant status in which they can seem simultaneously both insignificant and essential. A few lines concern a minor incident (albeit linked to the political history of the entire country of Italy) and a woman who affects Joyce. It is impossible to determine, though, which moments are essential, and which trivial:

> She thinks the Italian gentleman were right to haul Ettore Albini, the critic of the Secolo, from the stalls because he did not stand up when the band played the Royal March. She heard that at supper. Ay. They love their country when they are quite sure which country it is.
>
> She listens: virgin most prudent.
>
> A skirt caught back by her sudden moving knee; a white lace edging of an underskirt lifted unduly; a leg-stretched web of stocking. Si pol?[22]

Both the woman's presence and the narrator's desire are evoked by slight, fleeting touches; the reader finds herself faced with a series of appearances, moments that could just as well pass for a series of nothingnesses. Joyce presents reality as being composed of fine ends of presence, as well as of a multiplicity of discontinuous nothings.

> Who? A pale face surrounded by heavy odorous furs.
> Her movements are shy and nervous. She uses quizzing-glasses.
> *Yes:* a brief syllable. A brief laugh. A brief beat of the eyelids.
>
> Cobweb handwriting, traced long and fine with quiet disdain and resignation: a young person of quality.[23]

This would be, then, a text at once about desire and about nothing (about being): their presence brushes past, then escapes, the reader (all meaning is lost . . .).

> Unreadiness. A bare apartment. Torbid daylight. A long black piano: coffin of music. Poised on its edge a woman's hat, red-flowered, and umbrella, furled. Her arms: a casque, gules, and blunt spear on a field, sable.
>
> Envoy: Love me, love my umbrella.[24]

As its remainder, desire cannot render being present in its completeness. It is through distance that being and desire accord. They accord in their disaccord, by making the one correspond to the multiple. Being is shown to be a sum of nothingnesses, through the different moments of desire. Multiple desire becomes a graceful accord, necessarily dissonant, of its contradictory twinges. As Heraclitus put it, "Opposition brings concord. Out of discord comes the fairest harmony."[25]

While paradoxical, in the Husserlian outline, as in desire, the whole (being) reveals itself to be both different from and equal to the part (the outline, desire). In perception, an appearance presents an object as that which remains, in itself, unpresentable; similarly, desire's unveiling of being also veils it, for being can never be present in itself. Being is given as absence, is the lack in desire. The distance between desire and being cannot be covered, as being *is* in that distance.

Lack is not a question of the absence of an object: what is lacking is something more fundamental, at the origin of desire. Lack persists in desire, whether or not it has been attained. Lacan is explicit about this: "From its origin, its appearance, desire manifests in this interval, this gap that separates pure and simple, which is to say linguistic, articulation from speech, from what indicates that the subject thereby realizes something of itself that has import and sense only in relation to this emission of speech and which is, properly speaking, what language calls its being."[26] There is something that cannot be said in desire, and therefore also not of being—the words are lacking. Desire is not articulable,[27] is stricken by a fundamental inability *[manque]* at the level of saying, which Lacan indicates with the matheme S($\bar{A}$): signifier of the barred big Other.[28]

Desire's trajectory converges and closes on the unarticulable S($\bar{A}$), which designates the locus where the Other (the locus, again, of language, speech, and truth) ceases to exist. The bar over the "A" indicates the Other's incompleteness and inconsistency, and the "S," that in the face of this, there is nothing left to say. "S" (which is also the first letter of "silence") is the signifier of the big Other's disappearance, the signifier that remains when words are spent. This "S" can be written but not at all said, and in that sense is not articulable.

S($\bar{A}$) is the point of arrival of the trajectory of desire in Lacan's notorious graph of it (Figure 2).[29] It is the place of the *fading* of the subject, whose castration is laid bare by desire's route, a castration that is, for Lacan, nothing else but the truth of desire, which is that it is articulated in lack.

Desire is the desire for (and of) what the subject lost by having to speak: it is this being, whose signification is always sexual, that the subject seeks to rediscover in each phrase and word that it utters. Desire is the desire for nothing, as the Other does not consist of anything. This desire for nothing corresponds to a desire for completeness, a situation in which our being would, at last, satisfy the Other—a last silence, equivalent to death.

If words call and follow each other, it is because the Other is incomplete. The signifier of lack in the Other, S($\bar{A}$) is an indication of my own being: the Other is missing, and this lack of the Other constitutes the consistency of my being.

Desire is interval: there is always a gap between speech and being. Desire is situated in the gap—it *is* this gap—between the articula-

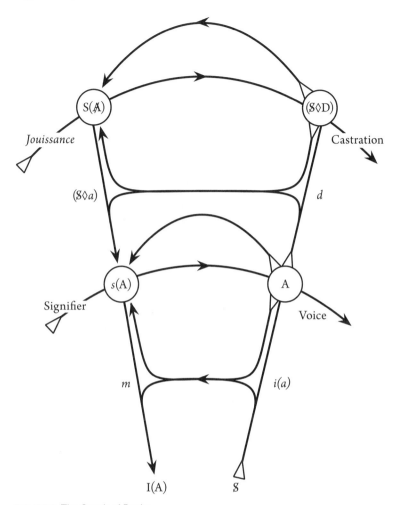

FIGURE 2. The Graph of Desire

tion of speech and the being of the subject, between everything that words can say and what cannot be said. That there are infinite words in speech, infinite possibilities of saying things, does not prevent their usage from being limited, their finitude. Everything is said but not everything can be; something is without the words to say itself. Desire is infinite possibility that is never sufficient.

Rilke made "cashmere shawls" the metaphor of infinite work of language in its will to symbolize:

the casually outspread center
of the cashmere shawl, reborn in black
from its flowered edge . . .
you realize that names would be forever
wasted on it; for it is the center.
As, whatever pattern may guide our steps,
it is around a void like this we wander.[30]

Being *is* in speech via desire—the real's irruption into the symbolic—
but in speech that cannot say, an impossible speech that is antithetical
to all revelation. Being, which is, according to Heidegger, inseparable
from speech,[31] is given, it should be repeated, as lacking—as a hollow,
which also corresponds to that of truth. Desire is what hollows out
the uncrossable distance, the gap between the speaking subject and
being.

The "speaking being" *[parlêtre]* then: where speech and being inter-
penetrate, but without completing each other. Speaking and being are
never unknotted: they modify each other, are mutually corrupted by
their divergence, and also encounter each other. We can therefore understand desire as establishing the gap between the speaking subject and
being while also being their hyphen.

It is on account of speech, which *marks* the lack in being, that the
subject becomes the "lacking-being" *[manque-à-être]* in desire.[32] Desire, qua the metonymy of being, is transformed into the metonymy
of the lacking-being, as Lacan says in "The Direction of the Treatment
and the Principles of Its Power."[33] Psychoanalysis speaks not of being
but of its lack, by which each subject is tied to the other[34]—by sex,
speech, demand, and also, of course, desire.

The lacking-being is the constitutive lack in being, the fundamental modality of the human condition: a lacking of substance and thus
a lacking-being in the sense of a complete and realized being—or, a
lacking "phallic" being. And this is both for itself and for the Other. In
itself and in the Other.

To conceive being as this lacking-being implies a certain structural
impossibility. Being cannot be considered universal ideality; it is neither transcendence nor plentitude. Lacan's "lacking-being" is close to
what Heidegger meant by a nothing *(Nicht)* more original than negation, and that always presupposes a first affirmation.[35] The lack-of-

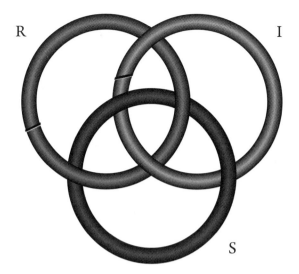

R   I

S

FIGURE 3. The Three-Ring Borromean Knot

being is an abyssal ground where being and nothing belong to each other: finitude as such as constitutive of being.

In *Anxiety*, Lacan supposes that "there is no lack in the real, that lack is only graspable through the intermediary of the symbolic."[36] The real is not a "lack of" and only becomes so when the signifier designates it as missing something: something that is missing from its place, the absence of which a signifier emerges to evoke.

Lacan defines the real as the impossible.[37] This is of course paradoxical, but what is impossible is also what anchors each existence. The real is that which resists,[38] is impossible to say (as well as to imagine), even though it can be thought of as a hole, emptiness, or lack . . . a lack for us, who lack nothing! The real is necessarily articulated to the dimensions of the symbolic and the imaginary.[39] In 1974, Lacan proposed as a model for the relation between all three—a relation involving permanent tension: the three-ring Borromean knot (Figure 3). This model conveys the near impossibility of unknotting each of them from the other two.[40] That unknotting can be produced when the symbolic ring ceases to stay bound to the others: it pops out, disordering the basis and continuity of the relationship between the three agencies [*instances*]. But that only happens in psychosis.

Lacan specifies that "there is no absence in the real. There is only absence if you suggest that there may be a presence there where there isn't one."[41] The symbolic and the real are in a relationship of reciprocal tension: the fact that the subject speaks expels the real from reality.[42] The real is not the reality organized by the symbolic, which is to say not a representation of the external world, but it is no more another world in the Platonic sense, or the transcendence of the phenomenal in Kant's.

The real returns to the place where the subject cannot assume it at a conscious level: it is presented in dreams, in hallucinatory form in certain kinds of psychosis, or still yet in trauma. The real is expulsed by the subject, and therefore regarded as a "hole."[43] But the real, it must be repeated, lacks nothing. By contrast, we speaking beings are lacking. Lacking what? Are we really lacking, or are we lacking in a strictly symbolic way? Or might lack be imaginary? In other words, to which of these three dimensions does it belong?

The notion of lack involves all three dimensions. Now there is of course a structural difference between each and the rest. In the symbolic, it is a question of a lack guaranteed by the signifier; in the imaginary, of the ideal of a complete self (of a form like Sartre's in-itself-for-itself) that has turned out to be lacking; in the real, lack is a hollow outside symbolization. The plurality of terms in play—gap, lack, castration—can cause confusion, as they can be synonyms or in contradiction with each other, depending on the context.

So then to which lack—symbolic or imaginary (both symbolizable) or real (outside symbolization)—is desire primarily connected?

There is an initial, active desire that is present from the subject's birth; pre-oedipal, it manifests in the newborn's hallucinatory dreams. And there also exists an oedipal desire that is tied to the fantasy of bisexednesss [bisexualité]—in other words, to castration.[44] According to Freud, during the first phase of that fantasy, the subject is active, and in that sense masculine. This first scene represents the desire for the father's death in the battle over the phallus. In the second phase, the subject is passive, enacting a fantasy of being feminized.

It should be specified that the father is necessarily castrated in the fantasy. This is first of all because a father who can die is symbolically castrated (death being closely related to castration, as Freud shows us). This is also, secondly, because the father gives the phallus to the child, through his name. That transmission of the name attests, among other things, to the father's love for the son as well as to the identification of the son for the father, which occurs through his taking of the latter's name. (This occurs alongside the son's imaginary holding of the phallus in fantasy.)

Symbolic castration activates the fantasy that sets desire in motion so that enjoyment might be possible for the subject. Under the influence of the fantasy, the subject is stretched between being and having/ not having the phallus. In other words, it is castration that binds enjoyment and prohibition together, and that constitutes the basis or foundation that maintains the structure of the fantasy.

The father is the pivot around which the fantasy's two phases turn, and castration, its central point:

—in the first, active phase, the subject kills the father, who is not invincible but *castrated*
—in the second, passive phase, the subject *gets castrated* by the father

Castration is not a matter of an organ but of desire. As Lacan clarifies, "at the very least, a minimum has to be retained to define what the castration complex is in its essence—it's the relationship of a desire to what for the moment I will call a mark."[45] Castration is much less the effect of some authority, a Chronos or ferocious father, than of our relationship to language. We are once again faced with desire's confrontation with the signifier. Desire, we already understand, must pass through the signifier, but what is its cause?

We have seen that desire is already there before symbolic castration, as pre-oedipal desire—prior, that is, to the father's intervention in fantasy. As Lacan affirms, "there is perhaps in this desire, from the outset, a gap that makes it possible for this mark to have its special effect."[46] Lacan is here referring to an original, intersubjective gap of distress *(Hilsflosigkeit)* which leaves the subject without words. The subject's anxiety becomes manifest as it faces this gap, and the same goes for its desire.

Desire that passes through symbolic castration does not efface this first gap. On the contrary, it stresses—*marks*—it. Desire results from the gap of the (pre-oedipal) real and is marked by symbolic (oedipal) castration, and these two lacks are what constitute structure.[47]

From Lacan's perspective, symbolic lack *[manque]* is associated with a mark *[marque]*. In other words, it is necessary to inscribe symbolically, with a mark—that of a primary identification that will later function as an ideal—the loss of a tip of one's own body. It is in this way that the subject loses its phallus. The subject can lose the phallus—*not have it*—because he or she has already given up on being it. To be symbolically marked by castration is to be resigned to not being the phallus for the (maternal) Other, and in this sense, castration is also a narcissistic wound. It is starting from this loss, which acquires symbolic value, that the subject has the experience of castration.

Throughout *Formations of the Unconscious,* Lacan insists on this mark. "Outside of analysis, in all its other interpretive or signifying manifestations, and certainly in all that embodies it ceremonially, ritually, or sociologically, the mark is the sign of that which supports the castrating relation, the anthropological emergence of which analysis permits us to discern. Let's not forget the religious incarnations in which the castration complex can be recognized, such as circumcision, to call it by name, or again in puberty rites, this or that form of inscription, marking, or tattooing which is linked with a particular phase that unambiguously presents itself as the accession to a certain stage of desire. All of that always presents itself as a mark and an impression."[48]

In this passage, we see Lacan situating ritual tattooing in puberty on the same plane as circumcision. Both kinds of practices, which are anthropological rites of castration,[49] introduce the subject into the real-imaginary-symbolic circuit of the experience of castration. Such symbolic marking, however, cannot be assimilated to "narcissistic markings," like tattoos and piercings, which function as imaginary supports of identity—marks that adolescents often resort to out of a need for admiration and in order to fill the lacunae of their identities.[50]

The symbolic mark is related to what Lacan calls a "unary trait," translating Freud's expression *einziger Zug.* This term designates an element of the object that the subject assimilates, and that allows for symbolic identification with that object. An example of identification by way of a unary trait is Dora's celebrated cough, which remanifested her father's cough by focusing on his symptomatic being.[51]

Lacan conceives the unary trait as a tattoo, by virtue of the relation between the (symbolic) mark and the (real + imaginary) body. In *The Four Fundamental Concepts of Psychoanalysis,* he maintains that with "the unary trait, the subject locates himself there *[le sujet lui-même s'en repère]*, and first he marks himself as a tattoo, the first of the signifiers. When this signifier, this one, is established—the count is *one* one. It is at the level not of the one, but of the *one* one, at the level of the count that the subject has to situate himself as such."[52]

For Freud, identification with the father is possible only after he has been incorporated: this is the father's *mark* on the subject's *body.*[53] And the subject identifies with a unary—symbolic—trait of the lost object, which is to say the father. (The unary trait effaces the object, the father, who thereafter exists as death in the trait, the symbolic mark.)

The trait incarnates the phallus in the form of a signifier and as a support of the image. In passing through the body, this first signifier, *"the* one [l'un],"[54] that Lacan speaks of, is constituted as the starting point of the symbolic chain. And *"the* one" becomes *"a* one" [un un], *one* signifier.

It is in the seminar *D'un autre à l'Autre* that Lacan explains that the unary trait and the signifier must be distinguished. Resuming with the matter of identification's relation to tattooing (the latter term should always be understood as the symbolic inscription of the trait on the body), he states that "this *one* is characterized by what is called numerical identity. Nothing is designated here by these terms; we are not at the level of any unary identity, that for example of a *one* that at some point could be put on your palm, like a tattoo by which you could be identified in a certain context, which has happened. It is a question, in each case, of a trait that marks nothing. We are strictly at the level of what is called numerical identity, which marks pure difference as nothing specific."[55]

As the support of the identity of the subject, the unary trait allows for this "count": for the *identity* of the signifiers, of *ones* that nothing specifies, and the *difference* of the signifier from itself when it is repeated.[56] At the level of the social, the subject, identified with the (unary) trait, is both *identical* to others (*some* ones) who have passed, like him, through castration, and *different* from them, because of the trait of the singularity (*the* one) with which he has identified.

Lacan insists on the inscription of the unary trait *in* the body: again, "a *one* that at some point could be put on your palm, like a tattoo."[57] In contrast, the signifier (*a* one, *some* ones . . .), qua some element of the chain, does not inscribe any mark on the body: it is a question, says

Lacan, of "a trait that marks nothing." The unary trait, the symbolic mark, is that which permits the subject to emerge, giving it identity.[58] Lacan represents (symbolic) castration in the same way as he does the phallus as signifier of (prohibited) jouissance, with a symbol, Φ.[59] (If the phallus is a symbol, it is necessarily lacking: a symbol is not an emblem, as the latter includes the representation of the thing.) Φ is linked to the law that forbids incest, that prohibits enjoyment from being absolute. It orders the modalities of enjoyment, authorizing and even commanding the enjoyment of another body while at the same time forming an obstacle to the possibility of the sexual encounter as a veritable unification. Φ furrows the hollow between man and woman: "It must be perceived," as Lacan affirms, "that in the relationship between man and woman, from the moment it is consecrated, a hollow [béance] remains open."[60] "There is no sexual relationship," he says elsewhere; in its place, there is lack, castration (Φ).[61] Or again, in still another text: "There is nothing excessive about what gives us the experience of making being or having the phallus responsible for . . . compensating for the sexual relation."[62]

The phallus is situated in an algebrization that radicalizes the asymmetry of sexual difference. Writing xRy is not going to account for the relation between the sexes. Thinking the phallus in terms of a "phallic function" thus allows the hiatus between man and woman to be precisely inscribed.

The encounter between a man and a woman is ordered by the phallus—that is, the phallus or castration—which is symbolic (Φ) but also imaginary: the phallus = φ, and castration = $-\varphi$. The imaginary phallus (φ) has the function of closing the distance between man and woman and thereby plugging up subjective division with an image of unity and possible completeness, which comes from the partner. The other will fulfill me right where I am lacking; the other is the object that is lacking in me. That idea is a lure, as the other cannot fulfill me— the distance between man and woman remains uncrossable, and unity impossible.

These are the positions of man as much as of woman in relation to the signifier in the order of the symbolic (Φ), as well as to the object in the order of the imaginary (φ, $-\varphi$), which makes their meeting impossible. The daily life of the couple consists in maintaining this impossibility, in watching over their share of dissatisfaction, as though it commanded them and enabled them to stay together.

Even in an atypical relation, like that established between the two protagonists of Bernardo Bertolucci's *Last Tango in Paris,* sexual relationship *[le rapport sexuel]* (in the term's Lacanian rather than empirical sense) is impossible. The film's denouement, which sees Maria Schneider (Jeanne) killing Marlon Brando (Paul), puts an end, on the one hand, to an impossible relationship, and declares, on the other, that it never existed. Schneider's final words, following Brando's death, are, "I don't know who he is . . . He's a lunatic. I'd never seen him before . . . he's a stranger. A lunatic. I don't know his name."

This man and woman were able to have, each in their own way, temporarily satisfying encounters, but they failed to heed that these could not last. A stable couple, by contrast, is founded on the dissatisfaction that stems from the absence of encounter. Between man and woman an impractical distance—a gap—prevents them from truly meeting.

But then why should we try to prop up this failure? "There is no sexual relationship" does not mean that a joining is impossible. Experience refutes this, as we can affirm that, empirically speaking, there are sexual relationships. Let us pause over the "there is no" and ask what sense Lacan gives it. To affirm that "there is no relationship" is to state the very property of relation, which is to be without-relation, that is, a separation, a distance, a difference between two bodies. The distance between the two subjects should subsist so that the sexual relationship, with the same going for love, can transpire. This between-the-two should be maintained, the two should remain two. The between-the-two, indeed, is the emptiness that allows the two to remain two; it is the gap, Lacan's non-relation. If there were to be "sexual relationship" in the sense of union and fusion, there would no longer be distance and therefore no difference between the two bodies. This is not possible—it is in this sense that there is no sexual relationship—and when fusional union is sought, it has catastrophic consequences.

"Relation" and "separation" are the same thing: relation exists, but only as non-relation. Sexual relation thus becomes the principle of the indefinite proliferation of differences. For Jean-Luc Nancy, "the non-unity and non-unicity of the one is the absolute condition for there being one: that is to say, one and the other, the one *singuli* (always in the plural) and not the one *unus.*"[63] The only unity possible is that deriving from the impossibility of unity.

That there is no relation means there are no returns, nor accounts rendered *[il n'y a pas de revenu, ni de compte rendu].* If relationship is understood as what this act brings, or what from it can be retained, recounted, calculated, and capitalized on and therefore registered, in order to be able to appropriate and determine it as "something," then the relation is not possible. The sexual relationship relates nothing, or better, it relates *the* nothing, the lack-of-being.

A love relation conceived as non-relation is a way of accepting solitude. The relation of the subject to the Other brings the process of the cleft *[béance]* into play, as it is the busting of the subject by the irreducible character of its scission that is the cleft itself. It is, indeed, in lack that the subject recognizes itself.

It was at the same moment as Lacan formulated his theory of the mirror stage—in 1953 and 1954, during his first seminar—that he first introduced the term gap *[béance]*, apropos the discrepancy between the child's experience and the image of itself it spots in the mirror.[64] This image is the one that it can never meet, and the child's impotence is inscribed in this gap. At the same time, the mirror image also functions to repair the originary gap, and for this reason causes the child jubilation. Yet the lack-of-being is only poorly concealed, and the gap thus redoubled.

Throughout this seminar, Lacan affirms that "the *Urbild . . .* [is] the first model in which man's delay, the unsticking of man in relation to his own libido," and "this gap means that there's a radical difference between the satisfaction of a desire and the pursuit of the fulfillment of a desire."[65] The pursuit of desire does not end in satisfaction, and an infinite desire insists beyond its enjoyment. In *Beyond the Pleasure Principle,* Freud wrote that "it is the difference in amount between the pleasure of satisfaction which is demanded and that which is actually achieved that provides the driving factor which will permit of no halting at any position attained, but, in the poet's words, *'ungebändigt, immer vormärts dringt'* [presses ever forward unsubdued]."[66]

In the sense of complete satisfaction and the representation of an original or final fusion, enjoyment is impossible. As Freud notes, "something in the nature of the sexual instinct itself is unfavorable to the realization of complete satisfaction."[67] There remains only ambiguous, partial, and limited enjoyment . . . such as enjoyment of the symptom.

Yet the chase of the fulfillment of desire is still pursued, for something about satisfaction does not satisfy: there is a lack, and it is all the more shown when desire is satisfied.

But it is also from another perspective that desire cannot attain enjoyment, if the latter is understood as complete satisfaction. The enjoyment that desire pursues, says Lacan, "is not of nature for promising us desire."[68] Desire pursues something that it will not be able to reach. It is like the famous paradox of Achilles and the tortoise, the latter of whom cannot be caught owing to a *remainder* of distance that cannot be closed. Desire can in this way be maintained to infinity by maintaining the barrier to enjoyment while still seeking it. The remainder is always to be conceived of as lack, as if the true object of desire were always out of reach. Lack is in relationship with this remainder, which corresponds in Lacanian theory to object *a*, desire's cause. We will return to that later.

Desire is always desire of the Other; by consequence, the subject's enjoyment is tied to that of the Other. On account of that, to enjoy means, from a structural point of view, to become object, that of the Other and its enjoyment. As infinite distance from enjoyment, end point, and limit that creates obstruction—castration—desire protects the subject from the Other, from the anxiety of becoming the object of its desire.

When the subject identifies with the object of the Other's desire, it stops lacking, and the distance between subject and Other becomes what is lacking. In Lacan's words, "anxiety isn't the signal of a lack, but of something that has to be conceived of at a duplicated level, as the failing of the support that lack provided. . . . The most anguishing thing for the infant is precisely the moment when the relation upon which he's established himself, of that lack that turns him into desire, is disrupted, and this relation is most disrupted when there's no possibility of any lack."[69] Anxiety arises when lack is what is lacking, when desire can no longer play its normative, assuaging role, when it no longer provides its law.

To repeat: lack is *marked* by castration, which inscribes the distance between subject and Other, between desire and enjoyment. Yes, castration is a relief! For Lacan, desire should go toward castration, "because a desire is also suspended from the central lack that disjoins desire from enjoyment, the threat of which for each and every subject is only fashioned from having recognized it in the desire of the Other."[70] Finally, what threatens the subject is not its castration but the Other's desire. Anxiety comes more from the Other's will to enjoy than from the impossibility, which is *real*, that the subject could satisfy it.

Castration anxiety is foremost provoked by the image of castration. -φ is the symbol employed by Lacan to write imaginary castration: being cut, or separated—imaginarily—from an end of itself, from what Lacan calls the imaginary phallus (φ), the piece of flesh that the subject is afraid to lose and that leads it to believe itself complete, in order to satisfy the Other's desire. (The imaginary phallus is not necessarily tied to the image of the male organ. For a young woman, for example, it may correspond to the idea of a body that brings enjoyment [*faire jouissance*].)

At the heart of anxiety and the foundation of impotence is the impression of no longer being able to . . . do what? Satisfy the desire of the Other. But what is more anguishing: the impossibility of satisfying the Other's desire, or the feeling of becoming (on account of the ideal of completeness) the object of its desire? With castration, in effect, one loses . . . but also wins! To accept castration means to accept one's own lack, which raises the barrier between subject and Other.

In "On Freud's *Trieb* and the Desire of the Psychoanalyst," Lacan distinguishes between fear of castration and its assumption. The fear of castration is certainly normalizing in its prohibiting function, but it fixes the subject in a position of obedience to the father, which attests that the Oedipus complex has not been overcome. On the contrary, "the assumption of castration," writes Lacan, "creates the lack on the basis of which desire is instituted," a desire that ceases to submit to the paternal ideal, the superego, which often inhibits the subject.[71]

Lacan's position runs counter to that of Ernest Jones, who maintains that castration anxiety is just the fear that desire will disappear, *aphanisis*.[72] By that account, castration would be the symbolization of that loss. But the fear that desire will disappear derives not from castration anxiety but from the refusal to accept it. For Lacan, "the fear of *aphanisis* in neurotic subjects corresponds, contrary to what Jones believed, to something that should be understood from the perspective of an insufficient formation, or articulation, of a partial foreclosure of the castration complex."[73] The neurotic continues to believe in this ideal image (of itself), and that it must be met. The distance between himself and this ideal image is intolerable: if he fails to reach it, he risks abandoning his desire, and thus his capacity to act.

The ego ideal is the dream-image of a total (but possible) enjoyment that transports us beyond ourselves; although inaccessible, it haunts and determines us.[74] She who acts seeks to equal this image, and by approaching it, lacks it. Whence the suspension of the act.

When castration is refused, desire (which is always the desire of the Other) can become inhibited, in the sense that it can become blocked by the inhibition of its enactment. The subject is, on the one hand, afraid of failing to satisfy the Other, but it is also, on the other, (unconsciously) afraid of succeeding in that by carrying out its acts: of being made the Other's object and thereby disappearing with its acts. To not be spayed [châtré] signifies being the phallus (φ) that is missing in the Other: to do better, to succeed, imperils the subject, since the most immediate meaning of this is incest consummated, the disappearance into a maternal Other that has, at last, been sated.

Desire is the desire of the Other, and desires escape from this desire. Desire heads simultaneously in opposite directions, covering the distance corresponding to that between the subject and itself. The subject is divided by desire because it wavers between its aspirations to be made into the object of the Other and to self-affirmation as a place of rupture and disjuncture vis-à-vis the Other and its desire.

To desire while still welcoming its own condition as lack-of-being—while accepting castration—allows one to act while still supporting the (infinite) distance between itself and the ideal, between itself and the Other: to desire by lack confirms this distance. The subject finds itself again in its being unwitting to its act, in a beyond of the desire for completeness of self and Other.

Desire, when it passes through castration (that has been assumed by the subject), veers from its path, and affirms the subject's existence against the determinations of it coming from the Other. This entails the subject's loss of being, its phallic being for the Other. Desire then no longer consists in filling lack but in being this lack. Identification, in turn, is no longer with the phallus but with its absence, not with the ideal image but with its collapse. There exists a difference between the *enactment* of the fantasy that corresponds to the former, imaginary identification and the veritable *act*, which involves a "traversing" of fantasy;[75] it permits the subject to free itself from alienated identity.

This is the infinite finitude of the subject of drifting desire, its incapacity to find the final resting point by which an end can be brought to its drift. The lack-of-being is designated, in Lacan's algebra, by the bar over the subject ($\math$) as well as by the bar over the Other ($\mathcal{A}$).

If it is possible to desire via the incompleteness of oneself, is it also possible to do so through the incompleteness of the Other? That is, by stripping [destituant] the Other of all its knowledge and power?

In October of 1967, Lacan spoke of "disbeing" [désêtre] with respect to the moment that one passes from the position of the analyzed to that of the analyst. "The passage from psychoanalyzed to psychoanalyst has a door whose hinge is the remainder that divides them, for this division is nothing but that of the subject, whose cause is this remainder. In the change of tack by which the subject sees capsized the assurance he took from this fantasy, by which each person's window on the real is constituted, what can be perceived is that the foothold of desire is nothing but that of a disbeing."[76] He further specified, in December of the same year, that "the psychoanalyst is always in the end at the mercy of the psychoanalyzed, and all the more so since the psychoanalyzed can spare him nothing if he stumbles about as psychoanalyst, and if he does not stumble, even less. At least that's what experience teaches us. What the psychoanalyzed cannot spare him, [the psychoanalyst] is this disbeing affected through the terminus to be assigned to each psychoanalysis, and which I am surprised to find echoed on so many lips (as though it were they who spelled it out) following my proposition, that one is in the pass only to imply a destitution of the subject: the psychoanalyzed."[77]

Lacan draws here a distinction between a "disbeing" that corresponds to the position of the analyst, who has been disenchanted of the ideals of his position and his knowledge, and "subjective destitution," which concerns, in contrast, the subject undergoing analysis.

Again in that same year, a few days later, Lacan will speak more generally on the destitution of the subject, associating it with desire in the same condition. "What they demonstrate," he says while commenting on the drives, "is the structure of this desire, which Spinoza formulated as being the essence of man. That desire, which is of the desideration that he avows to the Romance languages, suffers here a deflation, which leads it to its disbeing."[78]

When the subject perceives both himself and the Other structurally lacking, by undergoing the experience of lacking-being [manque-à-être] in his speech and the accomplishment of his acts—of subjective destitution if he is in analysis, and of disbeing if he is an analyst (by destituting the Other, just as he has himself, of all knowledge)[79]—then what place, or which, will desire occupy for him?

Part II
THE PAINFUL DIALECTIC OF THE OBJECT

4

The Object Slips Off,
a Signifier Takes Its Place

The Lacanian gap suggests a trait common to both the lacking-being [manque-à-être]—the fundamental structure of the divided subject— and the concept of nothingness, particularly Heidegger's, Sartre's, and Plato's versions of it.

Metaphysical discourse should be distinguished from the discourse of the unconscious. Where philosophy thinks nothingness, psychoanalysis instead discerns original repression. The point at which knowledge stops is not nothingness but the repression of the phallic signification of the subject's body.

To conceive being as nothingness is just another way to think being. The thought of nonbeing has nothing to do with nonbeing in itself, which is death. Every thought about death is a relief, a bit of an antidote to it, as well as a means of denying it: from the moment that I am thinking (about it), I am, if Cartesian ontology is to be followed. Such rationalist convictions about existence and death do not, however, allow me to remove myself from the enigma that is life, which I am forced to contend with each time I speak or think.

My true question is found here, in each and every thought. But it always comes disguised, transformed into a general—metaphysical— question. I forget its sexual origin:[1] if I encounter the real of the drives [le réel pulsional][2] that nourishes every desire for knowledge, I find myself facing castration once more. And castration makes me feel the anxiety of nothingness. I live it as a threat—that of my disappearance.

The savant's search for objectivity and his aspiration to the absolute end up erasing him, as he disappears into his thinking: the subject becomes the object of the desire of the Other (Knowledge, Science, Philosophy, etc.), without knowing it. In Gérard Pommier's estimation, science "doesn't want to know anything about the mainspring of its action, beginning with the incestuous desire of the subject, who seeks to erase himself by transitioning from hypothesis to thesis. This objectness of the subject realizes the Other's desire, and the scientist's enjoyment begins when he takes the leap toward it."[3] Knowing [connaissance] has no end: the realization of Being implied by the ideal of complete knowledge (with the same going for enjoyment) is impossible. The absolute does not exist: if that were the case, the death drive would be carried to its conclusion. Speech, likewise, comes up lacking when it tries to say everything, as it is what engendered the repression of the sexual thing in the first place. Psychoanalytic discourse is the line of questioning about the repression at the origin of all thought.

Freud explains that the child begins by hallucinating what it desires, even if the object is within reach. It follows that any object can become an object of desire, even while not being one in the structural sense: the object of desire transcends all the forms of the object: perceived, felt, lived, found, and so on.

The subject discovers itself in lack. This first nonbeing should be viewed not as the origin of being but as the effect of original repression. For Freud, that primordial repression is a way of shutting out a signification that refuses to be under the jurisdiction of conscience.[4] This signification is none other than the phallic signification that the subject's body has for the (maternal) Other. For Lacan, this unconscious sidelining concerns a signifier that has no signified and that instead designates the ensemble of effects that the signified(s) have: the phallus.[5] (We will come back to this.)

The being of the subject is destined for repression, and the subject is even its effect. The lacking-being, from which desire results, depends on the repressed sexual "thing." The emptiness of being at the origin is thus not nothingness but the impossible identification of the subject with the phallus. In this sense, the phallus—whether as, per Lacan, a signifier, or, per Freud, a phallic signification—is at the center of all psychoanalytic theorization, qua the object of original Freudian repression.

For Freud, the phallus is the symbol of libido for both sexes: "for both sexes, only one genital, namely the male one, comes into account. What is present, therefore, is not a primacy of the genitals, but a primacy of the *phallus*."[6] But this primacy of the phallus is not the primacy of the penis as an organ.[7] As Lacan shows, "the phallus, the woman does not have it, symbolically. But not having the phallus symbolically is to participate in it as absence and therefore to have it in some way. . . . This is entirely independent of the inferiority that she can feel on the imaginary plane about her real participation in the phallus."[8] This is not a matter of realizing that there are beings fortunate enough to have it and others to be pitied because they don't. The phallus is not an object, in the sense of a piece of flesh. As it happens, the penis will for men be just as insufficient as the clitoris is for women: inadequate to the phallic symbol. This inadequacy makes no discrimination between boys and girls in causing castration anxiety.

The importance of the phallus is only justified by the symbolic operation executed on the organ: the latter is raised—Lacan employs the Hegelian term *Aufhebung*—to the dignity of a *signifier,*[9] the signified of which is nothing else but the infinite question of desire. The phallus cannot, then, be considered an object, even if it is incarnated in imaginary objects; it does not designate any reality, but only the transition into signifying form.

In the 1958 text "The Signification of the Phallus," Lacan stresses the symbolic import of the phallus in the unconscious, and its place in the order of language.[10] The phallus, he says, cannot be assessed with respect to its own value, since it is a signifier that is significant only in its relation to other signifiers.

Lacan distinguishes in that text between φ and -φ, the imaginary significations, respectively, of the phallus and castration, from Φ qua signifier: phallus and castration in the symbolic. He treats the meanings of enjoyment—the forbidden, the barred, the mortifying, and so on—as signified by the signifier of desire, the phallus (Φ). Soon after, in "Subversion of the Subject and the Dialectic of Desire," Lacan attempts to recuperate impossible, nonsymbolic enjoyment in the form of the big phi (Φ), and this marks the outer extreme of his attempt at integrating enjoyment into the signifying system.

By 1972, Lacan is maintaining something else: that of all the signifiers, Φ is the only one that has no signified.[11] Yet if that is the case, how can it be paired with another signifier? What is a signifier that is not enchained to others, but that is their point of departure?

The phallus indicates its own lack, along with the impossibility of making it an object: it is always excluded, lacking, elusive.[12] It is in this way that the phallus is neither a fantasy nor an object, and still less the penile or the clitoral organ. It can only fulfill its function if veiled, exactly as happens in the myth of Psyche and Cupid. There, Cupid has to refrain from showing himself while satisfying his wife. When Psyche finally uncovers him, she finds only flowers where his penis should be. The flowers render the nothing evident instead of hiding it; that is, the nothing of the phallus, its inexistence in the same way as its insignificance. (Jacopo Zucchi represented this scene in a painting preserved in the Villa Borghese in Rome.)

Lacan also defines the phallus as a semblance, in the sense of an appearance to which no substance corresponds.

A signifier without a signified, the phallus also holds, paradoxically, an imaginary function (φ -φ): the phallus is the imaginary object—Lacan calls it the "imaginary signifier"—that the mother is lacking; the *object* of her desire. It is, quite obviously, not empirically an object but that through which the object of the mother's desire is symbolized. The child, whatever its sex, believes in the primacy of the phallus as symbol of its mother's desire.

The mother-child relation always passes through the imaginary dimension. Theirs is a specular relation: certainly important where affect is concerned, but incapable of making desire to circulate. For there to be desire, a third term is necessary:[13] the father for Freud, and the phallus (Φ) for Lacan. This third term is an element that transcends the specular relation, and thus allows the subject-object relation to be kept at a distance.

The phallus responds to the desire attributed to the mother by the child, who himself wants to be the phallus in order to satisfy her. Every child desires this. It is a necessary condition of existence, and the reason that castration and death are often associated in our thoughts. The child can thus believe the mother to be endowed with the phallus,[14] as he has himself incarnated this symbol. There would in that case not be any castration, whether for himself or his mother.

The child *is* because he can be the phallus of the mother: a way of being, *being-object,* which contradicts its life as subject. In order to be subject, its identification with the phallus must falter. Failure—castration—is the price of freedom, of taking and keeping distance from the (maternal) Other and her desire.

If the mother experiences satisfaction through her child, it is because she finds in it something that fulfills her. But that satisfaction, of course, can only be incomplete: the mother's, because her lack can never be filled, and the child's, because he proposes himself as object of satisfaction. Following Lacan, "it is only after the second instance of imaginary specular identification with the image of the body, which is at the origin of its ego and provides its matrix, that the subject can realize what is lacking in the mother. The specular experience of the other as forming a totality is a prior condition. It is in relation to this image that the subject realizes that he can lack something. The subject carries beyond the object of love this lack, for which he can be led to substitute himself, to propose himself as the object that fills it."[15]

In identifying with the object lacking in the mother (symbolized by the phallus), the child seeks to fill lack—both the lack in himself and that in his mother. In attempting this, the child, in lieu of equating himself with Being, equates himself with nothingness. For the phallus is nothing more than a symbol. By identifying itself with the phallus, the subject annihilates and effaces itself. The *all* becomes *nothing*, the nothing of the phallus, which is made present as absence: the subject once more finds itself facing castration, both its own and the mother's.

Yet through this meltdown brought about by the encounter with castration, the subject reappears. And it can identify itself with the lack, the lacking (of)-being that forces it to desire elsewhere, outside of the specular loop of maternal desire. The confrontation with castration makes the subject pass from endogenous desire to exogenous desire.

To avoid disappearing during primordial repression, the child ejected the phallic signification of its body.[16] The body qua phallus, the veritable object of the drive, is repressed. The body will henceforward be a total mystery to the subject, as he will be entirely in the dark about the function that it originally fulfilled. Repression is necessary, even at the cost of the subject's loss of his body, of living thereafter outside himself. (It should be remarked that in 1974, Lacan conceived the body as imaginary,[17] and then two years later, in 1976, the imaginary as a "confused image of the body";[18] but he also maintained, in "Le troisième," that the body, the body as real, is what we fear.[19])

The subject finds himself obliged to look everywhere, says Pommier, for "the secret of a body that escapes him: in the stars, under the earth, in the infinitely small, over the seas, volcanoes, the ice—everywhere."[20] The drive to know is similar to all the other drives (the oral, the anal, the scopic, the sexual, etc.). Every drive aims, but in a different way, to respond to the desire of the mother's phallus: in this sense, every desire

is unconsciously sexual and incestuous. It is the body in its phallic signification that is sought after and immediately repressed.

It is both at once: I want to be and I don't want to be the phallus.
And above all, I don't want to know about it. I can't know, or I'm a
goner. However, knowing nothing does not ameliorate the situation:
desire leads, inevitably, to the loss of oneself, as the Other's desire is at
the origin of every desire. That does not mean that the subject ceases
to desire but that it does so by way of compromises, like fantasies and
dreams.

Reality will be dealt a finishing blow so that our fantasies remain
fantasies, impossible and unrealizable, while the desire realized in
dreams is immediately annulled upon waking.

Desire brings into play a series of prohibitions and feelings of fault
that oblige the subject to repress. The debt toward the mother remains
unfulfilled, for the subject says no to the mother, refuses to be her
phallus, the object supposed to be fulfill her desire. Guilt is the fruit of
repression, and is present each time that the subject desires.

Desire offers no relief but is instead a vicious circle: I desire to be
the phallus, but also I don't want to be it, because I don't want to add up
to nothing. If I am not it, I feel guilt for having given up on *my* desire,
which is, in reality, the desire of the Other.

But I am also guilty of being, the phallus. If I *am* it—if I have the
illusion of being it, or do everything I can in order to be it—then I also
feel guilty. I have gone to a forbidden place, that of incest.[21] And here
again, I am giving up on *my* desire, completely submitting myself to
the Other's desire and making my desire correspond, without the least
compromise, to the desire of the Other. Lacan emphasizes the tragi-
comic dimension of desire when he says it is directed by the phallus: "A
preliminary sounding of the space of comedy shows it is less a question
of a triumph than of a futile or derisory play of vision. However little
time I have thus far devoted to the comic here, you have been able to
see that there, too, it is a question of the relationship between action
and desire, and of the former's fundamental failure to catch up with
the latter. The sphere of comedy is created by the presence at its center
of a hidden signifier, one that in ancient comedy was there in person,
namely, the phallus."[22]

The repressed returns via the symptom. The symptom guarantees
enjoyment for the subject, while at the same time functioning as a pro-

hibition. In one single trait, these two opposite movements condense incest and its impossibility through punishment: the symptom is lived as a punishment, and it occurs as though incest had been realized. In passing through suffering, the symptom is in the end opposed to incest, after having attempted to realize it. A bulimic subject, for example, realizes the Other's desire through eating, makes itself an object by being devoured by the drive. But it is rapidly punished with the suffering that this dependence-enjoyment involves: its body is abysmal, having lost its phallic function. The body annihilated after a session of gorging has stopped being a body; the self-destructive thrusting demolishes a body that can no longer be a phallus for the Other. Or then it will be, but in the form of waste: a trash-body, demolished by the Other's desire. Thanks to the bulimic symptom, the body enjoys and suffers, is given and not, is and is not the phallus. The subject says at once yes and no with its symptom, the painful compromise with an impossible desire.

It is only with difficulty that the subject rids itself of its symptom, as the latter is an enjoyable [jouissive] repetition of a desire that insists in its will to reduce the body to nothing. The symptom is the "witness" of the repressed body. The body, as Lacan says, that scares us, and that is made present in its function for the drives; the avatar of the rejected and then repressed phallus.

The phallus (Φ) directs two apparently distinct systems which analysis shows to be tightly linked: the body of the drives [le corps pulsionnel] and the signifying machine. The presence of speech results in a profound change to the needs of the child. By listening to its cries, the mother transforms them into the signifier of demand, which in itself concerns something else. Through demand, the child always "wants" something different than what has been demanded. Lacan writes of demand that "it is demand for a presence or an absence. This is what the primordial relationship with the mother manifests, replete as it is with that Other who must be situated shy of the needs that Other can fulfill. Demand already constitutes the Other as having the 'privilege' of satisfying needs, that is, the power to deprive them of what alone can satisfy them. The Other's privilege here thus outlines the radical form of the gift of what the Other does not have—namely, what is known as love."[23] The question here bears on the signification of demand.[24] What is it that the child wants from its mother? Naturally, that she feed, play with, and walk him . . . but what the child foremost demands is that she leave him in peace. Demand is for a break from all demands!

The child's demand is linked to that of the mother. What is it that the mother wants from him? To please her, it suffices to be the phallus. So the child searches for the signs that might make the Other's desire legible. But its effort is in vain, for, as Moustapha Safouan put it, "the only knowledge is that which, by virtue of the structural primacy of the imaginary in the order of appearance, remains withdrawn in primary repression."[25]

The law of pleasing the mother is implacable: *one must* be the phallus. And that is an exigency impossible to satisfy. The subject succumbs to anxiety, which is about its identification with nothingness, by which the hard truth of its lack might be exposed. To quell this, it is necessary that the subject transform the *one must* into *one must not*. It is here that the symbolic function of the father is revealed to be essential. The father introduces the negative form of the imperative; he introduces, symbolically, an order that relieves: *one must not*. The paternal superego enables the subject to be rid of the *one must be the phallus,* the destructive imperative erected from the maternal superego.

The father is a savior, although he is unbearable. For he is, for the child, the agent of the mother's castration—he demolishes the child as phallus—and, finally, the one who wields the phallus and can satisfy her. But above all, the father is a seducer at the level of fantasy.

In identifying with or seducing him (these actions are equivalent for the unconscious), the subject fantasizes eliminating him, by taking his place in the first case, and by stripping him of his role in the second. But when the father is brought down, the subject also falls . . . because it is no longer protected from the mother! The father then has to be resurrected, both through guilt—the subject pays, with his symptom, for the crime of parricide—and through love. The father must be reconstructed, as a "dead father" (= Name-of-the-Father [Nom-du-Père]) to which one pays homage for protection from the incestuous universe of the mother. The subject is left with no other choice but to love, by forgetting that hidden beneath its love is hatred, toward he who seduced and abandoned it.

The father has succeeded in his function if the subject accepts castration: he gives up being the phallus for the mother and the ideal of omnipotence that is entailed. This is where the desire of the subject begins to be structured. But this is not always the case, as the subject may sometimes prefer to sacrifice its desire in order to shelter its phallus.[26] The subject cannot break with the Other and its desire: it resumes wanting and infinitely persists, to be the its phallus. The child dreams of *being* the phallus because she senses that what she *has* is never sufficient. Each time that the subject returns to this regressive life, it refuses its castration and denies every desire that is not for power, and determined by its idealization and its phallic aspirations.

In its imaginary function, the phallus is a precious object. The masculine homosexual yields it: the phallus conjoins the signifier of desire with the sign, the erect penis. The phallus functions as an object that is always absent or elsewhere: it is at once what the subject does the most to preserve and that of which it believes itself deprived.

In *Desire and Its Interpretation*, Lacan explains that "the function of the object—which is uniquely the object of desire in that it is the endpoint of fantasy—is to take the place of that of which it has been symbolically deprived. . . . What is [this function]? It is from the phallus that the object gets the function that it has in fantasy, and that desire, with fantasy as support, constitutes."[27] Later in the seminar, he further states that "the character of the object inasmuch as it is the object of desire, we should therefore go look for it where human experience points us, indicating it in its most paradoxical form—I am naming what we commonly call the fetish. . . . There is indeed a community of sense in the usage of the word fetish, but for us, that which should be given priority is the accent that must be preserved on the object of desire, which is something that defines it first and foremost as being borrowed from the material signifier."[28]

In fetishism, an arousing, imaginary object becomes the phallus: the phallus is identified with this object, which moves into the place of its absence.[29] The fetish is, as Freud states, a substitute for the mother's phallus, which the small child believes in on account of identifying with it.[30] The subject is in need of a fetish in order not to be the phallus. Finally, the fetish, which plays the role of providing a phallus for the mother, distances and protects the subject from the identification with the phallus. The fetish takes the subject's place, saving it from this annihilating identification. In this sense, the fetish also holds a function that is symbolic, not simply imaginary, as seemed to be the case on the first reading.

We find ourselves back before the mother-child-phallus triad. As we already saw, the child is hung on the mother by its desire for her desire that it identify with the imaginary object of the latter desire, inasmuch as the mother symbolizes that object with the phallus. The phallus emerges, then, not as a symbol but as an image, a quasi-lure, that enters the place of lack and occludes—disclaims—maternal castration. In this sense, objects of desire always somehow possess the structure of the fetish. As Lacan explains in *The Object Relations* seminar, every metonymic object is a lure, in that it acts as a screen.[31] Desire is always somewhere else.

The imaginary phallus functions to dissimulate castration. In his adoration of the object, the fetishist denies castration. But not entirely: although the phallus is supposed to fill lack, it ends up exposing it. In fetishism, castration is thus at once affirmed and denied.[32] The fetish reveals the true nature of the phallus: an agitated nothing underneath a pair of panties, a camouflaged cleft *[béance]*.

The Lacanian conception of the phallus shows the vanity of idealizations and dreams of power. Because human beings speak, their needs deviate into desires. The subject is barred ($), and the phallus represents the bar that divides it. The phallus is the signifier of the Other's desire, but it is also the symbol of the loss of the other—the ideal—suffered by the subject during primordial repression. This loss corresponds to castration, after which it is no longer distinguished from the phallus as signifier of absence and nothing. "The subject is the phallus, but the subject is, of course, not the phallus," as Lacan maintains in *Desire and Its Interpretation*.[33] He then adds that "it can be said that the decisive moment, around which the assumption of castration turns, is this: yes, it can be said that [the subject] is and is not the phallus, but he is not without having it."[34]

Lacan stresses the close relation between the phallus and castration (both of which, it should not be forgotten, are represented with the same symbol, Φ). For both sexes, the assumption of castration means saying no to the possibility of *being* the phallus. And it is only secondarily that *having* it becomes possible. Having it requires a "lack of being it" *[le manque à l'être]*. This lack of being *it* is displaced, in metonymic fashion, by a lack of having it *[l'avoir]*. In order to be that which is lacking in the Other (or in the other) of love, what the subject is not (-φ) leads it to seek a supplement for being at the level of having, *a*.[35] But this supplement of enjoyment (*a*) will never compensate for the initial deficit in being, which results from castration.

Having (it) is not better than not having (it) when the problem concerns being (it). Being the phallus is a structural impossibility. But love consists of this mirage of fantasy structured in a phallic dialectic of being and having, in which the more the subject is on the side of being (the phallus), the less he has it, and the more he is located on the register of having, the less he is the phallus that the Other lacks. As Lacan writes in "The Direction of the Treatment," "the phallus, its receiving and giving, is equally impossible for the neurotic, whether he knows that the Other does not have it, or that the Other does have it, because in both cases the neurotic's desire is elsewhere—to be it. And whether male or female, man must accept to have and not have it, on the basis of the discovery that he isn't it."[36]

There is, then, a relationship between castration and the things of this world. Paradoxically, it is only when the subject comes to accept castration—in other words, when he manages to leave behind his phallic being—that he encounters and succeeds at acquiring the plurality of objects of the world.[37] Objects that he can have or not have, and (perhaps) enjoy—or at least desire.

5
That Singular
Cause of Desire

Cézanne wants to represent the *object* in painting. Not in the sense that he wishes to imitate it, rendering the objects he paints similar to those in reality. Rather, Cézanne endeavors to show what an object is in itself, whether an apple, a mountain, or someone seated at a table playing cards.

When Heidegger speaks of what makes a thing a thing, he states that "thingness must be something unconditioned *[Un-bedingtes]*."[1] Thingness is present with the thing and also in the thing, but it at the same time escapes us. We can only draw near to the Thing by being distanced from it. In other words, the Thing presents itself to us by slipping off. The paradox is unavoidable. "The thingness of the thing," as Heidegger says, "remains concealed, forgotten. The nature of the thing never comes to light, that is, it never gets a hearing. . . . not only are things no longer admitted as things, but they have never yet at all been able to appear to thinking as things."[2]

The real of the Thing is within the thing, but remains unknown. This real of the Thing is what Cézanne seeks to represent in painting: his technique of suppressing precise contours and of prioritizing color over line makes it so that the object is no longer covered, in the impressionist fashion, in flecks and as though it were softly illumined from inside.[3] Light emanates from the object, giving it an impression of solidity and materiality. By passing through the sensations of the artist, the object reveals itself. This is what leads Maurice Merleau-Ponty to say that Cézanne's painting is a paradox: it searches for reality, the objective, but without leaving sensation, the subjective.[4] There is no break in his work between subject and object: the subjective is blended with the objective, or better, the objective, the order of thought, can only be revealed by the subjective, the perception of the artist. The result is that Cézanne's apples are truer and more real than apples found in reality.

How is it possible for an artistic representation to unveil the real of the Thing more than the thing itself? From Lacan's perspective, the artist raises the object to the dignity of the Thing, the object of art not having the same value as the object of reality. The art object in its absoluteness is withdrawn from the field that the symbolic elaborates in conformity with the pleasure principle, and then deported to an absolute place.

In *The Ethics of Psychoanalysis,* Lacan states that "a work of art always involves encircling the Thing."[5] He adds, soon after, "Of course, works of art imitate the objects they represent, but their end is certainly not to represent them. In offering the imitation of an object, they make something different out of that object. Thus they only pretend to imitate. The object is established in a certain relationship to the Thing and is intended to encircle and to render both present and absent."[6]

In Lacanian theory, the Thing is the real, the real in tension with all the representations, both symbolic and imaginary, of the subject. The Thing is neither any more knowable nor any more symbolizable than the Kantian thing-in-itself *(Ding an sich),* although it is not the outer limit, as is the case in philosophy, of transcendental thought.

Access to the Thing can be had only in an illusory way. Yet artistic creation, or sublimation, makes an incursion beyond the pleasure principle possible: something of the order of the real is re-presented in the artwork. Lacan offers that "at the moment that Cézanne paints his apples, it is clear that in painting those apples, he is doing something different from imitating apples—even though his final manner of imitating them, which is the most striking, is primarily oriented toward a technique of presenting the object. But the more the object is presented in the imitation, the more it opens up the dimension in which illusion is destroyed and aims at something else. Everyone knows that there is a mystery in the way Cézanne paints apples, for the relationship to the real as it is renewed in art at that moment makes the object appear purified; it involves a renewal of its dignity."[7]

It is not simply a question of rendering the object more beautiful, in the Kantian sense of the term. Kant distinguishes the beautiful from the agreeable, that which pleases and gives pleasure by virtue of purely subjective causes. But the beautiful remains linked to pleasure and satisfaction, even when this is disinterested. Kantian beauty is always of the order of perfection: ideal, moral, and pure in some way.

The sublime, in contradistinction, can be encountered in an un-formed object. "The sublime is awe-inspiring greatness *(magnitudo reverenda),*" Kant affirms in *Anthropology from a Pragmatic Point of View,* "in extent or degree which invites approach (in order to mea-sure our powers against it); but the fear that in comparison with it we will disappear in our own estimation is at the same time a deterrent. And if we ourselves are in a safe place, the collecting of our powers to grasp the appearance, along with our anxiety that we are unable to measure up to its greatness."[8] Kant is referring here to the sensations sparked by natural phenomena, but his remark equally applies to artis-tic production.

The sublime is something that surpasses us, that is beyond what can be imagined. It nonetheless touches us, making us participate in its greatness.[9] Yet Kant speaks in this passage as though we could wit-ness the phenomena of the sublime from the outside, in safety; that we could look at one of Munch's paintings, or watch a storm or a per-formance of *Hamlet,* at a remove, detached from nature or art as spec-tacle. But we are of course never entirely safe before art.

In "Psychopathic Characters on the Stage," Freud observes that there is displeasure in watching tragedy, and that this results from our resistance to it—or at least from the resistance to it put up by our unconscious.[10] Freud interprets this resistance as the direct effect of repression. The artwork exposes us to the manifestation of some-thing that belongs to the real, and on account of which repression is undertaken. But the real cannot be evaded, and re-presents itself in the enigma of the artwork; this is why we are so attracted, even over-whelmed, by certain instances of art.

Lacan's notion of beauty is entirely different, as it is always of a piece with pain, devastation, decay—with destruction.

Let us look again at Cézanne's apples. They are at once represented apples—red, green, and in a particular arrangement in the painting—and something else, another thing. Is this other thing the Thing? Not quite: as Lacan states, the art object is made "in order to encircle and to render both present and absent" the Thing. The apples do just that; or better, they render the Thing present in its absence. Cézanne's ap-ples are the synthesis of the Thing and the represented objects, the apples in reality. In other words, they are that other thing, the "some-thing of the real" in the work. But that raises the question of what

synthesis means here, of how the unity of two elements of a heteroge-
neous nature can be realized. How to join, that is, an a priori element,
the Thing, to an empirical element, the representation of apples?
The art object recalls the object-cause of desire, "object *a*," in Lacan's
theory. This object-cause is, to continue speaking in Kantian terms, a
synthesis,[11] a mediating element: on the one hand, it is homogeneous
with the faculty of a priori desire—it proceeds from the uncondi-
tionedness of the Thing—and, on the other, it is linked to the object
that we desire in reality, the metonymic object of the signifying chain.
The function of this mediating element is to render empirical objects
desirable: in its absence, no object will be desirable, and desire will lose
its anchoring in reality.[12]

Just as Cézanne's apples are irreducible to imitations of real apples,
the object-cause of desire is not the object desired in reality. Desire
derives *[dérive]* from the Thing, which is not an empirical object but
the condition of possibility of every desire. The Thing is never given as
an object of desire. Enjoyment is structurally impossible: the Thing is
not accessible to desire.

In *The Ethics of Psychoanalysis,* Lacan states on this point that "the
Thing . . . is, by virtue of its structure, open to being represented by *[est
ouverte dans sa structure à être représentée par]* . . . the Other thing."[13]
This "other thing" is, according to my hypothesis, the object *a*. The object *a really* represents the lacking Thing. As the letter *a*, the Thing, in
being absent, in yielding its place to its absence, ends up being identified with that absence, the object *a*. For this reason, the object *a* is
the real representation of the Thing, as it contains the *presence* of the
Thing, even if it only constitutes the *absence* of the Thing that it pretends to represent. The object-cause of desire, like the art object, is
made, it should be repeated, "to encircle, to render both present and
absent" the Thing.

The object *a*, it should be specified, is the real elaborated in the
symbolic, namely, enjoyment that has been poured into the place pre-
scribed to it by the signifier, modulated in a hole, in the cavity already
prepared for it. The very concept of the object *a*, which of course is
not a signifier, nonetheless belongs to the regime of domination of the
signifier. The object *a* is necessarily bound to the signifying chain, indissolubly joined to the object desired in reality, and yet it is also at the
same time somewhere else. The object *a* is not itself an element of this

chain[14] but is instead intimately excluded from the signifying chain: it is "extimate" [*extime*].[15]

Lacan invents this neologism, "extimate," in order to define the character of the object *a*: what is most alien and most disturbing for each of us, but also the most intimate. And it is in anxiety[16]—that way of encountering the pure lack of the Thing—that the subject touches what is most intimate and originary in itself, this cause of desire.[17] Lacan writes that "the true, if not the good subject, the subject of desire—seen as much in the light of fantasy as in the hiding place beyond his ken—is nothing other than the Thing, which is and of itself is what is closest to him while escaping him more than anything else."[18] It is in the lack-of-being [*manque-à-être*] that the subject rediscovers itself in its incessant lacking of lack. The subject at the same time appears and is abolished, as if the lack-of-being is lacking to itself.

The subject sustains itself on account of its lack—that is, its desire. Recall that in "The Direction of the Treatment and the Principles of Its Power," Lacan speaks of desire as the metonymy of lack. In correlation with lack, the little "a" appears, an essential, radical positivity. (Lacan never writes "minus little *a*," i.e., (*-a*).)

Lacan indicates that "on the plane of the unconscious, *a*, which is not a symbol and which is a real element of the subject, is that which intervenes in order to support that moment, in a synchronic sense, when the subject fails to designate itself at the level of an instance which is, precisely, that of desire."[19] The object *a* is the cause of desire: the desire of the subject cannot be reduced to an empirical object, as it results from the structural lack of the Thing. The object *a* animates the entire symbolic and imaginary drift [*dérive*] of desire, but without ever being identifiable with any of the signifiers of the symbolic chain, nor with an image or ideal: desire remains equal to itself in the variability of all its forms.

In the era of the seminars *The Object Relation* (1956–57) and *The Formations of the Unconscious* (1957–58), Lacan attributes an infinite dimension to desire that he subsequently rejects. He is already affirming in *Desire and Its Interpretation* (1958–59) that "desire which is floating along, somewhere, but always in the beyond of the Other, is subject to a certain regulation, to a certain level, one might say to a fixation—that is determined."[20] But it is above all in *Anxiety* (1962–63) that Lacan definitively spells out his position. "It is even insofar as we, subjects of the unconscious, are stamped in this way by finitude that *our own lack can be desire, finite desire*. It looks to be indefinite, because lack, participating as it always does in some emptiness, can be filled in several ways. . . . From this perspective, what I would say is that the classic, moralistic, though not really theological, dimension of the infinity of desire has absolutely to be cut down to size."[21] Finally, Lacan will further state, in *The Four Fundamental Concepts of Psychoanalysis* (1964), that "if, in the register of a traditional psychology, stress is laid on the uncontrollable, infinite character of human desire—seeing in it the mark of some divine slipper that has left its imprint on it—what analytic experience enables us to declare is rather the limited function of desire."[22]

Lacan's two theses are equally valuable, and also complementary. The cause of desire is always the same: the object *a* is connected to the real, which sets desire in motion. It is, in this sense, a fixed point for the subject, which means not that it interrupts the infinity of the desiring quest but rather that it can stabilize desire, once and for all, fixing it on a goal or object which then becomes immutable.

The cause of desire, the object *a,* is nonsubjectivizable, as it cannot go out of us with speech. It is permanently docked in the unconscious: we cannot make it conscious in the same way as the will can be. What can be said belongs to the infinity of desire; one can express desires to have children, or to live in Paris, or to be a hairdresser or actress. That is, desires and objects that change can be expressed, but the *cause* of desire, its unconscious kernel, stays the same: the fixity of the cause of desire does not entail the fixity of desire and of the objects pursued in reality.[23]

Object and signification are structurally equivalent. Every signification is phallic: because of metonymy, the chain is structured such that signification flees. The phallus is the aspect of the imaginary that represents the elusive, and it is above all not the cause of desire. In *Transference,* Lacan speaks of the *agalma* as "the peak of the obscurity" into which the subject plunges in relation to its desire. And he remarks, in "Introduction to the Names-of-the-Father Seminar," that the "*agalma* is that object which the subject believes that his desire aims at, and through which he presses to an extreme the misrecognition of the object as cause of his desire. Such is the frenzy of Alcibiades, and Socrates's dismissal of him: *Concern yourself with your soul* means:

Acknowledge that what you are pursuing is nothing other than what Plato will later turn into your soul, namely your image. Realize that the function of that object is in the order not of a goal, but rather of a cause of death, and prepare your mourning of it. It is only your image. Then will you know the paths of your desire."[24] The *agalma* is only the imaginary face of the object of desire, not its cause. The object *a* is an object without image and without consistency; it is equivalent to its own lack. It is the object as an incarnation of lack (*a l-φ*) that turns the missing object into the object that is more real than all the rest. Lacan will even say that "the object *a* is that object which supports the subject's relation to what is not."[25]

In *Anxiety,* Lacan conceives the object *a* as a "remainder": "I've been teaching you to bind desire to the function of the cut, and to bring it into a certain relationship with the function of the remainder. This remainder is what sustains desire and animates it, and is what we have learnt to ascertain in the analytic function of the partial object. The lack to which satisfaction is linked, however, is something else."[26]

There is a difference between *the lack of satisfaction,* that which is never satisfied with satisfaction, and *the remainder as cause of desire.* The object must be forbidden for it to be desired. The enjoyment of the object, however, brings no satisfaction. On the contrary, it can induce disgust.[27] Infinite desire (for the object) unfailingly *[immanquablement]* leads back to dissatisfaction. But lack is not a lack of the object, as it is not the object that the subject is lacking[28] but the reverse: lack is revealed by satisfaction.

The child, as we have seen, desires by way of the desire of the mother. This desire has no other object than the signifier of recognition, or in other words, the phallus. The object *a* is the remainder of what in the desire of the other is symbolized by the phallus. Lacan explains that "the *a,* the object of desire, in its nature is a residue, a remainder. It is the residue left by the being to which the subject is confronted as such, in every possible demand. . . . And it is through it that the object rejoins the real."[29]

The infinity of desire, impossible desire—which objects in experience never satisfy—is not the cause of desire. That, again, is the object *a,* the remainder of the desire of the phallus as well as the remainder of the Thing (the Thing is completely ignorant of any limit or relinquishment), which is its mover. For the desiring subject, all that is left are

phantasmatic objects—"other things," as Lacan calls them—that turn
out upon attainment to be marked by difference, deception, and loss
in comparison with the Thing. The residual and compensatory enjoyment of the object *a* is indica-
tive of enjoyment "through lack," for enjoyment must be negotiated
with the Other, who gives only by leaving. The object *a* as, per Lacan's
expression, surplus enjoyment [*plus-de-jouir*] becomes the measure of
the lack of enjoyment, and it is in this sense that it is the cause of desire. Surplus enjoyment is a remainder of the enjoyment spared from
signifying mortification, but of which the signifier nevertheless con-
serves the imprint. (But again, we will proceed in order.)

Marx's theory of surplus value is repurposed by Lacan in his further development of the object *a*.[30] According to Marx, the processes
of capitalist production undertaken in order to yield profit instead produce only surplus value. Surplus value is not synonymous with profit
or enjoyment, as enjoyment is lost in those processes, transformed into
work or supplementary productive machines (hours of surplus work
for the worker and the purchase of better mechanical equipment for
the boss's factory). Note that no one enjoys in the capitalist system:
profit is infinitely reinvested.[31]

Surplus value regulates, in a sense, the question of enjoyment's relation to desire. The object *a* is surplus enjoyment *(Mehrlust),* the "homologue," Lacan says, of Marx's surplus value *(Mehrwert)*:[32] "*Mehrlust*
[is] obviously homological in relation to *Mehrwert,* not analogical."[33]
If analogy is situated between the univocal and the equivocal, on a
degree of proportional magnitude,[34] Lacan prefers to use "homology"
to qualify the relation between surplus value and the object *a*: the homology between surplus value and surplus enjoyment is located on the
register of the processes of the leaking and loss of enjoyment.

Mehrlust and *Mehrwert* alike denounce a loss of enjoyment, but
they cannot be identified.[35] *Mehrlust,* as an effect of the loss of enjoyment, becomes the cause of desire and eventually (but only partly)
recuperates it. In contrast, *Mehrwert,* as Marx shows, is only class exploitation, a consequence of capitalist organization against which the
proletariat must struggle.[36]

Surplus enjoyment, the residual enjoyment that reveals that total
enjoyment is lacking, is the motor of desire: the sur*plus* [*plus*] that is at
the same time what the subject loses, its *less*—that is, the "less *x*," the

debited usurary value, what is delivered to the Other and its insatiable desire. Surplus value, too, is a motor, but of the capitalist machine. It is the surplus of value produced by the worker and immediately snatched away by the Other, the capitalist, as stipulated by the labor contract. The Other allows the laborer a remainder of pleasure only in the form of his wages, so as to relaunch the process and compel him to return to work the next day.

Surplus enjoyment is obtained from the transfer of enjoyment— enjoyment as "surplus," "fulfilling," but which never compensates for the loss of enjoyment. Surplus enjoyment brings enjoyment while maintaining lack, and it is for this reason that the subject escapes from the alienating machine of the search for total enjoyment, when surplus value remains entangled in the capitalist machine, as means of reinvestment.

If Lacan spoke, in 1969's "D'une réforme dans son trou," of a homology between surplus value and surplus enjoyment, he identified them in that same year, in *The Other Side of Psychoanalysis*: "If by means of this relentlessness to castrate himself that he had, he hadn't computed this surplus enjoyment, if he hadn't converted it into surplus value, in other words, if he hadn't founded capitalism, Marx would have realized about surplus value that *it* is surplus enjoyment."[37] If one can speak of surplus value and surplus enjoyment as homologous processes where the loss of enjoyment is concerned, they nonetheless remain unamenable to being identified.

At the moment of that seminar, Lacan does not regard surplus value as the effect of relations of production (labor-capital) and the exploitation of the proletariat. There is not for him any remainder in surplus value: the capitalist machine turns relentlessly, and the lost enjoyment is reinvested in the infinite process of accumulation, which denies any possibility of lack. The same does not apply, however, for the object *a*, as it is both a remainder and it sets desire back in motion, a desire that passes through castration and makes the subject falter over its lack.

Although its exact worth would be difficult to calculate, surplus value in the capitalist machine is completely taken up and accounted for, whereas the object *a* exits the field of measure and calculation. In capitalism, everything is *more more more [plus plus plus],* while desire stumbles against a *less* that persistently returns.

In *D'un autre à l'Autre,* Lacan insists on the value of the wager:

"Whatever [I stake] in a game . . . I have already lost, or I am not at all playing."[38] Now that which is staked is desire, the object *a*. That stake wagered, the object *a*, is worthless, as desire has neither use nor exchange value.[39] But can it then be said that desire has no value at all, since it does not enter the dynamics of use or exchange value?

An estimate of desire cannot be provided. In this way, the value of desire rejoins that of proletarian labor, whose worth, as the fruit of effort and suffering, is unmeasurable.

The Thing is of course the unconditioned of desire, pure lack, and the unsayable, but it is not a transcendent entity. In "The Freudian Thing," Lacan refers to the Latin *res*, "thing" in the sense of a material entity as well as that of a cause.[40] The unconscious always speaks to us of the Thing, of the subject's real. For instance, the dream, as Freud says, opens the road to the unconscious and is in connection with the traumatic real.[41]

Lacan, for his part, recalls Freud's famous sentence "Wo Es war, soll Ich warden": "Where it was, there I shall be" *[Dans le lieu du ça, le sujet doit advenir]*. In Freud's second topology, this "it," aka the id, is defined as the locus of the drives and is thus closely related to the object *a*. The Freudian id tallies with the *a* of Lacanian script: there is nothing literal that might correspond to Freud's id, just as the cause of desire resists the signifier.

The id and the unconscious are in a relation of reciprocal implication. "It speaks," Lacan says, adding, "it is not about him [the subject] that you must speak to him, for he can do this well enough himself, and in doing so, it is not even to you that he speaks. While it is to him that you must speak, it is literally about something else—that is about some-thing other than what is at stake when he speaks of himself—which is the thing that speaks to you. Regardless of what he says, the thing will remain forever inaccessible."[42] There is, then, a linkage between Thing, real, id, and the unconscious.

According to Lacan, "the unconscious shows us the gap through which neurosis recreates a harmony with the real—a real that may not well be determined."[43] Of course the Thing is not the unconscious; the subject preserves no trace of the Thing, whereas the unconscious "is written."

In his first topography, Freud calls "the unconscious" the agency constituted of repressed elements that have been refused access to consciousness. Repression is a process that is accomplished twice-over, through a "primal repression," *Urverdrängung,* and "repression properly speaking," *Verdrängung.* The first instance corresponds to an expulsion *(Ausstoßung),* a pushing away of the phallic signification from the subject's body: the traumatic real is ejected to the outside by the subject. The second moment of repression concerns the ordering of the leftovers of this expulsion, namely, "the mnesic traces *(Errinerungspur),* which hold an indirect relation to what was put to the side."[44] (From a topographic point of view, these traced are pushed below by repression.)

In his second topography, the term "unconscious" qualifies the it (while being partially applied to the ego and superego).[45] But we should no longer confuse Lacan's "unconscious structured like a language" with the id; we may speak of a relation but not of an identity. There is certainly some continuity between the it of the second topography and the unconscious of the first, but it is really a question of two distinct modes: the it is a *disorganized* inscription, and the unconscious structured like a language is a writing that is, notably, *structured* and *organized* from traces, and that can be read from the construction/deconstruction of fantasy that occurs in analysis. Traversing the fantasy allows for the deciphering of mnemic trances and affects but not of *Ausstoßung,* the expulsed real—the Thing—which remains forever unrecoverable.

Lacan's formula "it speaks" unifies the it and the unconscious structured like a language. This is evident, for instance, in his neologism, from 1973, *lalangue*—"llanguage"—which indicates the space in the unconscious where "enjoyment is deposited."[46] Whence its tie with the it, the locus of the drives. In *Encore,* Lacan will say that "Language is, no doubt, made up of llanguage *[lalangue].* It is knowledge's hare-brained lucubration *[élucubration]* about language. But the unconscious is knowledge, a knowing how to do things *[savoir-faire]* with llanguage. And what we know how to do with llanguage goes well beyond what we can account for under the heading of language."[47] Llanguage is an unconscious writing that bears the traces of the real—the real of the body rejected during primal repression—the deciphering and interpretation of which always proves futile.

In contrast, the unconscious structured like a language undertakes a kind of ordering, which allows for movement across, which is to say the transcription of, different ways of writing the it—that, for example, of the dream: condensation/metaphor, displacement/ metonymy, and so on.

In sum, the unconscious executes the deciphering, always incomplete, approximate, and imperfect, of what remains of llanguage and enables interpretation, which makes meaning but is, at bottom, only a means of masking the truth and thereby shielding the subject from the impact of the real on the ego. Language is protective: enjoyment remains encrypted, even though language is supposed to unveil it.

The object-cause of desire is, as we have seen, a remainder produced by unconscious repression.[48] Repression concerns the Oedipus complex, and the cause of desire is its effect. Although it is paradoxical, the subject finds in the object-cause at once prohibition and desire. That cause, as Gérard Pommier points out, "puts the action of the subject before itself as if that action came first, although it does not but is deduced from being put into relationship with an ensemble,"[49] an ensemble composed of the oedipal triad of mother, father, and phallus. The phallus, as the signifier of absence, takes on as well the function of castration. In its dialectic with the three elements, the phallus makes them hold together.

The remainder, as cause of desire, is there each time that we desire: it sends us back to the first, structural cleft, which is connected to a knowledge that does not know: the *Freudian thing*, from Lacan's point of view. What results is a subject who stumbles over the rock of castration. He cannot know the cause of his desire, the effect of unconscious knowledge. Inasmuch as that subject advances in knowledge (unconscious knowledge as much as knowledge of other kinds), he encounters castration: neither the word that could make him understand it nor the object that could fill it exist. Castration and the cause of desire work move in tandem. The fantasy that responds to desire includes castration, the -φ joined to the object *a* like its shadow. As Lacan states, "the object *a* is most evanescent in its function of symbolizing the central lack of desire, which I have always indicated in a univocal way by the algorithm (-φ) [castration]."[50]

My analysis here has so far concerned desire as it is related to castration, lack, and disbeing—in short, to the limit—but desire is also a force that goes beyond the pleasure principle. It is in this sense that desire makes for such anxiety:[51] it is opposed to pleasure to the extent that it participates in excess, in a perturbation of the homoeostasis that governs pleasure. Desire exposes anxiety to the risk of the encounter with the originary cleft, the real. It proves itself threatening to the subject, who thus feels the need to defend herself.[52]

The danger lies in neither the infinitude of desire nor the deceiving character of an enjoyment that is in truth not one, but rather in the lacking-being [manque-à-l'être] that we encounter in desire and that is constituted, as we saw, by virtue of the fact that desire is desire of the Other. The confrontation with lack is conceived of as imperiling, but it is also our only possibility for encountering our being, which is given as lack and dispossession of self. The writer François Cheng recounts that during a session of his analysis with Lacan, he spoke to the latter of his "experiences of beauty and hell" and that Lacan intervened by saying, "You have lived the extreme gap, so why not widen it further and identify with it?"[53]

For Lacan, there is a correspondence between the object-cause of desire and the object of the drive (the object around which it turns).[54] If we take the breast and excrement as examples, we see that they are not the objects that the subject would have enjoyed and from which he would have subsequently separated. Separation is original; before it, there is neither subject nor object.

Lacan calls the object of the drive the "partial object."[55] For example, the breast, as object of the drive, represents from the subject's perspective only the object "breast." In wanting this "breast," the subject also wants an-Other thing. The object is necessarily partial, so total enjoyment (of no matter which object) is impossible. The partial object concerns the body in its real dimension: the body—necessarily—in pieces,[56] and hence partial.

The drive that brings into play the object a, around which it turns, originates in the body's orifices. The object a possesses the same structure as the orifices: a beating slit or cut. An object fallen from the body, lost. The orifice—mouth, anus, palpebral fissure—is always a cut, an absence. For Lacan, "the very delimitation of the erogenous zone that the drive isolates from the function's metabolism . . . is the result of a cut that takes advantage of the anatomical characteristic of a margin or border: the lips, the 'enclosure of the teeth,' the rim of the anus, the penile groove, the vagina, and the palpebral fissure, not to mention the hollow of the ear."[57]

The objects of the drives participate in the trait of the cut like the bodily orifices: the mammary gland, excrement, phallus, urinary flow, phoneme, gaze, the voice, and the nothing. Lacan pares that list, in the *Anxiety* seminar, to breast, feces, gaze, and voice. This is a reduction done for structural reasons; in reality, the objects of the drive are indefinite.

The drive is not satisfied with the simple possession of an empirical object; it circulates around the object, turns on its inconsistency. "This object," Lacan explains, "which is in fact only the presence of a furrow, of an unoccupable emptiness, Freud tells us, for whichever object, and which we know is only the instance under the form of the lost object small *a*. The object small *a* is not the origin of the oral drive. It is introduced not by way of primitive feeding, but by the fact that no food will ever satisfy the oral drive, if it does not circumambulate the eternally lacking object."[58]

The drive circles the object and remains, even when satisfied by an empirical object, necessarily unsatisfied. It is this impossibility—incompleteness, partiality—that represents, paradoxically, the satisfaction of the drive: failure is success, the only satisfaction.

In "Instincts and Their Vicissitudes," Freud shows that the object is what is most variable in the drive, that the latter is not originally linked to it and that it can be replaced and displaced: "highly important roles are played by this displacement of instinct *[Trieb]*."[59] The drives can replace each other, and exchange their objects as well as their original aims.

Freud also refers to sublimation, the psychic process that accounts for the sexual drive's aptitude for replacing a sexual object with a nonsexual object (scientific, artistic, other socially valuable activities). In sublimation, the initial sexual goal of the object is exchanged for another, nonsexual goal but without any decrease in intensity.

But why does the drive deviate, of necessity, from its path? It seeks to respond to the Other's demand,[60] its goal of reducing the body to the phallus for the Other. Sublimation—the diversion of the drive away from its sexual goal—means to get rid of the annihilating identification with the phallus. In what way? By keeping the phallus at a distance, even while exhibiting it through the work *[oeuvre]* thereby produced. That work takes the place of the body and indicates the gap between phallus and subject.

Lacan calls both the object of the drives (the one that art sublimates) and the object causing desire "object *a*." Should we conclude from this that these two objects are the same? They do have the same origin, which is the Other's desire, but drive and desire are distinct. There has to be voice and gaze, and food and the relation to excrement, if maternal demand is to find expression. But desire manifests beyond this demand.

Desire and drive are knotted, but they also antithetical. The drive turns indefinitely around an object that cannot placate it; it wants enjoyment and knows nothing of castration. But the body rebels against supporting this enjoyment, even as it relentlessly seeks it out (by way of the symptom). The body rejects the possibility of total enjoyment, recoiling in disgust. Inversely, desire, in its tie with prohibition and the assumption of castration, renounces once and for all this same impossible enjoyment; this is where desire is located, on the side of limit and finitude.

The cause of desire is never caught, as the object of the drive is. The cause of desire is impenetrable, which is Freud's scandalous discovery. Spinoza speaks of the misrecognition [*méconnaissance*] of cause in our acts. Like a stone moved by an external cause and persevering in its movement, man believes himself free while proceeding unaware of the cause that determines him: "Conceive . . . that while the stone continues to move, it thinks, and knows that as far as it can, it strives to continue moving. Of course, since the stone is conscious only of its striving, and not at all indifferent, it will believe that it is very free, and that it perseveres in motion for no other cause than because it wills it to. This is that famous human freedom that everyone brags of having, which consists only in this: that men are conscious only of their appetite and ignorant of the causes by which they are determined."[61]

Spinoza's thought invites its rapprochement with the revelation of the analytic cure: the subject knows not the cause of his desire. For Spinoza, this ignorance arises from a lack of knowledge [*méconnaissance*] of absolute determinism rather than the existence of unconscious knowledge. If the unconscious is in large part determined, the subject can all the same loosen that which seems fixed and unshakable: this is the unconscious's *open* character, the unconscious as process and functioning entity, not as substance. The cause of desire, which we do not know how to name, is nevertheless well known to our unconscious, as we are confronted with it in each of our actions: speaking, reading, writing, eating, working, playing, loving . . . At bottom, we mistake ourselves for it, but unwittingly. Life turns around an inaccessible cause—that of desire. The cause of desire is what is most singular, and most impenetrable, in each of us.

6
"Oneself" as Object of Desire and Love

To desire oneself is first of all to desire one's own body. To desire, to love, one's own body as if it were an external (sexual) object—that is, by Freud's definition, narcissism.[1]

To have a body is by no means something self-evident. In *De Anima*, Aristotle regards the *psyché*[2] (which is translated in French as *âme,* soul, as derived from *anima*) and the body as distinct but absolutely indissociable, each being unable to proceed without the other. He demonstrates this throughout the treatise, and provides this very clear example: "We can dismiss as unnecessary the question whether the soul and the body are one: it is as though we were to ask whether the wax and its shape are one, or generally the matter of a thing and that of which it is the matter. Unity has many senses (as many as 'is' has), but the proper one is that of actuality."[3]

Aristotle's theory of hylomorphism shows that there is a "collaboration" between the soul and the body, an accord, something like a "realization" or accomplishment of the two, that is capable of granting unity to form *(morphe)*[4] and matter *(hyle).*

The unity of the body and the psyche can be realized only at an imaginary level. That does not mean that the two agencies *[instances]* are radically separated, per the Cartesian conception. Of more interest to us is the Spinozist theory of "parallelism," according to which body and soul are the same substance, which is expressed, alternatively, as the attribute of the psyche and that of the body.[5]

From a psychoanalytic perspective, body and psyche are not, as hylomorphism states, in harmony with and do not mutually complete each other. They are articulated together owing to the drive, a limit concept introduced by Freud in his metapsychological writings.[6]

The body will always remain inaccessible, foreign to the subject: recall that the body, qua phallus for the Other, is expelled *(Ausstossung),* and language—language that institutes the processes of repression—would make the subject forget its "phallic" body. Psyche and body constitute not the unity or realization of the subject, as Aristotle would have it, but rather its disaggregation: the subject, as Lacan says, is barred (8). The narcissist desires his or her own body, which is unknown, expelled, and repressed, in order to escape the Other's desire.

The body is not its image. The child's body is a body in pieces: broken, fragmented, disaggregated, deprived of motor coordination and the power of speech, and entirely dependent on the Other. The specular image[7] enables the child to find a unity, a *Gestalt*, a kind of ideal achieved form. Through what Lacan calls the "mirror stage": something divided—carved up—in the corporeal real is ideally recomposed at the level of the image. The action of the *imago* offers the divided body a possible solution, remedying the latter's real division with an imaginary unification and mastery. The child identifies itself with the image of its body, loves itself through it. To love its body is to love its own image; body and image are thus confused in the mirror. The subject effectuates on itself or, more exactly, on the image of itself with which it is identified, its drive-investment.

The mirror stage gives the child a body—an imaginary body—to love. "Body" means mastery, power, recognition from the Other, libido, enjoyment . . . Yes, as the imaginary power given by the specular body is the cause of enjoyment. The image of the body is a spot invested with libido: it is the ego ideal, the ego-unity that poses itself as libidinal object.

In the theory of the mirror stage, Lacan combines the Freudian theme of narcissistic identification with the Hegelian theme of recognition as the foundation of the constitution of subjectivity (the "I"). The subject is not constructed, as per Kant, on the basis of some power of synthesizing representations but instead is realized, as per Hegel, through the mediation of the Other. The subject believes itself capable of existing only if it sees itself in the Other. It should be stressed along with Lacan that the Other attests to, certifies, the mirror image: "It is within this see-saw movement, the movement of exchange with the other, that man becomes aware of himself as body, as the empty form of the body. In the same way, everything which is then within him in a pure state of desire, original, unconstituted, and confused, which finds expression in the wailing of a child—he will learn to recognize it inverted in the other."[8] The image of the child in the mirror that its mother carries, which gazes back at the child, is turned toward her with the request that she authenticate its discovery: "It's you!" thus becomes for the child, "It's me."

The child assumes its image on the basis of its identification with itself, but the relation between subject and image is never binary. The child never sees itself with its own eyes, and does so only through those of the Other: "seeing itself" turns into "being seen." Desire is caught in a relation to an imaginary *other* who becomes *Other,* which is how desire acquires its alienating dimension: it is as another *[une autre]* that the subject lives and experiences, as its desire is found on the side of the Other, which dispossess and alienates it. The subject loves another *[une autre]* in the image of itself (that is wanted and recognized by the Other); that is, it loves its ideal double. For the child, then, the Other is not only the different and the external but the alterity that constitutes its identity. It is a question of a fictive identity, one that does not hold up since it is founded on an image rather than on the name—the latter being authenticated through the joint action of recognition (of the Other, of others)[9] in the social bond, on the one hand, and the act (of the subject), on the other.

The image of the body fails to prop up the subject: something in the image is lost, detached from it, as if the ideal unity that recomposes the fragmentation of the body arrives too early for the real of the body, which remains split up and disjoined. This is a passage from a *less*—the body in pieces—to a *more*—the unity realized by the image—back to a *less*: behind the well-constructed image, the body is unmade, decomposed in its inadequate temporality. As Lacan specifies, "the mirror stage is a drama whose internal pressure pushes precipitously from insufficiency to anticipation—and, for the subject caught up in the lure of spatial identification, turns out fantasies that proceed from a fragmented image of the body to what I will call an 'orthopedic' form of its totality—and to the finally donned armor of an alienating identity that will mark his entire mental development with its rigid structure."[10]

The ego *forms itself* by way of the image of its own body, which is only, says Lacan, a surface.[11] Unyieldingly wanting *to be,* carnally, this body entails its disaggregation: the subject again finds itself, through the cutting of regression in the drives, to be a carved and sectioned body, a functional meat destined for the Other's enjoyment (at least if a Name-of-the-Father does not intervene). Desiring to be the body in the mirror—to recognize oneself in it, to identify with it, to love it and thereby to love oneself—demonstrates once again the dependent tie established from the subject to the Other.

In *The Formations of the Unconscious,* Lacan stresses the importance of identification with the signifiers of the paternal matrix ("unary" signifiers), a process that leads from the *Urbild*—the original, phallic image—to the ego ideal. As Lacan's schema R shows (see Figure 4), the child transitions from identifications with different imaginary figures stuck in the relation with the mother (vector *i*-M in the figure) to identifications with signifiers (vector *m*-I) that evolve into the paternal identification that is the ego ideal.[12]

The intervention of the symbolic on the specular axis reveals itself to be fundamental: alienated in its image, the subject can only be reintegrated in the world through speech. "The desire of the Other," Lacan contends, "which is the desire of man, enters into the mediation of language. It is in the other, by the other, that desire is named. It enters into the symbolic relation of *I* and *you,* in a relation of mutual recognition and transcendence, into the order of a law which is already quite ready to encompass the history of each individual."[13]

The mirror stage involves a transition from a relation of equivalence and reciprocity (a passive relation) between the individual and its image to a causal relation: *a′* plays a formative role on *a*; in other words, there is a *real* effect of the image on the body. The subject produces this image that in turn determines it. But in the imaginary, not everything is imaginary: there is symbolic determination on the plane of the imaginary, or in other words, the big Other has a (nonreciprocal and asymmetrical) causal effect on the subject, albeit retroactively inscribed.

The mirror image is thus not only alienating. For Lacan, "the body can't be . . . given to us in a pure and simple way in the mirror. Even in the experience of the mirror, a moment can come about when the image we believe we abide by undergoes modification. If this specular image we have facing us, which is our stature, our face, our two eyes, allows the dimension of our gaze to emerge, the value of the image starts to change—above all if there's a moment when this gaze that appears in the mirror starts not to look at us anymore. There's an *initium,* an aura, a dawning sense of uncanniness which leaves the door open

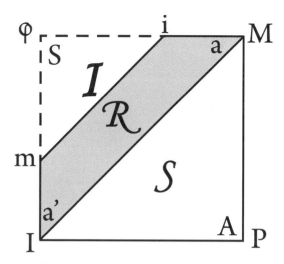

FIGURE 4. Schema R

to anxiety. The passage from the specular image to the double that escapes me is the point at which something occurs."[14]

The gaze, then, is not vision. "What one looks at is what cannot be
seen," Lacan says in *The Four Fundamental Concepts of Psychoanalysis*.[15]
There is manifest visibility, vision, and secret visibility, the gaze.
An unobjectifiable "unobjectivizable object" secretly animates the
movement of seeing. It is no longer me, the ego [*moi—le "moi"*], whom
I see via the gaze of the Other but the nothing that is hidden behind
the surface that is my body, the egoic surface. When discovered, the
nothing—"my" nothing—triggers anxiety. Being looked at makes me
anxious, and yet I want it, and seek the gaze of the Other/other. I wish
to find my body again for a brief instant, before the nothing begins
appearing to me again.

When facing the mirror, the subject contemplates what it forgets
in each moment: a body that does not exist if it is not desired by the
Other, a body that lives solely by virtue of the Other's gaze. The gazing
of the subject at its body becomes the gaze of the Other, and subject
and Other are joined in this latter gaze—the mirror-body is the product of this fusion. For the subject, becoming this body that results from
this double gaze (that of the subject and the Other) signifies being
erased from, falling out of, the image in the mirror—the self-image

that is, as soon it appears, an artifice, a constraining and servile image assembled for the Other.

The subject enjoys this body that attests to the union, via the two gazes, with the Other. The subject enjoys, and then just as quickly disappears: its jubilation about viewing its own body confirms that it is absent (§). "Seeing oneself" becomes "being seen" . . . enjoyment is always fleeting and prohibited. To see oneself is to look for the gaze of the Other, in order to enjoy it: an Other that sees, at the same time as it does my body, my lack.

In Freud's analysis and Lacan's completion of it, narcissism is not assimilable to the myth of Narcissus (such as Ovid's account of it in the *Metamorphoses*). The Lacanian mirror is an orthopedic remedy for the dismemberment [*morcellement*] of the body, whereas Narcissus's mirror is the origin of the drama, of his ruin and death. When Narcissus is sucked into his image, he becomes despondent, loses the exultancy of the child before the mirror.

Narcissus realizes that he is in love with an object that he can never possess. "In his tears," as Gérard Wacjman puts it, "Narcissus in truth embraces the image, that is to say the memory of the object."[16] He jumps into the water because he identifies with the lost object and wants to re-merge with it: like a melancholic who suicides, Narcissus's self-realization is in his death. The drama of Narcissus is that of the One, of the One of the body that was unified in order to become the object of the Other's desire. Narcissus cannot separate from himself, nor therefore can he from the Other. His act of stabbing himself in the chest is little else but an attempt to cut himself in two—to detach his being from his image.[17]

In contrast, the child before the mirror is separated from its image: being outside the mirror, the *I* does not partake in the reflected image. The subject is not made One with its image—the subject is *other* [*autre*] and can encounter the *other*—while Narcissus is prisoner to his mirror image, and can only ever know narcissistic love. The Other is always itself; the One—phallic plenitude—is entirely realized. Narcissus thus does not stay infatuated with himself for long, as he is soon devastated by the fact of being the object of both his own desire and, by consequence, that of the Other.

If the tragedy of Narcissus is that of the unified body, the tragedy of narcissism is that of unity lost. In narcissism, unification is imaginary, the body remains partitioned into several detached pieces that irremediably seek reunion. The Renaissance conception of beauty was formed in response to fragmentation [*morcellement*] and recalls the mirror stage. The painter task's was to reunite the most beautiful parts of a series of bodies, and thereby form an ideal, phantasmatic unity.

The mirror stage is a sort of *bricolage,* and constitutes the antechamber of subjectivation. In the narcissism of the mirror, the subject recognizes itself through its misrecognition of the reality [*du réel*] of its state. Just as the ideal of beauty remains unattainable for the painter, so the image of its own body is always incomplete, impotent, and insufficient for the subject. The image of the body fails to sustain to the last the identity of the subject. Something in that image is lost by the subject, and becomes detached from him: the ideal unity that recomposes the fragments of the body arrives too early for the real of that body, which thus remains discordant [*desaccordé*] and in pieces.

The mirror image's dependence on the Other has already been stressed: subject and Other merge in the mirror—the moment of jubilation—and the body of the mirror is the product of this imaginary fusion. But the subject is not its image, as the two do not make the One of Narcissus's body!

The symptom that is inscribed on the body enables the subject to break the corporeal surface of the mirror image: the body can exist, finding life at last in suffering its symptoms. This suffering is also enjoyment, as the symptom shows the enjoyment-suffering of a body pulled between providing and refusing the Other's enjoyment. The symptom's contradiction simultaneously realizes and destroys the copula with the Other. But the subject is saved: the fictive unity of the body is unequivocally demolished by the symptom.

In 1905, while editing the texts gathered as *Three Essays on the Theory of Sexuality,* Freud draws an opposition between drives that are sexual and those that are self-preserving, which he also calls "ego drives." The ego drives are not sexually invested but are in conflict with those that are. Now if the ego drives are not of the same kind as the sexual drives, then how can one speak, in the context of narcissism, of narcissistic libido or ego libido?[18] Even while preserving the duality, Freud introduces a new distinction between object libido and ego libido.[19]

The ego of "On Narcissism: An Introduction" (1914) is not the ego of the "Project for a Scientific Psychology" (the function of which is inhibiting), nor is it the psychic agency of *The Ego and the Id* (1923). It is nevertheless in this latter text that Freud affirms that "the ego is not sharply separated from the id, its lower portion merges into it. . . . The ego is that part of the id which has been modified by the direct influence of the external world."[20]

Freud conceives of the id as the "great reservoir of the libido," and the part of the ego merged with the id participates in it.[21] Freud had already stated, in *Beyond the Pleasure Principle,* that psychoanalysis, "by studying the libidinal development of children in its earliest phases, came to the conclusion that the ego is the true and original reservoir of libido, and that it is only from that reservoir that libido is extended to its objects. . . . A portion of the ego-instincts was seen to be libidinal; sexual instincts—probably alongside others—operated in the ego."[22] We are thus forced to admit the thesis that "narcissistic libido," as the word itself indicates, is sexually invested.

The unity of the body before the mirror, which the child builds because of the Other's approval, corresponds to the stage of the construction of the ego in Freudian theory. For Freud, the ego is closely related to the corporeal envelope: "The ego is first and foremost a bodily ego."[23] For him, too, the ego is the unified body that the child constructs in the mirror before the Other. As Freud puts it, "a unity comparable to the ego cannot exist in the individual from the start; the ego has to be developed. The auto-erotic drives, however, are there from the very first; so there must be something added to auto-eroticism—a new psychical action—in order to bring about narcissism."[24]

In the autoeroticism of precocious infantile sexual behavior, the partial drives finds satisfaction without recourse to an external object or making reference to the image of the unified body.[25] Narcissism, on the other hand, designates the retroversion of libido onto the ego: libido is withdrawn from objectal investments and affixed to the ideal image of the subject. This phase is contemporaneous with the appearance of an initial imaginary unification of the subject—that is, of the construction of the ego. In autoeroticism, the sexual drives are satisfied in anarchic fashion and independently of each other, while in narcissism, by contrast, it is the ego in its totality that is taken as the object of desire and love.

In Freud's texts from 1910 to 1915, the phase of primary narcissism is situated between that of autoeroticism and that of (external) object love and corresponds to the mirror stage in Lacan. After elaborating the second topography, Freud defines "primary narcissism" as an initial state of life that is prior even to the constitution of the ego, and the archetype of which would be the intrauterine state. At this point, the distinction between autoeroticism and narcissism is discarded.

Freud conceives of two separate moments in narcissism: primary, which we just saw, and secondary. It is on the basis of an original identification of the subject with its ego that the other imaginary identifications constitutive of the ego emerge. Fundamentally, this ego, this—surface—image that is the ego, is outside the subject, other to it. Secondary narcissism is secondary to this operation:[26] the subject invests in an object external to itself, an object that cannot be confused with its identity. Nevertheless, this object is supposed to be itself: an external object that is confused with its ego, which is, in turn, the image for which the subject takes itself, along with all the blindness and alienation entailed.

The ideal ego is built up on the basis of this desire and lure. Freud writes, in "On Narcissism: An Introduction," that "this ideal ego [Idealich] is now the target of the self-love which was enjoyed in childhood by the actual ego [das wirkliche Ich]. The subject's narcissism makes its appearance displaced on to this new ideal ego [dieses neue ideale Ich], which, like the infantile ego, finds itself possessed of every perfection that is of value. . . . [Man] is not willing to forego the narcissistic perfection of his childhood; and when, as he grows up, he is disturbed by the admonitions of others and by the awakening of his own critical judgment, so that he can no longer retain that perfection, he seeks to recover it in the new form of an ego ideal [Ichideal]. What he projects before him as his ideal is the substitute for the lost narcissism of his childhood in which he was his own ideal."[27]

The transition from the ego ideal—the mythical state of unbreached narcissism, which is confused with autoeroticism—to the future ideal ego creates a fracture in that narcissism. The child must come down from its pedestal. Perfection is suddenly discovered to be beyond itself; it has to desire and love a perfect image of itself that does not yet exist, and that can only be realized in the future. The ideal ego may give the impression of continuing the ego ideal's labor of reconstituting the lost position of perfection of the beginning of infancy, but it is, in reality, in strong conflict with that state.

The ego ideal pulls the subject backward, while the ideal ego projects it ahead; that is, the subject identifies with the father in order to escape from maternal demand.[28] And it finds itself mired in this spatio-temporal locus that prevents it from exiting the loop of ego-love. The subject has to make do with these two egos, follow each of its ideas by pursuing satisfaction in the ways specific to each. It is as if an energetic scale existed between these two investments, and the subject, in search of a self-love that passes through both of these divergent ideals, ends up split between the two agencies.

We are now before the oedipal dynamic. For the girl as much as for the boy, a change of object occurs following maternal castration: the object of love is no longer the mother but the father. The child will also eventually renounce love for the father: the boy, because of his anxiety about being seduced by the father and feminized, and the girl, on account of her disillusionment about him not satisfying her. The child withdraws love and identifies with the emblems of paternal power, the ideal ego.

"When the ego assumes the features of the object," Freud writes in *The Ego and the Id,* "it is forcing itself, so to speak, upon the id as a love-object and is trying to make good the id's loss by saying: 'Look, you can love me too—I am so like the object.'"[29] Freud's position in 1923 is in apparent contradiction with what he had previously advanced, or more simply, he considers the ego ideal to be sexually invested, whereas in the ideal ego, the phase of self-love projected ahead into the superimposition of the image proper and that of the perfected ideal (of the paternal matrix), there would thus be no sexual investment . . . The question remains open.

The child cannot satisfy the mother, and thus identifies with the (ideal) father in order to respond to her demand. The father of identification is also the one who enjoys the mother, and by consequence, to identify with him is to suppress him in fantasy and take his place at the mother's side.[30] The libido is reactivated, as the father's death excites it . . . The incestuous goal is present from the outset in this second form of identification (with the father or the ideal ego); it is just misrecognized by the subject.

Masturbation is an attempt at extricating oneself from maternal domination. The masturbating child feels guilty, but independently of any prohibition or reproach. There are often future projects that feed onanism, as the subject unconsciously enjoys the death of the father via his identification with the ideal: he is able to realize this or that goal *as,* or better, *in place* of, his ideal.

The father, however, must be immediately resuscitated in order to prevent the subject from collapsing again into the maternal chasm: the guilt entailed by the masturbatory act induces punishment—phantasmatic reprisal—that demonstrates that the father has not gone anywhere. The symptoms that at times present themselves following a success in life are sometimes the punishment needed for evading its enjoyment, as achievement has, phantasmatically, incestuous traits: the subject possesses the phallus (for the maternal Other), having taken the place of the father by taking his name. But the name symbolizes the presence of the father, even if it is that of the dead father, and tempers enjoyment of the success. (The Name-of-the-Father dams incestuous enjoyment.)

The father is there to punish. To punish and to make one enjoy [*faire jouir*]. The idea of punishment both excites and brings enjoyment during masturbation. If there is punishment, there must also be infraction, the phantasmatic commission of incest—masturbation is the enjoyment of prohibition.

The painless realization of the subject's projects (those of the subject who would take the place of its ideal ego) is sometimes difficult, for the following reasons:

—The subject chooses an inaccessible ideal, and thus prefers to do nothing to reach it and to keep it permanently out of reach. His or her narcissism will never be wounded by the least failure, and she can love her future self infinitely, while hating the present.

—As the subject's goals are realized, its symptoms become aggravated. Danger: you are murdering your father! What then becomes of the ideal ego? Is it overcome once and for all? And is the father now dead forever? Sinner! The father may not be murdered! Every attempt at putting ourselves in the place of the father and at the mother's side is in vain, as the mother is (already) with him: the father, though dead, is invisible. The power acquired by means of the act is pure loss.

When love of the ego is too strong—of an ego that is pulled behind and/or ahead—the subject is left in an imaginary bind that may become fatal. The subject in that event lives on projection alone, outside all social ties and separated from the external world, which in the end offers it little of interest.

The word *narcissism* returns us to the myth of Narcissus, a story of love in which the subject becomes so perfectly conjoined with the ego that it ends up dead. The narcissistic subject can only love itself infinitely, meaning mortally. But such love is only a disguised form of hate: a hatred and fear of itself. Which is also an obsession with itself, one in which there is no possibility of forgetting, detaching from, or abandoning itself. "I would like to leave *myself,* let *myself* go, forget *myself,*" a patient once said to me. "If forgetting *myself* were possible, if I could only manage to forget *myself,* I would be free!" Loving oneself and hating oneself are the same thing when the Other is introjected into one's relation with oneself. So then how can one make an exit from this binary (I ←→ ego)? It takes triadic circulation (I ←→ ego ←→ Other) for desire to make its entry.

In narcissism, the subject does not detach from its ego, which obsesses and crushes it. No encounter with the other, in the sense of a loved and desired other, is possible. An object is desired and loved only if occupies one of two ideal positions: either it is the bearer of what the subject was and is now lost to it, or it represents what the subject would like to be and has never been. The encounter with the phallus, or the phallic compensation of the self through the other, encounters and seeks out images . . . which cannot be handled. For desire, as much as love, requires the *Other.*

When the narcissistic subject becomes infatuated with another without realizing that the latter is only itself, it loses in every regard—above all itself. Since the conjunction with itself is imaginary, the more it approaches the surface (of the skin or the mirror), the less it sees itself. Sucked into its own image, the subject disappears. Subject and image cannot adhere to each other: identification, whether ego ideal or the ideal ego, is not equivalence.[31] What the narcissist loves is only its external, specular surface, its ego, or still yet its future perfection. In reality, it loves nothing about its self, its own existence as subject (S).

In mourning, self-love, or better, the feeling of self (*Selbstgefühl*), becomes degraded. The feeling of self, caught in the object, drops: the ego is stricken, defeated, despairing. As Freud says in "Mourning and

Melancholia," "an object-choice, an attachment of the ego to a particular person, had at one time existed; then, owing to a real slight or disappointment, coming from this loved person, the object-relationship was shattered. The result was not the normal one of a withdrawal of the libido from this object and a displacement of it on to a new one. . . . The object-cathexis proved to have little power of resistance and was brought to an end. But the free libido was not displaced onto another object; it was withdrawn into the ego. There, however, it was not employed in any unspecified way, but served to establish an identification of the ego with the abandoned object."[32]

In mourning, the object is incorporated.[33] The choice of object was made on a narcissistic foundation, and now the subject is deceived by this object about self-love: this object, which has become stained, soiled, and impure, falls onto the ego, disqualifying and destroying it. Through identification, the ego is transformed, and it too becomes provisionally stained, defiled, and impure . . . It become nothing, a nullity, a complete zero . . . at least until the next encounter, which makes the ego (under the emblems of narcissism) rise again in all its splendor.

The subject does not lose the object but its narcissistic image, the ego. "Why has she left me? Why me? I, who am so good?" a mourning analysand, left by a woman for another man, said to me in a session. "Why him and not me? What does he have that I don't? What am I missing?"

His loss of self brought this mourner to assume a position of general renunciation, of abandoning desire and resignation, which might have ended in suicidal acting out [un passage à l'acte suicidaire]. This was pure free fall: the subject went from loving to hating himself. His ego, his beautiful phallic image, left him with the object!

Every other can be the condition of the loss of the object in melancholia. Lacan furnishes us with an absolutely essential reading of "Mourning and Melancholia" in the final lecture, "The Mourning of the Analyst," of his seminar Transference. His commentary shows that the structural distinction between (neurotic) mourning and (psychotic) melancholia is already present, although inexplicitly, in Freud's writing.

In melancholia, the subject is not haunted by the specular, narcissistic—egoic—problematic. His question does not turn around narcissism but the radical, existential defect that afflicts the desire of the subject. Lacan underscores this in the lecture apropos melancholia:

"There the object is, curiously enough, much harder to get a handle on, even though it is constantly present and triggers infinitely more catastrophic effects. For these effects go so far as to dry up what Freud calls the most fundamental *Trieb,* the one that makes you want to go on living."[34] And, he adds, "'I am rubbish.' Observe that his specular image is never involved in his self-criticism. The melancholic never tells you that he looks bad, that his face is at its worst, or that it is contorted; instead he tells you that he is the lowest of the low, that he brings on one catastrophe after another for his entire family, and so on."[35]

If the melancholic does not invest in the external object, then she likewise does not invest in the self, which is to say in the ego as imaginary phallus. The opposite is instead the case, as the melancholic treats herself as an object[36] that is foreign, hostile, and detestable:[37] she considers herself the lowest of the low, trash, rotten . . . Her ego is entirely demolished. (This is amply verified in the clinic, where melancholics tend, when in crisis, to let themselves entirely go, not speaking, eating, washing, etc.)

Melancholia is not a narcissistic passion. That is, it is a passion not of the self but of being: its position is that of pain in its pure state.[38] The melancholic cannot mourn, as the lost object is not missing to him at an unconscious level but rather fulfills and engulfs him, and prevents him from being able to desire outside himself. The melancholic's lost object, in contrast with that of the neurotic, is the object on which no flaws have been found: "hallucinatory psychosis of desire," as Freud says. Or lack that has been found lacking, as Lacan might have said. The melancholic possesses its object, for it is this object. And this possession suffocates its desire.

The death grip in which the narcissistic subject finds itself caught confirms, as Freud discerned, the tie between masochism and narcissism. In "The Economic Problem of Masochism," Freud offers that the masochist "binds himself" because the libido has taken itself as an object.[39] There is a turning around of the drive in masochism.[40] Why does the drive drives reverse into its opposite? Why would pleasure become unpleasure, and the inverse? Masochism is an activity whose goal is passivity, and of which the subject is simultaneously the director and the actor, subject and object. It is the retroversion of the drive into its opposite, and thus the act of a subject who is no longer swallowed by the drive's passivity. The masochist releases her object and this yields a narcissistic effect; like the narcissist, she is exalted at the same time as she is disillusioned with herself. She loves and hates herself.

Masochism constitutes the ground of ambivalence at the origin of narcissism,[41] an ambivalence of which all self-love consists, and in which love is confounded with hate, enthusiasm with disgust, and passion with destruction.

Part III
DESIRE AND
BEYOND DESIRE

7

Conatus and/or
the Death Drive

Lacan's inspiration for saying that the drive is a question of being is Spinoza's notion of *conatus*, "the endeavor to persevere in its being."[1] A certain contemporary reading of the *Ethics* consists in saying that there is nothing in Spinoza's theory of *conatus* that might allow for the possibility that an individual could cease to be of its own accord. Destruction and death can only come from the exterior, from the Other, such that the *conatus* produces movements that have the effect of maintaining it in existence, and that will maintain it indefinitely if no external cause emerges to oppose it. Does such a notion not run counter to Freud's idea that the individual perishes from inner conflicts? And more crucially, how might Spinoza's doctrine, which radically excludes the possibility of destruction due to internal processes, be reconciled with the notion that repetition compulsion is a mortifying process?

Spinoza writes that "no thing can be destroyed except through an external cause."[2] This is, in fact, not in contradiction with what Freud says in the early phase of *Studies on Hysteria*: the mass production of excitation due to an external event—a trauma that penetrates the psychical apparatus, as well as any social, erotic, or psychic element that threatens to burst through it—is the essential pathogenic factor, an extreme danger for the individual. The theme of a threatening exterior will eventually lead Freud to conceive the psyche's strategy as centered not on welcoming a foreign body but rather on reinforcing a barrier by which excitation can be kept out.

In 1920, in *Beyond the Pleasure Principle*, Freud writes that "this little fragment of living substance is suspended in the middle of an external world charged with the most powerful energies; and it would be killed by the stimulation emanating from these if it were not provided with a protective shield against stimuli. It acquires the shield in this way: its outermost surface ceases to have the structure proper to living matter, becomes to some degree inorganic and thenceforward functions as a special envelope or membrane resistant to stimuli. . . . *Protection against* stimuli is an almost more important function for the living organism than *reception of* stimuli."[3] The forces of destruction are therefore situated outside of the psychical apparatus, and this amounts to a return to the Freudian hypothesis that connects pathology to an externally provoked trauma, which Freud regards as penetrating and irruptive in *Studies on Hysteria* and as extremely destructive in *Beyond the Pleasure Principle.*

Freud's position here is in accord with Spinoza's, but it should nonetheless be stressed that even if the destructive cause comes from the outside, excitation, which is deleterious for the individual, is produced by itself, that it therefore also comes from the inside. We should remember that from Freud's perspective, the psychic apparatus is dominated by the pleasure principle, and is deduced from the principle of constancy: the tendency to keep to a minimum the quantity of excitation in the individual, or at least to keep it level. Everything that increases excitation, as every external event does, is necessarily felt as displeasure.

Excitation also derives from the struggle between the individual's power of self-preservation and the external event. When the subject does not manage to maintain his barriers against the latter, tension is released, and we can thus say with Freud that the individual perishes from his internal conflicts. One has to keep in mind the two naves, one external and the other internal—the exterior event and the interior excitation—of the destructive enterprise.

Furthermore, Freud establishes a distinction between the self-preserving, or ego, drives (narcissistic libido) and the sexual drives (object libido): "the analysis of the transference neuroses forced upon our notice the opposition between 'sexual drives,' which are directed toward an object, and certain other drives, with which we were very insufficiently acquainted, and which we described provisionally as the 'ego-drives.' A foremost place among these was necessarily given to the drives serving the self-preservation of the individual."[4]

The self-preserving drives designate the ensemble of needs tied to the corporeal functions necessary to conserve the life of the individual. In contrast, Freud characterizes the sexual drives as forces that can be educated only with difficulty and that relentlessly pose a threat to the psychic apparatus.

Beginning with the second topography, the sexual drives become forces that work toward the constitution and maintenance of living unities. Freud associates the drives with the mythological figure of Eros and christens them the life drives. These are the ego-drives that become death drives, by obeying the principle of seeking total discharge.[5]

So then how should we understand the paradoxical idea that the same thing that contributes to the self-preservation of the individual corresponds to the death drive? "The hypothesis of self-preservative instincts," Freud states clearly in *Beyond the Pleasure Principle*, "such as we attribute to all living beings, stands in marked opposition to the idea that instinctual life as whole serves to bring about death. Seen in this light, the theoretical importance of the instincts of self-preservation, of self-assertion, and of mastery greatly diminishes. They are component instincts whose function it is to assure that the organism shall follow its own path to death. . . . [T]he organism wishes to die only in its own fashion. Thus these guardians of life [the self-preserving drives], too, were originally the myrmidons of death. Hence arises the paradoxical situation that the living organism struggles most energetically against events (dangers, in fact) which might help it to attain its life's aim rapidly—by a kind of short-circuit."[6]

The death drive is not the desire to die; it silently undertakes its labor, going largely noticed. That labor is to delay: its goal is not pursued directly but has to be approached by detours and circumvented, as the destination must be kept far off in the distance. In fact, the death drive seeks to prevent the arrival from ever being reached, pushing it ahead to infinity but without making it vanish. "It is as though the life of the organism moved with a vacillating rhythm. One group of instincts rushes forward as to reach the final aim of life as swiftly as possible; but when a particular stage in the advance has been reached, the other group jerks back to a certain point to make a fresh start and so prolong the journey."[7]

It is a slow return to zero, to the inert, the nothingness that is at once the point of departure and that of arrival. Or a passion for zero, the neutralization of excitations, a desire to return to the inanimate: "the aim of all life is death," Freud tells us.[8] For a long time, it appeared to Freud that the pleasure principle and the nirvana principle regulate the psychical apparatus.[9] In 1920, however, he will revise this view and state that in reality, both of them are at the service of the death drive.

But we must return to Spinoza's *conatus*. The concept itself is not Spinoza's alone, as Hobbes also employed it, albeit only in a static way that denoted an instinct for self-preservation. In Spinoza, by contrast, the term takes on a dynamic connotation that concerns the degree of activeness of a being: everything endeavors to preserve itself in its being, through the sort of self-affirmation that is specific to it and in order to increase its power.

When applied to the condition of living beings, the *conatus* is given the less abstract name of appetite, or desire. The latter manifests in the two indissociable modes of being that are "matter," the power to act and to produce effects, and "mind," the power to think.

Being is, indiscernibly, body-spirit: an affection of the body is also at the same time a correlative modification of thought, and, reciprocally, an instance of thought is simultaneously an affection of the body. There is not, however, any transitive causality running from body to mind or mind to body. Their relation, of course, is rather one of "parallelism," which "consists not only in denying," as Deleuze characterizes it, "any relation of causality between mind and body but of prohibiting any eminence of one over the other."[10]

The concept of *conatus* is, in Spinoza, determined by the affects of joy and sadness. A joyous affect, such as a fortunate encounter with a thing or a being, will incite anew this happy feeling and thereby play a determining role in *conatus*. Inversely, a sad affect reduces the power to exist and thereby weakens *conatus*.

Now the concept of *conatus* can be related to that of the death drive, as it, too, has the individual persisting on its path—that of the obstacles toward death.

Death is not simply the end of life but the dead moment of life, in the sense from painting of *la nature morte,* or better, "a still life." A still life is, we know, irreducible to the structure of its lines and colors, and refers to that which lies outside the harmony and surface on the canvas.[11] Death is present in the moment at which fruit matures or a flower blooms, in the instant at which the life in nature expresses itself the most manifestly—when life has reached the threshold of decline *[décadence].* That is when the *conatus* augments its power to persevere in its being—at the moment of the joining between life and death, between, in Freud's language, Eros and Thanatos.

What seduces us in a still life is its intense blending of life and death—of the blooming and the wilting—of represented things. Its fruits and flowers are already a little rotten in their efflorescence, somewhat dead at their opening. Intertwined with death, they represent the most profound expressions of beauty and of life. As Lacan observes, "the aesthetic phenomenon where it is identified with beauty—beauty in all its shining radiance, [is] the beauty that has been called the splendor of truth. It is obviously because truth is not pretty to look at that beauty is, if not its splendor, then at least its envelope. [Beauty] stops us, but also points in the direction of destruction."[12] Beauty is the ultimate barrier separating, while also bringing together, the subject and that which is at once the most intimate and the most disturbing to it: its desire—its radical desire, Lacan tells us[13]—and desire is always close to destruction, death, and the impossible.

The primary drive in man, says Freud, is to return to the inanimate, to the state anterior to life, the nonlife that was there before life.[14] In its actual realization, this relentless return to the inert is not direct, and its continual forward pushing endows it with a trajectory that is the reverse, or at least the slowdown, of its original logic. The death drive draws from or inherits all the forces that have resisted this tendency, the sexual or life drives. The search for an end to excitation turns into a search for excitation itself, but in order to make it end once more. Such is the cycle of the drive: the pursuit of the occasion for excitation in order to enjoy *[jouir]* its subsequent drop. The return to the point of departure is also always a return toward and through all the vital forces that first distanced the organism from that starting point; it is a return to the origin but by way of all the detours that lead away from it, and thus also a return to vital forces. There is, in truth, no short circuit.

If there is an imbrication of the sexual drives and those of self-preservation (or of death and of life), Freud nonetheless maintains the distinction between them. This happens during the moment of his dispute with Jung, as Freud has need of distinguishing himself from the former's use of libido to signify a generalized drive, and he does this by means of a dualistic conception of the drives. However, there remains some ambiguity as to the relation between the sexual drives and the drives of self-preservation or death: the sexual drives, Freud says, "are conservative in the same sense as the other instincts in that they bring back earlier states of living substance; but they are conservative to a higher degree in that they are particularly resistant to external influences; and they are conservative to in another sense in that they preserve life itself for a particularly long period."[15]

So if Freud affirms in the first topography that the sexual drives hasten toward the goal—the end—of life, which is death, he appears here to be proposing the opposite. In effect, the sexual drives seeks to sate pleasure in the same way that life is moved by the quiescence that death alone will bring. There is an ambivalence in every sexual drive, and Freud is not trying to conceal it. "The possibility remains," he writes, "that the instincts which were later to be described as sexual may have been in operation from the very first, and it may not be true that it was only a later time that they started upon their work of opposing the activities of the 'ego-instincts.'"[16]

Freud also conceives of an ambivalence between love and hate in romantic *[amoureuse]* life, and the hypothesis allows him to reveal the death drive that impels every love.[17]

Now the question of the relation between life and death was broached prior to Freud by Schopenhauer, who evokes, in *The World as Will and Representation,* the conjunction of death and sexuality. There is a tension between sexuality as it is individually lived through the erotic activity of the subject, and sexuality in service to the species. The subject is active when in its "acts" and passive when trapped in the game of reproduction. Schopenhauer maintains that the sex act is undertaken for the conservation of the species rather than the individual. Every sexual act successfully undertaken for reproduction renders the individual eternal by making him continue beyond himself and at the same time effaces him to the benefit of the species. "Man is sexual instinct [impulse] that has taken a body," Schopenhauer writes, "for his origin is an act of copulation, and the desire of his desires is an act of copulation, and this instinct alone holds together the whole of his phenomenal appearance. It is true that the will to live manifests itself primarily as an effort to maintain the individual; yet this is only a stage toward the effort to maintain the species. The latter effort must be more intense in proportion as the life of the species surpasses that of the individual in duration, extension, and value."[18]

To think as the species is to be annulled as subject; if my life continues in the species, I am no longer a subject, as I *am* the species in which someday I *will no longer be*. Lacan appears to be inspired by Schopenhauer when he writes that there is a symbolic lack that "takes up the other lack, which is the earlier, real lack, to be situated at the advent of the living being, that is, in sexual reproduction. The real lack is what the living being loses, that part of himself qua living being, in reproducing himself by the way of sex. This lack is real because it relates to something real, which is that the living being, by being subject to sex, has fallen under the blow of individual death."[19]

Sex opens both to the infinite and to death. To think that one lives through the individual who comes after oneself is equivalent to thinking oneself to be infinite. But infinity is death, not life. To think through the infinity of the species is like thinking oneself to be already dead.

The death drive is not a leap to the death over all obstacles. It demands, on the contrary, retreading the course formed by those obstacles, a path that the subject stays on for its entire life and that is repeated in all the subject's constructions (which then add to the obstacles). The death drive operates not so much by abolishing forms but by constructing other forms to abolish them; it is the detour through all the forms of life taken in the patient pursuit of death. And that torturous pathway is strewn with singular obstacles. To each his death, as Freud says.

The particularly speculative dimension of the Freudian theory of the death drive ought to be emphasized. Speculation may not lead to as much certainty as theory based on direct observation, but such induction provides no greater guarantee of the validity of its hypotheses. One part observation, one part speculation is the formula for Freud's approach to discovering that which founds the real; even his highest speculations rely in this way on clinical evidence, such as his investigation of the repetitive character of the negative experiences of his patients.[20]

The death drive is what it is only as a concept: in its realization, it is just as much the "life drive," a dimension of the vital impulses. Everything that stands opposed to the return to the inorganic (the anterior state of life) is merely a phase of that very movement. And the return should be understood not only in chronological but spatial terms: all the moments of its development are at the same time the immobile points at which life aims. Life and death can no longer be conceived as disimbricated.

From a topological perspective, *conatus* can be envisaged as a movement that always comes back to the same point: to "persevere" is to insist and to persist in the return to being, and being becomes nonbeing, nonlife, anteriority, nothing. Spinoza's concept should not necessarily be conceived as a rectilinear impulse (a directional and finalized straight line), because when the *conatus* is conceived in light of Freud's thesis, it becomes a kind of entropy! And this link between the death drive and entropy is something that Lacan, too, perceived: "At the level of material systems considered to be inanimate, and thus up to and including that which intervenes in the form of the material organization internal to living organisms, the operation of an irreversible tendency that proceeds in the direction of the advent of a terminal state of equilibrium is, properly speaking, something that in energetics is known as entropy. This is the first meaning that can be given to the death drive in Freud."[21]

Conatus is not a positive and guided force but the drive of life *toward nothing,* and therefore a drive for death. *Conatus* is life, but detour-life, life whose purpose is necessarily the return to zero. Life that perseveres for nothing, that perseveres for—desires—death. In Lacan's view, "that is what life is—a detour, a dogged detour, in itself transient and null, and deprived of signification."[22] He also affirms, in the same early seminar, that "life is taken into the symbolic only parceled and decomposed. The human being itself is partly outside of life, participating in the death drive. Only from there alone can he attain the register of life."[23] Life, parceled and decomposed, and in constant connection with death.

In relation to the pleasure principle, the death drive expresses itself in two, contrary ways. The first remains on the hither side of the pleasure principle; it presses on to the point at which the subject would rejoin the degree zero of excitation, the limit where life becomes indistinguishable from death. The second way is beyond pleasure, on the side of an infinite augmentation of excitation that overcomes the limit at which excitation becomes compatible with life. These two ways can become confused.

Conatus is desire. Desire, as Deleuze writes, "is nothing else but the effort by which each thing strives to persevere in its being, each body in extension, each mind or each idea in thought *(conatus)*."[24] But desire is not paradise (it is the desire of the Other); it is not constructed exclusively from the vital impulses of the subject: *conatus* is the desire of/for life that aims, structurally, for death.

Something that persists in human beings is the indestructibility of desire. The subject seeks to realize its desire without being able to succeed, and yet also without being able to renounce it. This desire that never lets the subject relax is not an organic, automatic machine but a power that impels it forward and that can, in its persistence, cross over its limits and set off catastrophe. Desire seeks to annihilate and destroy itself, to disappear. It is in this persistence that it encounters the drives, that is, the death drive.[25] For the death drive, too, persists, insists, and never stops—even in desire, which turns out not to be, as has been believed, its antagonist. If for Spinoza joy is opposed to sadness because when one passion is active, another is canceled, for Freudian psychoanalysis the death drive and desire act simultaneously (given that desire is the Other's desire).

There is a will to annihilate and destroy in the death drive: the subject responds to the desire of the Other and makes himself its object. Lacan envisages the death drive as a "will toward destruction" that exists beyond the tendency to return to the inanimate. For Lacan, that will to destruction is opposed to the tendency toward equilibrium of the nirvana principle: "The death drive is to be situated in the historical domain; it is articulated at a level that can only be defined as a function of the signifying chain, that is to say, insofar as a reference point, that is a reference point of order, can be situated relative to the functioning of nature. It requires something from beyond whence it may itself be grasped in a fundamental act of memorization, as a result of which everything may be recaptured, not simply in the movement of the metamorphosis but from an initial intention."[26]

The death drive presses beyond the pleasure principle (the eponymous title of Freud's essay makes this explicit). When observing destiny neuroses[27] and war neuroses, Freud is unable to account for why their psychic systems more favorably obey some other tendency distinct from the pleasure principle; why, he asks, did his patients have the tendency to repeat disagreeable experiences instead of avoiding them?

Such forms of repetition evince a logic not accounted for by the pleasure principle. One is beyond pleasure and also beyond desire: it is the acephalic drive that aims at enjoyment, annihilating it.

When an event transpires that is almost impossible for the subject to face—one that he can neither integrate into the sequence of his representations nor abstract from his field of consciousness via repression—the event acquires the value of a trauma, an "unhappy encounter" or *tuché*, as Lacan says. It is the real that makes trauma. If the subject is to be liberated from its yoke, trauma must be reduced; in other words, it has to be symbolized, that is, *subjectified*. Its relentless return in the form of images, dreams, and acting out has precisely that for its task: in other words, the integration of the symbolic organization of the subject. One of the functions of repetition is therefore to reduce trauma (in the sense of "reducing hemorrhaging"). But the automatism, Lacan's *automaton*, only causes the misfiring of symbolization to repeat and ends up perpetuating it infinitely. It is a bit like a child constantly asking to be told the same fairy tale, in exactly the same way: unfortunately, the tale's construction is never clear enough in the child's memory to allow it to retrieve the particularities of the first telling, its significance as such. Once repeated, the tale cannot but differ from the version she initially heard, which is forever lost.

Repetition thus has a ritual function: something is repeated in order to commemorate a "nonrememberable *[immémorable]* encounter."[28] But to what end, in that case, is repetition put in place? Something of the order of the impossible is pursued in the automatism of repetition. Think back to the symptom: what is sought after by way of it is always enjoyment, an enjoyment that can eventually replace another, annihilating and traumatic enjoyment, and that, in the symptom, is delivered in the form of suffering. Or as punishment, which, we have seen, brings enjoyment *[fait jouir]*.

The subject prey to his repetition compulsion suffers—or better, he enjoys his suffering. The death drive as drive to destruction is what is acting: the subject makes himself the object of the Other's enjoyment.[29] But in the repetition of the symptom, something can be constructed otherwise, through destruction and suffering; something changes in the subject's position vis-à-vis the original trauma that it had passively lived and consequently sought after, unconsciously, via the symptom.

There is a sexual dimension in trauma: the real is incestuous. It should be specified that there are accidental, objective traumas that are structurally different from those that are sexual and subjective, which have a structural status for the subject that corresponds to the *Ausstossung*: the subject's rejection of the phallic signification that its body has for the Other.[30]

This repression of the desire of the Other (the *Ausstossung*) is a subjective and sexual trauma, and correlative to the birth of the subject. It should be specified that the subject has no direct representations of this subjective trauma but only recollections *[souvenirs]* and sensations that accompanied it and that were memorized at the moment of the trauma and inscribed in the unconscious as "memory-traces," *Erinnerungspur*.[31] Such traces are found in the writing of dreams and some types of psychotic hallucination, as well as in certain corporeal experiences, that is, affects (affects that have been detached from unconscious representation, according to Freud).

Although an objective trauma can be recalled easily, no words or images are able to bespeak or picture subjective-sexual trauma. Objective trauma covers over sexual trauma, which thus remains non-subjectified; the subject relives it in repetition, but unwittingly.

The original, subjective trauma is revived by the subsequent objective traumas produced in the subject's life. The subjective trauma is camouflaged by objective traumas in the formations of the unconscious, and it is the latter that are most often represented in nightmares, waking dreams, or disturbing memories. For instance, the subject may dream of a car accident in which she was involved or of an erotic separation, or of a loss, a harm, a mistreatment, an abandonment—every kind of situation in which she occupies a *passive* position. In the attempt to reverse the trauma, the subject unconsciously relives (sees, imagines, thinks, etc.), in an *active* way, what she has undergone.

It is not the recollection of trauma that forces repetition but the subject, who is in fact not absent from the unconscious operation carried out by means of nightmares, waking dreams, memories, affects, and so forth. In repeating the trauma, the subject of the unconscious works an inversion, seeking to relive in an active way what has been otherwise lived passively.

Freud gives a famous example of repetition in its relation to the death drive, which is, of course, that of a child engrossed in playing with a bobbin. He recounts witnessing his grandson occupy himself with a little game each time his mother left him for a period: he would cast the bobbin away from himself while cooing the words *fort,* gone, and *da,* there, in order to repeat the painful experience of being separated from her. Now why is it that the child renewed, a virtually infinite number of times, those disagreeable events of maternal separation?[32] There is, of course, a certain gain in enjoyment that comes from this form of repetition. But more crucially, the child's attitude about his mother is transformed by means of his play. After discovering himself in a passive position within the event of his mother's departure, he changes his role to an active one, and makes himself its "master";[33] he reneges on being his mother's object so as to become the subject of the game—thanks, it should be noted, to the intervention of language (the *fort-da*).

Repetition in play (of which the game of the bobbin is of course merely an example) is distinct from certain kinds of traumatic repetition, which lock the subject into a state of paralyzing immobility, a suffocating real from which there is no exit and that leaves no room for contingency. There is quite a difference between a traumatic event that is repeated throughout the course of life and the repetition that occurs in a game created by the subject, even when it reiterates a disagreeable event.[34] The game of the bobbin is pleasurable, even if its pleasure appears in the guise of unpleasure, and the subject takes an active position: the traumatic event thus remains to some extent within the framework of the pleasure principle.

The child can play at making himself an object, as his game protects him from the real. On the other hand, he can at the same time master his separation from his mother. His use of language renders that separation into something independent of him, subjectivizes it. The signifier is the first mark of the subject, and language does not create a barrier but can bring enjoyment: *fort* and *da,* owing to their sonorous value, become captivating, seductive words—they are given value by the drives.

The child is an actor, and therefore "passive"[35] in the game: he is the here-and-gone-again bobbin itself, the object of the mother with which she is confused. And he is also, simultaneously, this whole scene's director—this is the active role—as it is always he who controls the play, through the string(s) *[ficelle]* that he manipulates for his pleasure.

He is, then, at once dependent on and independent of his mother, and it is repetition's variation of itself that quells the situation of his indebtedness to her. Lacan characterizes this situation by saying that "repetition demands the new. It is turned toward the ludic, which finds its dimension in the new. . . . The adult, and even the more advanced child, demands something new in his activities, in his games. But this sliding conceals what is the true secret of the ludic, namely the most radical diversity constituted by repetition itself."[36] It is in this sense as well that Lacan's notion of the death drive should be understood: "Will to destruction. Will to make a fresh start. Will for an Other-thing, given that everything can be challenged from the perspective of the function of the signifier. . . . [The death drive] challenges everything that exists. But it is equally a will to create from zero, a will to begin again."[37]

Another case of painful but nonetheless creative repetition is the symptom.[38] Repetition is in this sense progress, as it succeeds at providing a way to avoid fixation—the symptom does not always linger but comes and goes (and this is even more the case during analysis). And symptomatic repetition is even progressive when its cycles become discouraging, as dullness is necessary if something unanticipated is to come about.

Now completely different from this is repetition in neuroses of destiny or melancholia, which both reveal an inefficacious attempt to annul the trauma at the same time as they do a vain commemoration of this missed encounter. What is repeated responds, at the level of the unconscious, to the Other's desire, notwithstanding the subject's bid to change its position relative to it. It is the drive that seeks to fix the equation body = phallus.

The labor of the death drive manifests destructively in these and other such forms of traumatic repetition. Conversely, the death drive's action on the repetition of signifiers or symptoms reveals that it indeed travels its path by simultaneously moving in opposite directions: destruction and/or self-preservation, or even annihilation and/or renewal.

According to this perspective, repetition is the seal of original trauma; the rejected real, impossible to bespeak or imagine, of the (phallic) signification that the subject has for the Other. It is the signature of the death drive: the permanent return to original trauma. But that return is what allows for an immediate restart from somewhere else. Repetition contains the change, the unexpected . . . or, the entropic force of the *conatus*![39]

Does masochism reveal the destructive tendency of traumatic repetitions? Freud distinguishes three forms of masochism: "erogenous masochism," which manifests when sexual pleasure is bound up with pain (this is masochism as perversion properly speaking); "feminine masochism," which is expressed in the desire of certain subjects, whether men or women, for castration, sexual submissiveness, and giving birth; and also, finally, "moral masochism." In this third form, the subject does not await the suffering procured by a partner but arranges it himself in order to obtain diverse sorts of circumstances in life. Moral masochism can express itself in an apparently totally desexualized way, revealing a need for self-destruction that is itself referable to the death drive.[40]

Now the specific action of the death drive in moral masochism stems from the drive's attempt to respond to the demand of the maternal Other by satisfying it. The drive is incapable of this, but keeps insisting and repeating at aiming after a target that it always misses. Its goal is not attained by its own pacification *(Befriedigung)*, via peace *(Friede)*, but by again loosing its arrow, by the arc of its aspiration, which is always under tension. "Every drive is virtually a death drive," says Lacan.[41]

If we follow Lacan, every desire is the desire of/for the Other; but in that case, how can desire be autonomous? Subjective desire is the act of the subject, even as it at the same time puts him in danger by pressing him onward, beyond the pleasure principle.

Can any distinction then be made between desire and dependence? How can one desire to be an object (to aim for enjoyment) while remaining the client, the subject, of the operation? Here again we arrive at the impasses of desire, its irresolvable antinomies, that it involves, that it is, psychic simultaneity . . .

This structural impossibility of desire is shown in dreams. The dream is charged with representing the subject in a position in which he becomes object (the satisfaction of desire), while continuing to take the initiative. It is the subject who decides to dream when she can longer tolerate passivity in the extreme.

In dreams, desire lends its hand to repetition: that which repeats, which is sexual trauma, has already assumed a different form apropos the original Thing by being bound to the subject's desire. In other words, dreams reconfigure trauma, making the subject at once active and passive. Desire is of course involved in this new construction of the subject, as it is not fixed on, not blocked by, the original trauma and also takes a new form and undergoes an expansionist boom by way of this new psychic configuration, whose possibility is owed to repetition.

Every dream reveals itself to be masochistic in character. To assume the masochistic position is to act for a passive end: an act of the subject in relation to what she should suffer. The subject resists the death drive, which wants to destroy it for realizing the desire of the Other. The masochist's existence lies in giving in to and putting up resistance against that desire: both at the same time. She takes an object, a sexual partner, who takes her place—her place as a subject—and chooses to make herself into an object. In masochism, as with all perversion, a kind of depersonalization occurs, and it is capable of provoking anxiety in the masochist. Yet at the same time, the masochist is in a more active position than is the sadist: the former plays the initiating role and is in fact the agent of her objectness, whereas the sadist serves the Law of the Other, to which he is a mere, wretched acolyte.

We can see by extension that on account of the physical, psychic, and moral blows dealt to it, any subject can reclaim life, and exit from its identification with the maternal phallus. At the same time, these blows are the signs that its enjoyment is being procured through punishment. Lacan indicates that "enjoyment is the real" and that "it's clear that the enjoyment of the real includes masochism, which Freud noticed."[42] Freud defines the dream of "A Child Is Being Beaten" as a masochistic fantasy. To be beaten by the father is to announce that enjoyment is contradictory, but possible.[43]

All subjects have an inclination toward masochism. Each inquires about the meaning of her existence, but the Other remains completely unresponsive. In the absence of the Other, the subject vacillates. For she is never as assured that she exists in the Other's eyes as when she suffers.

8

The Laws
of Desire

Man would seem to have always fought against his enslavement to desire, to master and to order it, so as to be able to remove it when it becomes a source of pain.

Plato, Aristotle, and the Epicureans and Stoics tried, as we saw, to distinguish legitimate desires from those that they considered violent and dangerous. Since dangerous desires, such as those for power, wealth, honor, and sex, cannot be eliminated, they must be moderated. They therefore concluded that a limit capable of blocking excess should be established. But prohibition, as we know, does nothing to prevent desire.

Desire and prohibition regulate the subject's life, when it is viewed as a cycle: each time its impulse to realize its desire runs up against a limit that stops its movement, preventing satisfaction even in its realization. But the impulse of desire persists, going beyond every object, every prevention, even every dissatisfaction . . . Prohibition infinitely relaunches desire (desire's objects being, of course, metonymic), is tied in a structural knot with the cause of desire.

It is somewhat like breathing: just as we inhale and exhale, we need desire and its prohibition, if not as well the movement of its interruption. But the rhythm of the desire-prohibition relationship is not as regular as that as of breathing. If the accent is placed on the power of prohibition, the very object of desire (for power, richness, honor, sexual pleasure) loses its importance and the prohibition becomes the stake, the center, the desire itself.

For Bataille, prohibition founds desire. In *Erotism*, he famously affirms that "prohibition is there in order to be violated."[1] In erotic experience, desire concerns not only sexual activity but comprises the gamut of the phantasmatic life of the subject. On account of this transgression of prohibition, sexuality is taken to the limit: the limits of consciousness, of the law, and of language (since for Bataille, as is well known, eroticism is a silencing experience).[2]

Transgression is for Bataille initially disorder and confusion, a violence against the order of the world, which is the order of labor and the sexual order, the latter of which presumes sexual behavior that is well organized and submitted to precise rules. Eroticism, then, has nothing to do with animal sexuality, which, while free, is nonetheless limited to a simple, natural need that allows for the perpetuation of the species. Such natural and purposive activity, which is permissible even to the church, is of no interest to Bataille. It is sex proper that Bataille transgresses,[3] and not sexual transgression in the sense of perversion, which is, in this sense, the crux of the matter: sex that serves to "go elsewhere."

Bataille's difference from de Sade is clear. Sade undertakes an exploration of combinations that are free of every structural constraint and that do not at all entail sexual transgression in the above sense. Bataille, on the other hand, wishes to find a way to go beyond sexual enjoyment, and even past perversion. In *Story of the Eye*, the male protagonist affirms that

no doubt existed in me. I did not care for what is known as pleasures of the flesh because they really are insipid; I cared only for what is classified as "dirty." On the other hand, I was not even satisfied with the usual debauchery, because the only thing it dirties is debauchery itself, while, in some way or another, anything sublime and perfectly pure is left intact by it. My kind of debauchery soils not only my body and my thoughts, but also anything I may conceive in its course, that is to say, the vast starry universe.[4]

For Bataille, desire is the desire for limits as well as the desire to go beyond them: transgression crosses the line and never ceases crossing it again. But transgression cannot go beyond the "starry universe." Transgression is only imagination, and the limit does not exist outside of the impulse to cross over and deny it.

This limit that prohibits and also becomes the object of desire necessarily calls to mind the father, who not only appears as the prohibiting agency but also becomes the object of desire.

The daughter *wants* the father,[5] but at the same time she wants him to forbid incest. The father himself is sexually prohibited, and it is therefore necessary for her to take her desire elsewhere. She can then have the feeling that by desiring other persons, she betrays her father. Desire in this case becomes an offense against him, and the desire to offend (the father) a form of transgression. This offense allows her to enjoy a partner who is not her father, but without risking incest in any way.

The transgression, the offense, against the father is imaginary as long as there is not a duty or sentiment that he could accuse the daughter of having neglected. On the contrary, having a relationship with a man who resembles her own father is not transgressive: it is incestuous, and, far worse, the incest is achieved twice over, along two routes—those of the father *and* the mother.

The "replica" of the father is confused with the biological father, and they become one: but a father who lets himself be seduced by his daughter is no longer a father. The father erects the barrier against incestuous desire but foremost functions as the cause of desire. In the absence of the father, which is to say in the absence of someone who can take on that function,[6] desire is blocked. Many cases of impotence—on the side of both men and women, and whether in bed or as expressed through inhibition in life—can be explained in this way. Incestuous enjoyment is intolerable, so the subject rejects it. Excessive enjoyment flips into its opposite. Disgust, which is mixed with guilt, then seizes the subject. Desire is suffocating when it becomes detached from the prohibition that delimits and marks it.

In transgressing, the daughter will go so far as to fantasize the father's murder: she will remain unable to enjoy unless she manages to kill him. And things get even more complicated: her guilt about deceiving the father, about having wanted to kill him, can lead her into a masochistic fantasy (see again Freud's "A Child Is Being Beaten"). She experiences the desire to be aggressed, battered, and violated by a man who fulfills two roles: to move her (by forcing her), on the one hand, to betray the father, and to be the father, on the other hand, who punishes her for this bad action. The father, by virtue of the blows he inflicts on her in the fantasy—and also on her body, with the help of her symptoms—is immediately resuscitated: the punishment he metes out is the evidence that a father always lives.

In *Story of the Eye*, Marcelle wants to be humiliated, and more importantly, she enters by her own initiative the humiliating situations.

The scene in which she retreats, desperate and crying, into an armoire is emblematic.[7] When she decides to offer herself to the violence of two individuals, one who forces her into sex and another who punishes her, her apparently passive attitude also returns much of her own violence back to her. The two characters who mistreat her, the narrator and Simone, fulfill the functions of the protagonists of her fantasy (it is Simone who orchestrates the three-way sexual encounter). Marcelle decides to position them as subjects, and herself, via the humiliations to which she is subjected, as an object. Marcelle's role is simultaneously active and passive; she at once acts and directs the scene. That is, she enjoys incest and its prohibition; she enjoys and is punished for her transgression of the law.

Desire is in itself violent—in *Erotism*, Bataille affirms this in several reprises—but it is also the desire for violence; a violence against someone else, the father, but also against oneself. The roles in fantasy become confused: the father is the batterer, and the subject is he or she who is beaten; but the subject can also occupy the position of the batterer, through its identification with the father. This identification leads the subject into error: the subject who beats itself must be guilty of having taken the father's place, for the blows are there to attest to it. The violence against the father is confused with and added onto the violence against the self: this is violence against the subject's own ideal image, transferred back onto itself.

Another way of saying that the subject is at the same time beating and beaten is that the father is at once dead and alive. The subject is beaten for the murder he has committed, but the father remains, miraculously, alive—he does the beating—and will continue to be alive the more the subject identifies with him. Identification at once kills and eternalizes the father, by turning him into myth.

The subject that identifies with the father believes himself to have taken the latter's place: he has, at last, pulled off his father's murder in fantasy. But the father is reborn in order to punish him. It should not be forgotten that it is the father who makes the law, and that the law in turn symbolizes the father. There must be a father—dead, living—if fantasy is to be capable of infinite reiteration: the father's death and rebirth lend desire its rhythm.

In what way can a woman kill the father? In cursing his proper name, the Name-of-the-Father [*Nom-du-Père*]. And it is the lover that is ordered to do this, symbolically, as the lover's name substitutes for her for the place of the father. In marriage, the woman *officially* replaces, which is to say symbolically substitutes, the Name-of-the-Father with the name of the man who makes her enjoy *[jouis]* (and with, in the case of marriage, society's blessing!). In *Story of the Eye,* Marcelle asks the narrator to wed her, a request that might seem to be a surprising capitulation to social conformity but that makes sense once the meaning of feminine fantasy is grasped.

Marriage is the official document attesting that the Name-of-the-Father has been *effaced*—it states that the father is symbolically dead. There is here a war of symbols: the Name-of-the-Father qua the name of the lover that is symbolized by the phallus, the power of which, qua absence, is in turn represented by the name. The symbolic gift of the name, or of any other form of symbolic recognition of the partner (as this holds the same value), quells the desire between lovers and makes the woman enjoy *[jouir]*.

For Lacan, language is of course intimately tied to desire: it constitutes desire's limit—language assumes the role of the law—that enjoyment runs up against. During the 1950s, Lacan entertained the hypothesis that enjoyment and language are mutually exclusive, but he altered his views at the beginning of the 1970s. In effect, he decided that words make one come *[jouir]*. Their sonorousness makes them seductive, in the way that bodies are, and they attain a beauty that is almost physical or material. Invested with value by the drives *[investi de valeur pulsionnelle],* they turn into "objects"—become erotic, enjoyful.

In the enjoyment of words, signifying material replaces the object of the drives. We can recall Lacan's notion of *lalangue,* "llangauge": in its aspect that is real (that falling under the purview of the drives), the body "speaks." Lacan said this in "Le troisième": "the unconscious [can be characterized as] being a knowledge that is articulated from llanguage *[lalangue],* the body that speaks there being knotted only by the real that it enjoys."[8]

Language is the lashing point of desire. Language is what maintains the barrier against enjoyment, as the prohibition on enjoyment becomes the enjoyment of prohibition.

Excitation is produced by the material absence of the object, an object that circulates through the (infinite) signification of each word.

Certain signifiers, by virtue of their sonorous value, graze the sexual real, or better, the "tips *[bouts]* of the real,"[9] thin extremities of enjoyment that incur into the signifier. Words bring enjoyment, but in a way that is impure and incomplete. In this sense, the enjoyment of words reveals itself to be transgressive.

Lacan states on this point that "to make this enjoyment possible is the same thing as what I shall write as j'OUIS-SENS [I hear/yes sense], the same thing as *ouïr*, to hear, a sense."[10] The unconscious engages in ciphering and deciphering in order to produce enjoyment, and this *j'ouis-sens* is outside sense, which is to say outside of every anticipatable semantic determination. The synthesis *ouïr un sens* [to hear a sense] does not necessarily mean "understand a sense," as the verbs "to hear" and "to understand" can hold contradictory meanings. That does not mean that it is impossible to understand and to enjoy at the same time (as philosophers know very well). *J'ouis-sens* is a bit, a tip of enjoyment that brushes the signifier, the little thing outside a signifier that is within that very signifier. (If we cannot grasp anything through words, even by the little tips of them that hang out of the symbolic chain and its fixed semantic determinations, then what good is psychoanalysis?)

Lacan points to Joyce as an example of symptomatic but enjoyful writing, as *Finnegans Wake* wrecks the order of words and endows them with signification.[11] Sometimes the text's words seem to exit altogether the syntagmatic chain. Joyce manages to liberate himself to some degree from the yoke of speech through his unique use of language, by which he hears and develops every possibility of enjoyment, in lieu of confining them to a single sense. That does not mean they have no sense, as there is instead too much, too many, senses. *Finnegans Wake* seems at first glance to be an extremely mad book, but for Joyce it is the continuation and radicalization of the body of work by which he warded off psychosis. It was through the word *[la parole]*—his own wording, which was a thing unto itself in the universe of literature— that Joyce managed to compensate for the deficiency of the father. Lacan states that Joyce *made himself a name,* and this is no metaphor: his literary symptom has the identificatory function of a proper name. Where his ego was concerned, it was not developed in relation to an image of the body, as Joyce gave it consistency through a style of writing that he was right to believe would long occupy his commentators.

In contrast with Lacan, Bataille thinks that enjoyment makes us pass beyond language. Eroticism is for him an experience of silence, and enjoyment would exclude words. It is therefore experienced only in extraordinary moments, when language is suspended. Bataille's corpus of literature is thus often a description of those moments as they approach.

The Law of Desire is a 1987 film by Pedro Almodóvar. The title's association of law and desire could seem paradoxical, as we commonly think that one follows either desire or the law—either I follow my urges and transgress the law, or I forbid myself my desires.

In the Oedipus myth, the father, who lays down the law, prohibits the mother: it suffices to rid oneself of the father and the law to be able to enjoy the mother. This is what Oedipus does,[12] but once the father has been successfully killed, it is no longer possible to keep waiting for enjoyment—it too departed, with the now-dead father.

The primitive horde's murder of the father in *Totem and Taboo* allows us to explain the imbrication of desire and law: the father is the key to enjoyment. Enjoyment is incarnate in the horde's father, who possesses all the women and has the exclusive privilege of enjoying them. His sons eventually decide to kill and eat him in order to have their turn at enjoyment—having suppressed the father, they also would have the law. But the totem also symbolizes the law of the dead father, a law that is metabolized by the son through their incorporation (the *Einverleibung*) of the father. This incorporation of the dead father is consubstantial with that of the law, the symbolic father: enjoyment afterward remains just as impossible for the murderous brothers. Their murder of the father only brings them guilt, and the law originates from his murder,[13] which entirely bans satisfaction: instead of disappearing, the prohibition of enjoyment is reaffirmed.

Now if the father represents the only obstacle to enjoyment, why does his death end up preventing it? The law symbolizes the guilt of the murderous assassin–sons, but is the cause rather the consequence of the absolute loss of enjoyment, which is symbolized by the death of he who incarnates it: the father.

Enjoyment and the dead father are therefore equivalent. It is the dead father who inscribes—incorporates—the law for the sons, a law that prohibits enjoyment; and it is always he who keeps it. Lacan offers that "this is what makes it possible to place at the center of logic this 'all men'—'all men are mortal'—the basis of which is precisely the non-knowledge of death, just as it is what makes us believe that that 'all men' means something, all men are born of a father, who, we are told, insofar as they, the men, are dead do not enjoy what is there for them to enjoy. An equivalence is therefore drawn, in Freudian terms, between the dead father and enjoyment. It is he who keeps it in reserve, if I can put it like that."[14]

The dead father *is* enjoyment. And yet how is it possible for the dead to enjoy? The dead father's enjoyment represents the impossibility that fixes the category of the real, which is in permanent tension with the symbolic, of which the dead father is always the armature.

Must the father be kept alive so that it will be possible to continue to fantasize about a possible enjoyment? (There has to be an *at-least-one* who enjoys . . .) It is the wish to kill the father that keeps him alive, as this is the ultimate proof of his existence. And enjoyment remains, as Lacan tells us, in reserve: the oedipal fantasy here drops the mask of artifice, by maintaining the horizon of enjoyment as the promise of desire, through the intervention of its very prohibition. It is the (symbolic) law which, at the same time as it symbolizes the guilt of the sons, engenders a fantasy of enjoyment. The father always leaves some hope that transgression remains possible (through his death), and the subject can continue to desire.

The law that originates from the murder of the primitive father bears the traces of the guilt of the sons. Now if I am guilty, I must have done something wrong! The sense of fault perpetuates the crime. In this sense, both the killing of the father—a killing that is certified by the guilt of the sons—and the enjoyment of the mother have essentially the same value in fantasy.

In another aspect of this fantasy, the father's infinite rebirth is central, as we have seen: the father is propped up and kept alive, which allows for desire, for the hope for enjoyment . . . by killing him afterward once more! This is not in contradiction with the fact that the father should bar the way to maternal enjoyment. In effect, the father plays both functions, as he promises enjoyment in the future while preventing it in the present.

All law, even when it is phantasmatic, is indissolubly bound to desire. What then is its function? Ought it to prohibit enjoyment, or instead prescribe it?

The law at once symbolizes desire, forbids it, and renders it guilty. Fault is co-present with law: it is the law that makes men sinners.[15] Fault is constituted after the fact, following the death of the father, and even after every trauma. This is a fault without name, as repression leaves the author knowing nothing about his actions. The murderous act is repressed by the founding of the law. The law is aimed toward the effacement of the traces of that act, while at the same time it obliges one to act as if the father were not dead: the father imposes himself in the name of the law as though he were it. The father and the law are in symbiosis with each other.

The father is living only at the level of the imaginary, which is how it is that the superego originates.[16] As Lacan writes, "Since the Other doesn't exist, all that's left for me is to place the blame on *I*."[17] The father is incorporated into the law, which in turn has been incorporated by the subject. It is the subject who will thenceforward carry the burden of enjoyment, and while enjoyment is impossible, that does not render it any less imperative.

The Freudian superego is similar to Kant's categorical imperative. "The superego—the conscience at work in the ego—may become harsh, cruel, and inexorable against the ego which is in its charge," says Freud. "Kant's Categorical Imperative is thus the direct heir of the Oedipal Complex."[18] For Kant, "it is . . . the moral law that first determines and makes possible the concept of the good.[19] It is the law that makes a moral action good, not the empirical end that it is supposed to serve. For philosophy, good will is that which acts according to the ought, and only according to the ought. Its imperative is not hypothetical, as is the case with the imperative to desire, but a priori, categorical, and absolute.

Contrasting it with the moral faculty, Kant conceives the faculty of desire as proceeding from the hypothetical imperative:[20] if an action ought to contribute to well-being, then the means by which it is achieved can be called good. The maxim "the end justifies the means," the very principle of immorality, is for Kant the principle of desire: the goal of every desire is related in one way or another to the *Wohl*, the well-being of the subject, rather than to an a priori law that takes no account of the subject's interests.

For an action to be moral, then, it should not be motivated by anything other than the moral law. It suffices for my action to be affected by the least pathological motive to not be moral. To act morally, I must recuse myself of every pathos, what Lacan calls the "radical rejection of the pathological."[21] For as Kant maintains, "apathy is an indispensable condition of virtue.[22]

Kant's moral law brings about the annulment of any enjoyment that might still honor the pleasure principle. It is in some way identical with *Das Ding,* for it has the same blind, absolute, and mute character. And just what is this will that orders the law to be carried out in an entirely apathetic way? For Lacan, that will is "the will of the Other," as it is the will not for pleasure but enjoyment—an enjoyment, it bears repeating, that is absolute and mortifying.

Just like the moralist, the Sadean pervert acts according to the categorical imperative of the Other's will, an other that imposes him to enjoy, and to enjoy at all cost.[23] The pervert transfers to the other the cruel effect of the Other's law, and through dissociation he is reduced to being only the apathetic agent of the law of the Other.

The idea of the pervert as the obsequious mandator of the Other's law of course contradicts the common idea that the pervert desires to be the law's transgressor instead of its delegate. As Jean Clavreul explains, "It is said that the pervert lacks a Superego, which is idiotic, or at least that he considers the Superego to be the law [of the community], but integrated, made his own. That the superego is ferocious and obscene is nevertheless what the pervert endlessly repeats to us, in allowing us the possibility of incarnating it, which in turn enables him to disavow what we pretend to do for him for both his protection and that of society."[24]

To be, like the pervert, in disavowal *[désaveu]* is not the same as having nothing to avow *[san aveu].* The pervert follows the law of his desire, not the law of the community of brothers. The pervert gives his desire the force of law, which excludes every fetter on its realization. Once the pervert succeeds at making his own desire into the law of his behavior, he institutes the only ethics to which he will thenceforward be able to adhere. "The pervert escapes," as Clavreul puts it, "the oppositions between law and desire by attempting to find in them a common vector."[25]

In *Bad Education,* Almodóvar provides a very subtle treatment of perversion. One of the film's central characters is a Catholic priest and teacher, Father Manolo, who teaches and seduces adolescents. That is, he compels through his position respect for the law even as he himself transgresses it. At the same time, we are shown that Father Manolo has his own law, which he cannot transgress: the law of his desire, a law beyond every law. This desire is encumbering, ferocious, absolute, and pushes him toward an enjoyment that is abulic, almost autistic. The horror we feel before Manolo is strong, and directly proportional to the sort of horror that triggers in us limitless enjoyment, the kind identified with the law of the Other: a horror that also attracts.

If the superego can be compared to the categorical imperative, it might be said that it does not necessarily seek with its commandments the good of the subject. The pervert's superego is a case in point, as his superego drives him beyond the pleasure principle. Yet in another of its faces, the superego is prohibiting: it banishes enjoyment that is ferocious, annihilating, and impossible. The superego holds an ambivalent position, and its law is double: it both prohibits and imposes enjoyment.

In its prohibiting side, the superego is a demand, in the form of an imperative, to which the subject must submit; it thus seals an alliance with the father: "You will not desire he who has my desire." The formation of the superego consists of a reinforcement of paternal love and the idealization of the father, both of which are in direct proportion to the wish for his death that accompanies incestuous desire.[26]

The superego other's side sees it command enjoyment, imposes the desire to go all the way, and to accept neither compromise nor accommodation. Lacan indicates that "were the law in effect to order 'Jouis!' [Enjoy!] the subject could only reply 'J'ouïs' [I heard]."[27] The law of the superego is speech that has become voice, the drive-object that transgresses the symbolic function of the father.[28] Language and speech act in concert in the superego that commands enjoyment.

The superego is revealed to be "obscene and ferocious" in both cases: in the first, the subject is submitted to the domination of a model figure, which opens the way to sacrificial enjoyment with respect to a father chosen as ideal; in the second, the subject is made to serve the Other's enjoyment.

Now, desire is in rapport with the two laws of the superego.[29] The law of the Freudian superego, the "small law," prohibits enjoyment of the mother and orders the subject to not cross the pleasure principle. This is the law that governs the symbolic order and the metonymic drift of desire: the small law forbids desire to ever find an object by which it could be fulfilled. In contrast, the law of the Other, the "big Law," is that of the Thing, law that commands enjoyment without mediation. The little law imposes a limit on desire, which the big Law then causes it to overflow so that it eventually becomes confused with enjoyment.

There is desire that goes beyond the pleasure principle, the little law, beyond any and every empirical object capable of providing it with partial satisfaction; such desire is not constrained by prohibition and castration, and is ultimately indistinguishable from the drives. It is desire completely "free," free of being confused with the desire of the Other. It is the Law for the Law, the moral law, the pervert's law that is enfolded with will of his desire (which is always the desire of the Other).

Lacan writes that in Sade "the freedom to desire . . . is a new factor, not because it has inspired a revolution—people have always fought and died for a desire—but because this revolution wants its struggle to be for the freedom of desire."[30] "Free" desire is incontestably a perverse desire, perverted by the Other's desire. So then which is more free, desire without limits, or desire marked by prohibition?

In "Kant with Sade," Lacan is still stating that "law and repressed desire are one and the same thing."[31] But he also stresses here, just a little after, that "this demonstrates from another vantage that desire is the flipside of the law."[32] The two sentences are not contradictory: one must always establish if it is the little law, which prohibits enjoyment, or the big Law, which commands it, that is being referred to; in other words, whether Lacan is speaking in any such case of desire protected by fantasy, that is, barred by castration, or of "pure," unconditioned desire, like that of the pervert. Lacan asks: "How far does Sade lead us in the experience of this enjoyment, or simply of its truth? For the human pyramids he describes, which are fabulous insofar as they demonstrate the cascading nature of enjoyment, these water buffets of desire built so that enjoyment makes the Villa d'Este Gardens sparkle with a baroque voluptuousness—the higher they try to make enjoyment spurt up in the heavens, the more insistently the question, 'What is it that is flowing here?' demands to be answered [*que plus proche nous attirerait la question de ce qui est là ruisselant*]. Unpredictable quanta by which the love/hate atom glistens in the vicinity of the Thing from which man emerges through a cry, what is experienced, beyond certain limits, has nothing to do with what desire is propped up by in fantasy, which is in fact constituted on the basis of these limits."[33] Apart from delighting us with its beauty, this passage tells us that desire that is supported by fantasy is restricted, "limited" desire, desire that is opposed to the law of infinite enjoyment. But Lacan also says that desire is "propped up by a fantasy that has at least one foot in the Other."[34] Such is the equivocal position of desire: it falls short of and also lies on the other side of the law.

Lacan establishes that Kant's moral law, the Law for/of the Law, and unconditioned, "pure" desire are equivalent. "Experience shows us," he says in *The Four Fundamental Concepts of Psychoanalysis,* "that Kant is more true [than Spinoza], and I have proved that his theory of consciousness, when he writes of practical reason, is sustained only by giving a specification of the moral law which, looked at more closely, is simply desire in its pure state, that very desire that culminates in the sacrifice strictly speaking, of everything that is object of love in one's human tenderness—I would say, not only in the rejection of the pathological object, but also in its sacrifice and murder. That is why I wrote *Kant avec Sade.*"[35]

In *The Ethics of Psychoanalysis,* Lacan presents Antigone's desire as an example of this pure desire, that is, a desire that is confounded with enjoyment and reveals itself to be incestuous, a desire for death.[36] Antigone "chooses" death after having defied the decree of Creon by providing her brother Polynices with a sepulcher. She transgresses the law of the city in order to follow the law of her desire: an intransigent, absolute desire that will lead to her death. Hers is a desire that is realized in the end, in the sense of the end of life, by way of death. "The way toward death is nothing other than what is called enjoyment," affirms Lacan.[37]

Three limit points, which together constitute the real as impossible, converge in pure desire: enjoyment, incest, and death. The tragedy of Antigone demonstrates this. Pure desire is traversed by an enjoyment that severs the generational line.

At the origin of the tragedy is the desire of her mother, Jocasta, a desire apropos of which Lacan asks, "What happens to Antigone's desire? Shouldn't it be the desire of the Other and be linked to the desire of the mother? The text alludes to the fact that the desire of the mother is the origin of everything. The desire of the mother is the founding desire of the whole structure . . . but it is also criminal desire. . . . No mediation is possible here except that of this desire with its radically destructive character."[38]

This is a disturbing origin for desire, this desire of the Other, which Lacan identifies with the desire of the mother (with the subjective and objective genitives alike applying), this duplicitous desire that both gives life and ushers destruction (the mother's desire is always criminal). This does not, though, entail making the mother a bad mother in Melanie Klein's sense, an obscene figure of the superego. Lacan instead endeavors to show that desire is caught in a precise structure that is independent of the specific behaviors of all the maternal figures that have been encountered by the subject. The variations within each psychic structure notwithstanding, the foundations of desire remain the same: it is desire at the incestuous, destructive origin. It remains to be seen in what way and to what extent the subject can oppose it. These lines from Bataille's novel *My Mother* are apropos here:

> "What do I want?" said my mother to me. "To indulge all my desires before I die."
> "Mamma, even the most crazy?"
> "Yes son, even the most crazy."
> She smiled, or rather, laughter twisted her lips. As if she might, by laughing, eat me.[39]

Desire, we have seen, is constructed on the basis of a primordial repression, the repression of the Other's desire. A limit impossible to cross, this is a foundational repression that pure desire wishes to uncover, through sacrifice and self-destruction.

"Indestructible desire" does not mean that the subject should destroy himself for it. Indestructible desire does not underlie repression, as the truth of unconscious desire. Intransigence is not a criterion for the truth of desire: sacrifice to a cause does not make it right.

Can we compare pure desire with the absolute desire of the pervert? In fact, they can be seen as two limbs of the same desire: purity on the one hand, and perversion on the other. The characters in *The Law of Desire* are perverse in their sexual habits and structure: homosexuals, transvestites, or even people who simply desire too much.[40] The big Law that governs them requires them to push their desire to the extreme, and this can (as we saw with Antigone) lead to death, whether their own or that of the other. Death, in that case, is no longer a consequence but a desire. The paradox is evident: desire that wants to be realized in the most intense point of life, that pushes past "banal, insipid homoeostasis," reveals itself to be a desire for death. The Law of desire lets death be bypassed, so that another will be met. Desire is satisfied by crossing life's limit. This proximity of death can be felt by the subject when it desires, which explains why it is quite often simply afraid to desire.

To desire or not to desire? "I propose," Lacan famously replies, "that the only thing of which one can be guilty is of having given ground [*cédé*] on one's desire."[41] Now which of the two desires is he speaking? A desire that is subject to the double law, both the little law, which refuses enjoyment and blocks desire, and the big Law, which grants desire an incommensurate, infinite measure. But if that is the case, then to which law should one submit? Must one remain short of or go beyond the pleasure principle?

The situation is quite tragic, as we end up guilty no matter what we do: if we pass to the infinite side of desire, we end up before the law that prohibits enjoyment, and if we stay with the finite, we remain under the law that decrees it. Both cases, then, deprive us of choice. Desire's infinite and finite sides are superimposed, and desire becomes impossible. Lacan again confirms it: "What needs to be unmasked . . . is nothing less than the impossibility in which we recognize the topology of our desire."[42]

Pure desire is tied to incest, madness, and perversion, for it is "pure" only from being submitted to a radical purification of the kind Sade called for: a rejection of everything that can be modified, altered, and to some extent overturned in one's original desire, that of the Other. In contrast, any desire that has been altered through its subjected to the little law, which is that of castration, includes death, even while not being death.

It is therefore impure desire that is conceivable, as betrayal is more beneficial than fidelity, the latter being possible only at the cost of sacrifice. Whenever desire is possible, some betrayal is always involved: infidelity to the Other's desire saves us.

The transgression of prohibition leads to enjoyment, which is thenceforward equivalent to death. Bataille sees a door opening itself from transgression. Yet for Lacan, "libido . . . at fleeting moments carries us beyond the encounter" between desire and enjoyment, between life and death, and "makes us forget it."[43] This is at once the same theory as Bataille's and its contrary, since while there is certainly for Lacan here the surpassing of contradiction, it engenders a moment of forgetting rather than heightened consciousness.

Infinite desire in Bataille's thought has already been dealt with here, but to reiterate: desire for him is infinite because it is the only path to enjoyment, and because it is already enjoyment. It creates neither a disconnection from nor an obstruction of enjoyment and eventually becomes confused with it, most notably in transgression.

So if we follow Bataille, erotic desire pursues and brings about a kind of enjoyment that gives one the feeling that life and death are indistinguishable but which of course does not involve any real risk of death. In this sense, Bataille's notion of desire is not pure, despite being unconditioned. Certain characters in his work move, like Antigone, toward death, but that does not require us to conclude that we are in immediate danger of death as soon as we are desiring. In truth, there is no need to go all the way to death for Bataille, as sex itself [le rapport sexuel] suffices to give us a certain experience of death.

For Bataille, like Lacan, desire is at once tempting and forbidden. But for Lacan, desire does not lead directly to enjoyment: "Seeing a door half-open," as he says in 1969, "is not the same as going through it."[44]

Enjoyment presents itself in desire, but again in tiny extremities, in tips. Brief, transient surges of enjoyment sometimes transpire in the life of the subject, during dreams or syncopes, or even in love, and this is always—here Lacan stands with Bataille—tied to horror.[45]

Desire is a strange conjuncture of the pursuit and prevention of enjoyment, which can happen only through its prohibition and the barrier against it—in other words, through desire (enjoyment is in need of contradiction). To enjoy prohibition involves the enjoyment of its impotence, which, by insisting, opens up a breach in enjoyment: to enjoy at the same time both its impossibility and its transgression, in fantasy.[46] This is ferocious enjoyment, enraged at being unable to go all the way, to push beyond the pleasure principle. Rage, anger, paroxysm: transgression always rhymes with violence. Such enjoyment is also incomplete, for it needs to be at once finite and infinite.

Unconditioned desire escapes from the subject but nonetheless grants the latter its singularity. Both Bataille and Lacan view desire as a challenge to all conceptions of a natural order, as well as to moral law and social pressure. For Bataille, though, desire qua interior experience sometimes seems to verge on metaphysics. Lacan differs by helping us liberate ourselves from our expectant wait for some Revelation, or at least from whatever "revelation" is awaited when one undergoes an analysis, which is at any rate more modest: that is, the analysand discovers the contradiction in his desire, one that he can only confront with difficulty since it has gone unperceived. He also discovers that all enjoyment is invariably tied to loss. And yet in the end, the stakes are not that modest, since that discovery can turn the analysand upside down and modify his behavior, or at least his affects.

9
Enjoyment:
All and Not-All

Novelty is always the condition of enjoyment.
—Freud, *Beyond the Pleasure Principle*

Freud showed that sexual enjoyment cannot be reduced to simple physiological pleasure, ejaculation or physical discharge—and that this applies to women as much to men.

And if feminine sexual enjoyment nonetheless remains enigmatic to Freud, Lacan eventually pinpoints its specificity (even if he is not exclusively referring to sexual enjoyment when he speaks of "woman's enjoyment" *[jouissance de la femme]*). Feminine enjoyment cannot only be Other—"Other than phallic," he says[1]—that is, beyond the enjoyment of an organ and even of castration: it is, rather, a question of a supplementary[2] enjoyment, not-all *[pas-toute]* phallic[3] and close to religious and mystical ecstasy.[4] An enjoyment of woman of which "she knows nothing, other than that she experiences it."[5] There is a hole in feminine enjoyment by virtue of the impossibility of saying it (an enjoyment that Lacan writes as S($\bar{A}$)).

Lacan rejected the question of feminine enjoyment that had previously interested psychoanalysts, which concerned the organic division between clitoral and vaginal enjoyment. That question was based on the conviction that to become a woman requires having experienced vaginal orgasm.

For Lacan, the other enjoyment of woman is situated between an enjoyment outside the body and another that is outside language, between castration (Φ) and enjoyment that is impossible to say (S($\bar{A}$)).

The comparison Lacan undertakes between mystical enjoyment and that of woman is, however, an unexpected and original notion that is not easy to verify. This is first of all because he treats the distinction between the two enjoyments as fundamental: mystical enjoyment is solitary, while that of woman need not be. Sexual enjoyment, of coitus, involves the other; the partner is present materially at the moment when the woman comes [jouit], even if the latter is smitten by her own body or fantasy as stimulating for the other.

Of course the mystic can enjoy the love of God in his or her own body, as the corporeal marks, stigmata, self-flagellation, and self-punishment of certain of the Christian mystics all attest. Yet it cannot be said that God holds for the mystic the same function as the partner in the sexual relationship: if it is God who feeds the fantasy of the mystic, he is not physically present during enjoyment! In this sense, masturbation, which is also solitary enjoyment, seems much closer to mystical enjoyment than that arising from sex acts.

For a woman, to enjoy man—to enjoy [jouit] in the presence of a man, or with a man, or for a man—is not the same as enjoying God, whether corporeally or spiritually, in his supposed presence or absence. It is not at all the same thing as enjoying a signifier of "llanguage" [lalangue], as is the case with Hadewijch of Anver, who, per Michel Bousseyroux's assessment, enjoyed via the neologism minne: "enjoying minne is," he writes, "enjoying the abyss of S($\cancel{A}$)."[6] Bousseyroux cites this passage from Hadewijch:

> But then wonder seized me because of all the riches that I had seen in him, and through this wonder I came out of the spirit in which I had seen all that I sought; and as in this situation in all this rich enlightenment I recognized my awe-inspiring, my unspeakably sweet Beloved, I fell out of the spirit—from myself and all that I had seen in him—and wholly lost, fell upon the breast, the fruition, of his Nature, which is Love. There I remained, engulfed and lost, without any comprehension of other knowledge.[7]

The feeling of annihilation, the abyss experienced by the mystics, is comparable to what the speaking being can feel during amorous enjoyment. Loss in/of the Other/other, convulsion, bewitchment, engulfment, abyss . . . The celebrated formula by which Breton ended Nadja is apposite here: "Beauty will be CONVULSIVE or will not be at all."[8]

We see, in this verse by Baudelaire, the feeling of the abyss and the infinite that can evoke amorous experience:

You are a candle where the mayfly dies
In flames, blessing this fire's deadly bloom
The painting lover bending to his love
Looks like a dying man who stokes his tomb.

What difference, then, from heaven or from hell,
O Beauty, monstrous in simplicity?
If eye, smile, step can open me the way
To find unknown, sublime infinity?[9]

In *Dark Night of the Soul*, John of the Cross compares amorous enjoyment ("material night") and the enjoyment of God ("spiritual night") while nevertheless celebrating the immense advantages of this latter form of love.

Oh night that guided me,
Oh night more lovely than the dawn.
Oh night that joined Beloved with lover,
Lover transformed in The Beloved!

The breeze flew from the turret
As I parted his locks.
With his gentle hand he wounded my neck
And caused all my senses to be suspended.

I remained, lost in oblivion;
My face I reclined on the Beloved.
All ceased and I abandoned myself,
Leaving my cares forgotten among the lilies.[10]

But we must return to mystical enjoyment, which is, according to Lacan, enjoyment *beyond* the phallus (Φ). In effect, such enjoyment can only with difficulty be conceived as nonphallic, as it is realized in the name of an idealized father and is in this sense bound up with the phallic symbol.[11]

Yet according to Lacan's hypothesis, the phallic symbol, qua the structural element of enjoyment of the speaking being, is "exceeded," crossed over *[franchi]*. The mystic would then experience a supplementary enjoyment specific to the order of S($Å$), what Lacan calls "enjoyment of the signifier of the lack of the Other," for his God would be *not-all [pastout]*.

But what is a *not-all* God? Bousseyroux tells us that through knowledge of God, the mystics undergo the experience of his absence. It is the Nothing that is lived via the excess of their passion, a nothing that makes them enjoy: "The mystics attest that God is the *not-all* and that he is identified with the gap *[la béance]* and the darkness of love in which they are annihilated. They are moved to say that in the excess of God is the Nothing that they enjoy!"[12]

By invoking God, the mystic encounters the Nothing, a process that is analogous to that of the neurotic who seeks the phallus and finds castration. This is inevitable, whether it is the omnipotence *[toute-puissance]* of God or that of the phallus that is at stake: neither one exists, for the neurotic just as much as the mystic is unable to encounter them as absences. Enjoyful absences of course: just as the Nothing does for the mystic, lack makes the neurotic enjoy.[13]

It should nevertheless be noted that there is a difference between mystical and hysterical enjoyment: the "lack of God" of the mystic is not the "lack of caviar" of the butcher's wife from Freud's famous analysis in the *Traumdeutung* and Lacan's subsequent commentary.[14] The hysteric enjoys the fact that the Other, being impotent, cannot make him or her enjoy: he or she enjoys nonsatisfaction. The mystic, in contrast, enjoys the lack of God, in the sense that God ends up *logically* lacking in the mystics' attempt to rejoin it: the Other enjoyment is an acceptance *[assomption]* of the absence of God, following Bousseyroux. One cannot at any rate think that the Other (God) is always—symbolically—present in fantasy qua absence, and as impossible (to be or to have).

Then to what does the big barred Other ($Å$) correspond? "Lack *in* the Other" (the barred Other) and "lack *of* the Other" (the inexistence of the Other) are not equivalent formulas. Is the Other, which the mystics regarded, per Bousseyroux's expression, as "the hole of a whirling abyss," lacking?[15] In other words, is it a *not-all* God? And is a *not-all* God an absent God? Whence the question: is there a difference between the enjoyment of the barred Other ($Å$) and the enjoyment of the Other that does not exist? Or more precisely, what is it that the mystic enjoys in her enjoyment of the "lack of God"? A God who is supposed to be missing (something), or the missing (absent) God?

According to Bousseyroux, for Hadewijch, "there is contiguity between enjoyment and the flaw in this enjoyment that one finds in the phonetic and semantic sliding of the Middle Dutch in which it is expressed, through the form of two paronyms, *ghebruken,* to enjoy, and *ghebreken,* to be lacking, at fault."[16] But what is it about the lack in the mystic's encounter with God (and with his perfect and inaccessible enjoyment) that structurally distinguishes it from the lack in the speaking being's encounter with the Other (and with its incestuous and impossible enjoyment)?

To accept *[assumer]* castration is not the same thing as accepting the absence of the Other.[17] For the speaking being, whether in analysis or not, two distinct experiences are necessary to be able to assume its desire and enjoy it (this enjoyment does not correspond to that of the hysteric's nonsatisfaction). If for the hysteric the destitution of the Other occurs through the experience of its incompleteness and inconsistency, for the mystic this destitution happens, by Bousseyroux's hypothesis, through ecstasy. How to carry out the transition from the all-powerful Other (God) to the barred Other (God) in ecstasy?

In another passage from Hadewijch, from a letter to a friend, she writes: "You must also live in joyful hope and strong confidence that God will allow you to love him with that great love wherewith he loves himself, Three and One, and wherewith he has eternally sufficed to himself and so shall suffice eternally. In contenting him with that love, all the denizens of heaven are and shall be eternally engaged. This is their occupation, which never comes to an end, and the incompletion of this beautiful fruition *[jouissance]* is yet the sweetest fruition *[jouissance]*."[18]

Bousseyroux remarks that it is through lack (of enjoyment, that of God) that another enjoyment happens: "there is," he writes, "another enjoyment, which is the most sweet, taken from this lack of enjoyment of God."[19] He also writes that "of this other, more sweet enjoyment, which resonates for us with the other enjoyment of which Lacan speaks of, [Hadewijch] says that she is in what is lacking in God's enjoyment, that it is in that lack that she comes."[20]

But in the passage in question, Hadewijch does not speak of the lack in the enjoyment *of* God (subjective genitive). There is no lack in the enjoyment that God experiences in loving himself: God "sufficed to himself and so shall suffice eternally," as she writes.[21] God lacks not (A), nor does he lack enjoyment (J(A)).

Hadewijch instead considers both her own enjoyment and that of heavenly beings that are lacking, and not that of God, who is, it must be repeated, complete and self-sufficient, non-barred ($J(A)$). "The lack of enjoyment *of* God" is in the mystic and the denizens of heaven but not in God himself, who does not lack an enjoyment of himself.

The mystic lacks (Φ) the possibility of rendering equivalent her love *of* God (objective genitive) and the love *of* God (subjective genitive). It is the impossible encounter with God that renders the mystic's enjoyment barred ($J(A)$),[22] and the latter, in this failure, becomes an "Other enjoyment" that is, says Hadewijch, more sweet than the enjoyment of those who are at pains to love God as he loves himself. But this Other enjoyment—the enjoyment of the lack of the encounter with God[23]—is still not more sweet than the enjoyment of God (subjective genitive), the enjoyment experienced by God himself—which, in Hadewijch's view, is a perfect and eternal enjoyment.

The comments of a psychotic patient in a mystical crisis can illumine this point. As he avowed to me during one of our sessions: "I feel like John of the Cross. My soul, like St. John's, is in a quest for God . . . for I have lost my God! I know what it means to lose faith, to lose God's support in life, and it's a state impossible to live! I can only see one way out now, and that's suicide, as I can no longer live without God, can't accept to doubt him, or his existence, his love . . . God wanted to test me. Just like St. John, I had to undertake a spiritual journey to find my God again. And I finally found God once more, and his immense love. The only imperfection is in me, me of little faith, not in God . . . God is perfect in his vast power and magnanimity, is entirely independent of the fluctuations of my soul."

This patient's words, which were directly inspired by John of the Cross, show that the lack in man (whether the speaking being or the mystic), who does not manage to love God in his perfection and permanence, does not at all depend on any supposed lack *in* God or *of* God. It is human imperfection that pushes him to doubt God's existence and love, while God himself is not at fault: from the point of view of a mystic or a psychotic in a mystical crisis, God remains perfect, immovable, omnipotent.

Enjoyment that passes through lack—through Nothing—is more sweet, for Hadewijch, than enjoyment that involves a hopeless attempt to become equal to the enjoyment felt by God. The sense of this *Other* enjoyment to the mystic is revealed to be an act of humility, a humble inclination toward the Above.[24] It is an affirmation of absolute distance of the mystic from God, a God again who is omnipotent and enjoys in a self-sufficient and eternal way. Man is in such a miserable condition that he seeks God but only encounters Nothing, which the mystic celebrates through spiritual self-flagellation—which is also enjoyful, of course.

Yet being unable to enjoy God does not, in the eyes of the mystic, bar him. To think, as Hadewijch does, that the Other (God) enjoys self-love in his omnipotence means that he continues to exist, in his perfection, consistence, and completeness (A).

For certain women, the question of enjoyment remains even more obscure than it is in the mystics. Pleasure, arousal, satisfaction, anxiety, submission, pain, love: what is the border between these different moments of sex *[le rapport sexuel]*? And what of the "unclassifiable" forms of feminine enjoyment, of enjoyment that corresponds neither to orgasm nor to phallic enjoyment, nor even to Lacan's Other enjoyment?

To draw clinical distinctions between the different enjoyments felt by a woman in sexual relations allows us to foreground both the complexity of her sexual behavior and the impossibility of treating her enjoyment as an idealized stereotype. The hypothesis that there is an enjoyment specific to woman risks making of it an ideal, a final end to be rejoined; in short, a "norm": there would be, on the one hand, good enjoyment—the true—and, on the other, its inauthentic, symptomatic, autoerotic, and neurotic forms.

In what follows, the extranormative character of feminine sexual enjoyment in the sexual relation will be analyzed with respect to its different forms, and how these relate both to the condition of woman as such and to subjective particularities among women. Stimulation will be taken up in its relation to frigidity and sexual enjoyment, and an attempt will be made to show that simulation is in rapport with the desire of the subject and is not antithetical to enjoyment.

An analysand once said to me, "I love to make love, and with X. it's really good, I mean, the sex is great. Actually, I don't know if I have come . . . no, I don't believe I ever did. Or maybe I did . . . I don't know. In any case, it's great with him!" How can one know in light of such statements if a sexual relationship *[le rapport sexual]* involves "true" enjoyment or only a semblance of it? And how ought one analyze a kind of enjoyment that has as a characteristic its confusion with its absence?

On the subject of the enjoyment of Teresa of Avila, the saint and mystic represented in Bernini's celebrated sculpture in Santa Maria della Vittoria, Lacan famously states: "You need but go to Rome and see the statue by Bernini to immediately understand that she's coming. There's no doubt about it. What is she getting off on? It is clear that the essential testimony of the mystics consists in saying that they experience it, but know nothing about it."[25] It must not be forgotten that this sculpture is the work of a mannerist artist who portrayed the fantasies of men, about the enjoyment of saints, women, and so on.[26] In any case, we can always ask whether a woman whose mouth is open, eyes closed, and body lasciviously splayed is coming [jouir] or faking it. In the same way, a man who watches his partner "enjoying" him is rarely certain if she is experiencing sexual ecstasy or only simulating.

In a monologue titled "After Love," which is part of a performance called *Farm Chickens*, the Italian comedian Giorgio Gaber reckons with the problem of recognizing woman's enjoyment:

> To summarize: I had an orgasm, but as for her . . . who knows! Anyway, nobody ever knows! Hell, it's a conspiracy. A man gets together with a woman once, twice, ten times, and he never knows! Basta! It's also pretty hard to ask. Most of the time, you just say, "Was it good for you?" [Ça a été?], and she goes, "Yeah, of course!" Of course what?! What does that even mean? Such insanity! I mean, for men, it's clear: when he comes hard, it's obvious! The proof is right there! But her . . . Basically, how do women function? Hell, there's no proof! That's why a man just lies there, naked, like an idiot, asking himself, "So was I good or was I not good?" And selfishness, withdrawing, staying present, the harmony, the bumbling gesture . . . Was she there, or not there? And the timing is off . . . Did he ejaculate or not? And there you have it: The double header of orgasms!

While sexual arousal is manifest for women and not just for men (in the sense that it is displayed in lubrication for women and an erection for men), female orgasm does not manifest itself through signs as evident as those accompanying male orgasm. This does not mean that the process by which a man is brought to climax *[jouissance]* is simple and mechanical. The assumption that male orgasm is self-evident can of course be doubted as well. As a patient once admitted to me, when speaking of his enjoyment in a sexual relationship with a woman, "I don't know if I had an orgasm with her . . . Okay, I think so . . . In any case, it was quite flat, certainly middling, and very mediocre."

"Physical" and "psychic" enjoyment must be distinguished, even though they can occur at the same time in sexual relations, particularly during orgasm.[27] Orgasm, however, is not synonymous with ejaculation or discharge: while ejaculation cannot be dissociated from orgasm, it does not necessarily include psychic enjoyment. Some men complain that their enjoyment of their partners is often not completely satisfactory—is just "modest," as another patient said to me—even as they manage to come *[jouir]* with them, in the senses of ejaculation and physiological release.

Although the term "psychic enjoyment" is doubtlessly unsatisfactory, it allows us to mark the importance to both partners in a sexual relationship of the way they *meet* in desire, a meeting that transpires at the level of fantasy and that is ostensibly favorable to enjoyment. Following Lacan, if something is to happen between a man and a woman, a "consonance of unconsciousness" is necessary.[28]

This meeting of two fantasies—a kind of meeting that is not synonymous with their accord, harmony, or fusion—is essential if one is going to talk of orgasm in the sexual relation. Discharge does not, though, necessarily imply such a meeting: the fantasy of the subject is of course always active in a sexual relation, but it is not always "consonant" with that of the partner.[29] Even if a sexual relationship involves both subjects, the sexual act is much like masturbation. It is for this reason that orgasm cannot be equated with physical release.

He or she who enjoys without any preoccupation with the enjoyment of the other remains much closer to masturbatory enjoyment than that specific to coitus. In fact, the sex act *[le rapport sexuel]* can become in certain cases equivalent to actual masturbation. Masturbatory enjoyment is not of the same order as orgasm, for the latter involves the presence of the other, the partner who brings release, and can take a particularly intense form when the other is truly implicated in it. The enjoyment of the other intensifies the enjoyment of the subject (provided, again, that their fantasies meet).

Feminine enjoyment includes physiological changes (muscular contraction, female ejaculation, etc.) that also become manifest during mere sexual arousal. It is for this reason that the nature of a woman's orgasm cannot be determined on the basis of physical changes, as they are not proof of anything. As for men, arousal and enjoyment are physically distinct phenomena: an erection is a clear indication of excitement, in the same way that ejaculation is of coming [la jouissance sexuelle] (unless a man is sufficiently disturbed as to lose his capacity for one or both).

For women, it is not the body that *speaks,* openly, of her pleasure; her body does not necessarily reveal what is taking place at the level of psychic enjoyment. Men may think that they can know, or at least sense, if their partner is reaching orgasm, but they are never doing more than making an assumption. For doubts can always crop up—was she excited or did she orgasm? The issue is not whether an instance of ejaculation corresponds to physiological discharge or psychic enjoyment, as the question is much more radical: is this woman coming [*jouir*] or faking it? Determining the answer is all the more difficult given that women can also blur the distinction between enjoyment and simulation.

Simulation is of course closely related to feminine frigidity, but not necessarily. According to the first of the above hypotheses, symptomatic enjoyment is alienating. But it also can become a form of opening to the other and its enjoyment: this is the second hypothesis that we have been considering.

Enjoyment is often feigned in order to create pleasure in a partner, a pleasure in the other that itself engenders (symptomatic) satisfaction for the subject. This "pleasure in the pleasure of the other" is contiguous with pain, eroticized pain which the woman hides—and "hides herself"—in order to present herself as an "occasion for pleasure."

The woman who simulates enjoyment responds to the desire of the other by means of a desire that is not her own. This desire nevertheless moves through her, making her into an object capable of responding to the other's need for enjoyment: an *other* who becomes *Other,* as the woman submits herself to it, making herself into the object of its enjoyment (by forgetting her own). But the sacrifice of her own enjoyment is still enjoyment, or enjoyment and its failure: an enjoyment that is empty, apathetic, uniform, and never discontinuous.

In order for there to be the sort of sexual connection [le rapport sexuel] that I have been calling orgasm, the *other* (the partner) has to be opposed to the *Other* and without any obsession with fusional unity: the meeting of fantasies frequently presents itself under the form of opposition, conflict, counteraction, and clash (the consonance of un-consciousnesses is not romance). In other words, the sexual relation is quite distinct from fusion, as if it were necessary to deny the disconti-nuity, intermittence, and fracture between lovers with orgasm.

The sexual couple becomes, paradoxically, a *trio*: the partner as-sumes the function of a third, but not in the sense of a witness or spec-tator. During sex, the partner is the element that at once allows for unity and breaks it (the *consonance* of unconsciousnesses necessarily includes a certain *discordance* between two fantasies), that institutes phallic satisfaction while at the same time undoing it: every orgasm, after all, ushers the end of physical tumescence[30] and suspends sexual desire.[31]

Enjoyment that involves simulation is lacking the third, and the subject forms a couple with herself (an autoerotic fantasy) in which there is neither disconnection nor any possible obstruction: "I fuse with myself," as a patient once told me when broaching the question of simulation. It is in this sense that simulation can be said to be a sort of enjoyment that verges on autoeroticism.[32]

Another patient admitted to me that she always simulated with her partners, her husband included: "I never knew what an orgasm was before I made love with a woman.[33] With men, I was always faking [semblant]. The men in my encounters never understood how my body functioned or how I might obtain pleasure . . . As if my body were basi-cally of no interest."[34]

So why does she simulate? "I want to give pleasure to my man," she told me. "And I don't want him to be disappointed in me. I've often thought that the problem is me, that I'm no good, and am not able to come [jouir]. I don't want my partner to see that I'm not able to make him come [jouir] . . . I always feel inferior around men. I always see men who are perfect, powerful, and completely self-realized . . . men who represent the ideal for me . . . basically, great men. So I should be

my best, or at least make it seem that way . . . I don't want to deceive—
I want to give them pleasure."

To simulate while forgetting her own pleasure—or while sacrific-
ing it to that of the other/Other—can be an indication of frigidity, of
an "enjoyable" frigidity. Frigidity is essentially solitary enjoyment, in
which the subject's desire is not supported and stimulated by that of
the other but instead only by the latter's demand (for enjoyment). This
patient sacrificed her orgasm for an ideal—the ideal (of) man as well
as an ideal of herself, the woman who causes enjoyment.

When simulating enjoyment, a woman will imagine and "represent," through the postures of her body and facial expressions, the
"perfect" sexual enjoyment. "The woman who enjoys herself" (like
Saint Theresa for certain psychoanalysts) becomes the icon, the model,
and the ideal of enjoyment. She also becomes the ideal woman, the
feminine representation of enjoyment outside all limits, a magnificent,
perfect, and complete enjoyment that cannot be tarnished by the prospect of castration: a feminine figure transformed into an omnipotent
woman, and accompanied by the risk that the enjoyment of woman
and that of the mother end up confused.[35]

The woman who has escaped castration and enjoys limitlessly is obviously the dream of certain men. This woman has the mother superimposed over her for enjoying without being castrated, and men thus
voluntarily accept to become her object, the instrument supposed to
furnish this woman—or to the mother?—an *Other* enjoyment, one
that is supplementary, unlimited, and infinite. This could be written
as perfect enjoyment = perfect woman = phallus. Here we find imaginary power: woman is transformed into the phallus, via simulating the
phallus.

Simulation may serve as a technique by which to fascinate man (and
fascinating man is usually pleasurable for a woman). For the Romans,
the word *phallus* did not exist, as what the Greeks named with the word
phallos they instead called *fascinus*.[36] "To fascinate" of course means to
force a person looking at something into not averting his gaze from it,
as happens with the man who sees a woman feigning enjoyment. Such
delight! So it goes with man who submits to the *fascinus* of woman.
Simulation is thus the expression of the (imaginary) omnipotence of
woman, a strange form of identification with the phallus. That identification is of course excessive, and excessive with respect to form, as excess cannot be felt in the body; it is the isolation, distance, and alterity

of woman. And it is also the negation of the other and of its desire, of an other who then exists only to be the spectator of a gleaming emptiness. All that excess is staged in order to deny castration.

Simulation gives a feeling of (imaginary) omnipotence while being at the same time a form of frigidity.[37] Such frigidity is not the negation of enjoyment but a kind of substitutive enjoyment—a symptom. It is a compromise between the possibility and impossibility of enjoying, being both at once but also neither (which is permissible by the impossible logic of the unconscious . . .). In other words, frigidity is the enjoyment of nonsatisifaction and of the symptom.

This form of substitutive enjoyment, which procures the symptom—frigidity—takes the place of sexual enjoyment—orgasm—which is difficult to obtain, as it requires that one pass through castration and the other. Orgasm is antagonistic toward the ideal (of the other, the self). "An 'end of the world' . . . is to be found at the climax of the ecstasy of love," Freud remarks, "and in this case, it is not the ego but the single love object which absorbs all the cathexes directed toward the external world."[38]

"Choosing" to enjoy by not enjoying, by way of frigidity, allows the woman to not lose control during sex. In order to remain phallic, it is better to simulate and enjoy (by) being the object of the enjoyment of the Other (other ≅ Other). The body becomes a *representation* of that "sexual thing"—orgasm—that is impossible to tolerate.

Orgasm in this sense is also intolerable for a young woman who cannot enjoy with her partner, and from whom there is no end, she tells me, to her responsibilities (she herself makes the connection between her professional life and her frigidity during sex [le rapport sexuel]). Not going all the way keeps one from taking any risks, and yet what is the risk in question—failure or success?

Frigidity provides protection against enjoyment, be it excessively strong or inordinately limited (but in either case necessarily leading back to lack). Both at once, the too much and not enough: the two unreconcilable motions remain psychically simultaneous, and expose the grueling, painful, and unlivable impasse of the subject under the influence of castration anxiety, as well as of anxiety[39] that transforms itself into a symptom: frigidity.

The line between enjoyment and its simulation is sometimes difficult to make out for she who faces it. Whether the experience is pleasure or pain, arousal or submission, the authentic or the imagined, enjoyment eludes words, and even sensations. "So how can I know when I am truly enjoying [*jouir*]?" a woman said to me during a session. "It's clear that I experience pleasure. But I don't know if I feel relief or not, whether it's truly satisfaction . . . I don't know what that is. And my boyfriend doesn't know or understand anything. He just keeps saying, 'You're amazing when you come!'"

In "Remarks on Femininity and Its Avatars," Piera Aulagnier analyzes the case of a patient who asked herself, after attending a lecture titled "Enjoyment: A Woman's Right," whether enjoyment is true, or a pure simulacrum. "I was led to ask myself," the patient concluded, "if my enjoyment is a simulacrum, a pretense; yet the pleasure I took from it would still then be real. It's as though I had been told that the most authentic part of me is just a lie, even though this lie had always seemed to be the height of truth." Aulagnier emphasizes that "the problem of feminine enjoyment always borders on the scandalous. . . . For woman, the path of the simulacrum is always available, and it should not be considered to be synonymous with imposture."[40]

Simulation can become a voluntarily chosen behavior for a woman, through devotion to her husband and submission to his pleasure and enjoyment. But simulation is also a form of autoerotic enjoyment capable of engendering a feeling of omnipotence: by simulating, a woman endeavors to take the position of the ideal woman, who is strong in her ability to make the other enjoy. The enjoyment that she thereby draws is symptomatic.

In the passage quoted above, Aulagnier alludes to another form of simulation. This sort of simulation is, on account of what one of my patients has called its authenticity and truth, already a form of enjoyment that is not necessarily symptomatic. Simulation is not in every case a lie, a form of the mystification of enjoyment: it enters, structurally, into the constitution of the orgasm for certain woman, and can even be an (almost) indispensable condition for it.[41] In this sense, simulation—the exaggerated expression of lived pleasure—is not antithetical to sexual enjoyment and can maintain a strong link with it.

Orgasm is not "pure" enjoyment, a pleasure confined to the subject, and detached from that of the partner. It instead requires renouncing singular, autoerotic enjoyment that would be separate and independent from that of the other. Sex is not a solitary experience like mystical ecstasy or masturbation, but rather an abandonment of the self that involves the other (i.e., involves its desire, fantasy, pleasure, enjoyment, and so forth).

Human beings, both men and women, are not monads encapsulated in fantasy and autoerotic enjoyment. A sexual fantasy is activated if it enters into "consonance" with another sexual fantasy that it stimulates (Lacan's "consonance of unconsciousness" once again). And then the subject lets go—forgets the phallus and the ideal—for its desire is borne by the partner (and by its partner's fantasy), and vice versa.

Simulation comes down to saying, "I'm going to show you that you make me feel great, that when I'm with you, I experience pleasure because of you, and that I can't get that pleasure by myself." This is a meeting that is not fusional but in disequilibrium, and discordant. Some women acknowledge that they always (more or less) fake it when they make love. That admission should not come as much of a surprise, as sexual enjoyment (orgasm) necessarily involves semblance.

To make the other enjoy is to belong to the feminine fantasy (that one can always make the other enjoy without renouncing one's own enjoyment), and simulation too is an effect of this fantasy. Displaying to the partner a pleasure that is not (yet) a meeting can nonetheless unleash desire in him, can stimulate him and thereby bring him to enjoy [*jouir*]: desire, arousal, and enjoyment that, through the other—according to the logic of *this* particular fantasy—can eventually be returned to the subject. Simulation is therefore not always a way of being alienated by the enjoyment of the other. Like a balloon, enjoyment bounces back and forth between a pair of subjects: simulation can stimulate and favor enjoyments in reciprocity, especially when orgasm is anticipated.

Distinct from masturbation, this form of simulation in the sexual relation proves that a woman, via the intervention of her fantasy, moves toward the other and seeks to meet with him, through her desire to make her partner desire and enjoy.

It is due to this mechanism of "reverse pleasure" that simulation transforms into sexual enjoyment. In this sense, simulation, the *simulacrum* of enjoyment, is not deception, as it lies beyond the true and the false. In the Nietzschean sense of the word, the simulacrum "pretends" to an appearance, behind which there is no substance, no pretense to ultimate or deep truth.[42] Everything is given at the outset, for truth, after Nietzsche, is not found in depth. The simulacrum is therefore at once true and false, or, inversely, neither true nor false. Not true: because truth is an illusion. Nor false: if truth there is, it is to be found only in the appearance of semblance. Something that Lacan said in 1971 in this regard should be remembered: "Semblance that is given as what it is, is the primary function of truth."[43] Semblance makes the subjective position of the speaking being apparent. If for Lacan, the signifier is semblance par excellence (the phallus, qua signifier, is also semblance), the field of semblance remains irreducible to that of the signifier.

Feminine enjoyment, like that specific to man, maintains a close tie to semblance, even if it cannot be reduced to the latter. Such enjoyment, being both the truth of simulation and the truth of the impossibility of grasping it, lies at a distance from satisfaction, as simulation simultaneously affirms and denies it.

To reiterate, physical enjoyment and psychic enjoyment do not necessarily accompany each other. Psychic enjoyment is difficult to discern, for the factors that produce it are not necessarily apparent in bodily responses. In simulation, enjoyment is independent of the body and its reactions, a body that intervenes either as semblance does (in order to support the fantasy of the enjoyment of the subject) or as pretense [faux-semblant] (in order to support the fantasy of the enjoyment of the other). This does not mean that there is no enjoyment of the body for women, nor that it would be particularly absent among women who simulate. A patient once confided to me that in order to obtain such enjoyment, she has to focus on a specific part of her body in an almost fetishistic way. But it is nevertheless in relation to the other—by way of his gaze, caresses, and attention—that she becomes aroused, and draws sexual enjoyment from that aspect of her body.

According to Lacan's thesis in *Encore,* there exists a feminine enjoyment that "does not pass through the body" but rather "results from a logical demand in speech."[44]

Sexual enjoyment is not foreign to language (with that going for men as much for women). The phrases uttered in the context of sex as well as in romantic love are arousing precisely because they depart from the rationality of discourse. It is as though language was no more: sexual and amorous words assume a corporeal value—a drive status—that is of course enjoyful.

But what is enjoyment that "results from a logical demand in speech"? Is Lacan thinking of an enjoyment that does not require physical pleasure, or even that would entirely exclude bodily pleasure? Or is it that he considers enjoyment to follow exclusively from fantasy?

The answer is that for Lacan, there is in feminine enjoyment "an Other who is incarnated . . . as sexed being,"[45] an Other "outside the body" and thus related to language—as well as with language, of course. The enjoyment outside the body and dominated by the Other of language is far closer to mystical enjoyment and that of simulation than that of feminine orgasm, which is, in all respects, in-bodied [*en-corps*].[46]

Just as Aulagnier's patient said, there is some truth in simulation: the scandalous truth of feminine enjoyment, for sure, but also the truth of fantasy, of desire, of the meeting of discordant enjoyments. Enjoyments remain divided at the level of fantasy, and even too at the level of the body. Simulation—nonsatisfaction and enjoyment at once—reveals itself to be the failure of sexual fusion, but it does not for that exclude the possibility of enjoyment via this failure, and not just through the symptom.

The search for *pure* sexual pleasure, free of every form of semblance, would still be of the order of the ideal, the impossible. Pleasure is always accompanied by nonpleasure, or at least by pleasure that does not reach its culmination; simulation exposes the flaws in feminine enjoyment, proving that an entirely realized enjoyment, without limits and beyond castration, is impossible—or only imaginary.

Simulation, when it is not manifested as a symptom, becomes a constituent aspect of feminine desire and enjoyment that bypasses castration: the remainder of a dreamed-of and inaccessible enjoyment, a barrier against the fusion of beings, an index of the impotence of the subject as well as of woman. Simulation poses an obstacle to the absolute encounter of beings, and yet not to enjoyment. A semblance of enjoyment is already enjoyment: the enjoyment of nonsatisfaction that bears the signs of incompleteness but not of impossibility. To repeat, simulation is a phase in the sexual relationship that brings enjoyment, but without preventing its intensification, as that occurs through the dissonant meeting with the other.

The little other (*a*)—the partner—is an important element in sexual relationship, as it allows the subject to emancipate itself (only partly, of course) from the big Other.[47] The subject enjoys . . . but not for the Other, in its honor, as happens via the symptom.

$J(\bar{A})$ is enjoyment of the *other*, not the *Other*. It is the little other that is to be found at the center of the whole affair. In sexual enjoyment, when it is revealed possible, the Other is already barred, *has been barred* from the moment of the entrance of the little other (a)[48] in the fantasy that gives the subject enjoyment, especially in the fantasy of love (since love is sexually arousing).

It is due to the little other that the subject is freed not only of the Other but also of the self, from the *ego*; the subject forgets itself. At last, finally, it loses itself. It is this destitution of the self rather than that of the Other which brings enjoyment in the sexual relationship, as distinct from mysticism, in which God is transformed into the Nothingness that procures ecstasy.

Sexual enjoyment requires the destruction of the ego. The subject of course tries to resist this by fleeing into its symptoms (simulation, frigidity, impotence, etc.) or by acting out. The ego, shattered to pieces, is exposed in sexual ecstasy to the most extreme weakness. The enjoyment here is of impotence, of the radical impotence of the subject when faced with the swelling of the other's power: the subject is ready to be invaded.

This passive attitude is not the same as that specific to masochism, even if every form of enjoyment is somehow related to it. The loss of self in amorous ecstasy is not a spiritual and intellectual quest as it is for the masochistic disposition; there, the ego is not disintegrated but reinforced by the subject's affirmative will, often conscious, to get itself destroyed by the other.

In amorous ecstasy, the process is almost inverted: the subject allows itself to be invaded, but not destroyed; it abandons itself, exposes itself to a risk in the unconscious, is sustained by the love that it feels coming from the other, a love that renders it phallic while at the same time giving it the strength to depose itself qua phallic power.

This is enjoyment in forgetting oneself, in self-loss, in the destruction of the ego. And this destruction is also a creation, and a disalienation. A destruction of all the armor, of the phallic being of the subject: in lieu of the ego and the phallus one finds the little object (a), which is beyond every stable phallic value (the little object that is exalted, admired, adored, sullied, hated, and on and on), and outside, too, that of exchange.

Loss. Forgetting. I am left nude—nude in my body, and also in my being. The bodies of lovers await on the other side of phantasmatic reality, and pierce the imaginary to *ex-ist* in the real of sexual enjoyment. Fantasy no longer functions as a screen for the body; the body *ex-ists* in amorous ecstasy. The more I lose myself (in the other), the more my body *ex-ists*. It exists—again, in the body *[en-corps]*!—in enjoyment.[49]

The body of the other takes me: I am dominated *[dominé(e)]*, crushed *[ecrasé(e)]*, eaten *[bouffé(e)]* by him or her. He or she who, in contradistinction with the phallus and God, is present *[présent(e)]* corporeally, in my enjoyment. I no longer exist, but I *ex-ist* . . . in him or her, I *ex-ist, in-bodied, again [en-corps]*.

The body *ex-ists* in sexual enjoyment—above all, the body of the other. If the big Other is a body that does not exist,[50] a figureless body, like the God of the mystics, the little other *ex-ists*: it *ex-ists* and it makes me *ex-ist*, as body, as being.

In the lovers' enjoyment, which difference is it—being or body? The ecstasy of lovers instead collapses the cut between being and the body, that between belief[51] and existence, and those between existence, the imaginary, and the real. It is a smashing, phantasmagoric event, to lose oneself in the meeting of bodies, to be lost in enjoyments. I enjoy my division, my destitution, my absence from myself, my nothing, my body, my other . . .

Mystic enjoyment involves a loss of self,[52] but this is brought about by the loss of the imaginary of God: neither a remainder nor the little other *(a)* persists. In amorous ecstasy, the little other that causes *(a)* does not belong only to the imaginary: the real of a body wrested from mine so as to make me find myself again, divided of course, in my enjoyment.

Conclusion
From Double
Alienation to Joy

Behind ourselves, we must not let the paths of desire become overgrown.

—André Breton, *Mad Love*

Desire is structured on the basis of a double alienation: the alienation in fantasy—the antinomy of desire that is written into contradictory scenarios—and alienation in the signifier.[1]

Alienation in psychic simultaneity, alienation in language. Lacan wrote in 1965 that "this alienating *or* is not an arbitrary invention, nor is it a matter of *how one sees things*. It is part of language. This *or* exists."[2] The subject is alienated in the signifying chain. In 1955, in *The Psychoses,* Lacan had already said that the subject is "pacified" [*passivié*] by language from the moment he becomes an effect of the signified, a signified situated beneath the signifier (S/s). This property, while first restricted to psychosis, was subsequently understood by Lacan as belonging to every subject.

From a symbolic point of view, nothing proves that the subject is alive; the symbolic "treats" the subject as being already dead. However, the use of language modifies the being of the subject, forming and deforming it, by way of and by virtue of the signifier. In this sense, the subject is neither a signifier nor a being but a rather a want-to-be [*un vouloir-être*]. But the subject is above all a "lacking-being" [*manque-à-être*] and "desire for being," to return to the Sartrean conception of desire. Lacan will say, as we have seen, that the subject is a "lack-of-being": desire is the metonymy of the lack of being (the infinite displacement of the effects of the signified).

As Lacan's teaching develops, subject and signifier are increasingly conceived as being mutually exclusive. The subject is represented by

a signifier for another signifier (S1/$). [3] No representation through
identification will be complete for the subject; the subject disappears
below the bar and becomes unrepresentable. As Lacan indicates, "The
signifier, producing itself in the field of the Other, makes manifest the
subject of its signification. But it functions as a signifier only to reduce
the subject in question to being no more than a signifier, to petrify the
subject in the same movement in which it calls the subject to function,
to speak, as subject." [4]

There is no subject outside language: the subject *ex-ists* in the signifier that it represents for another signifier, in the form of a discontinuity, a lack. The signifier is therefore at the origin of the constitution
of the subject, a subject alienated in an identification that freezes and
erases it. This is the paradox of language: the signifier allows for the
emergence of the subject while petrifying it in the imaginary representation that is thereby imposed on it, and that seeks to separate it from
its constitutive emptiness.

The symbolic Other is opposed to the real Other, seeks to encompass and limit it, as though it were possible through language to intervene in a real that opens a hole, that escapes us. We believes ourselves
able to take control of it by means of speech and to quell the tension
of the psychic simultaneity of fantasy: a tension between the subject-
being and the object-being in the relation with the Other, between
speech and enjoyment, or, quite simply, between the symbolic and
the real.

Language that pretends to give sense to the real only serves to add
a further degree of alienation. The subject is alienated by the symbolic
in its confrontation with a traumatic real—a *troumatique* [hole-matic],
by Lacan's neologism, [5] real—which always return to the same place, in
the symptom. But the repetition of the symptom includes difference:
the enjoyment linked to trauma is always repeated at a loss. One can
also think here of the function of the father. He constitutes a second
trauma for the subject, as the castrator of the mother and the seducer
of the son. But his seduction engenders his death (in fantasy), inscrib-
ing the symbolic function (castration) in the structure of the desire of
the subject.

The alienation of the subject in language is explained by Lacan
through the example of Freud's grandson's game with the spool from
Beyond the Pleasure Principle. After saying in *Anxiety* that the game is

an attempt at mastery on the child's part,[6] Lacan modifies his interpretation to "the function of the exercise with this object refers to an alienation, and not to some supposed mastery, which is difficult to imagine being increased in an endless repetition, whereas the endless repetition that is in question reveals the radical vacillation of the subject."[7] In repetition compulsion, the subject is confronted with enjoyment, and vacillates. Repetition is alienating: by trying to exceed—efface— the *troumatique* real, the subject inscribes it forever. The *automaton* commemorates the *tuché*: the *fort-da* game revives not only the trauma of the child's separation from the mother but also desire's anxious division of the subject from being/not-being her object (her phallus).

Desire in Lacan is articulated around two poles: the desire of the Other and that of death (i.e., pure desire). These two poles can meet, as we have seen. The subject is passively caught in desire at the same time as it actively affirms its singularity through desire. This is a combat without end, and not only against the dominant alterity, the threatening exterior (the Other is not exclusively, paternal, material, social, economic, political . . .).[8] The fight against the Other is foremost against the *Other* part of oneself. Desire divides the subject ($), pitting it against the interior of the self: the subject perishes from inner conflicts, as Freud said: the subject is alienated by its subjective division, says Lacan.

Alienation in desire results from psychic simultaneity, in fantasy, from two forces vectored in opposite directions: that of the subject-being, which wants to preserve itself (by the devices of the symbolic, and by being lashed by the imaginary), and that of the object-being, which wants to enjoy (on the side of the real). "Already, in 1884," Bernard Toboul stresses, "Freud is circling the neurotic kernel in an 'irreconcilable' (*Unverträglich*) submitted to repression, which he distinguishes from an 'unbearable' (*Unerträglich*), which is radically excluded in paranoia."[9] Psychic simultaneity in fantasy—the irreconcilable—is of the order of the cause of desire (the object *a*). If the symptom is conceived of as a compromise, a form of reconciliation between the contrary movements of desire (*Verträglich* = compatible, reconcilable, reconciling), fantasy is the *Unverträglich*. In other words, psychic conflict remains, at the unconscious level, unresolved.[10]

The subject's alienation, again, is double, being in psychic simultaneity as well as in the signifier. Everything conspires against the constitution of the being of the subject, leading instead to its destitution.

And it is right there that we find desire: at the point of the fall in being, in the crumbling of every assuring representation (S1). Lacan specifies that "alienation consists in this *vel,* which . . . condemns the subject to appearing only in that division, which, it seems to me, I have just articulated sufficiently by saying that, if it appears on one side as meaning, produced by the signifier, it exists on the other as *aphanisis.*"[11] When he desires, the subject is at once in *ex-istence* and in absence: it is *fading,* says Lacan. The binary structure of the signifier (S1-S2) is the cause of the disappearance of the subject. The signifier, through its signifying effects, is what makes the subject rise in its emergence. To put it differently, the subject finds its being only in the signifier, is "petrified" beneath it (the subject functions only as represented by a signifier for another signifier).

The decision of desire involves two simultaneous movements: the subject appears as *aphanisis.* On the one hand, *it is desire that decides*: the subject is determined by its unconscious desire (whence its *fading*). On the other, *desire is decided by the subject.* Desire does not need to be read in its common sense, as there is no question of a conscious and rational choice on the part of the subject: the decision of desire, as we saw, is not a matter of mastery. The decision of desire is an *opening* to desire at the same time as it is the relinquishment of enjoyment. Enjoyment is relinquished in order to be able to modify and render it, by way of a detour—not necessarily through symptoms—possible.

The subject opens itself, gives to itself the possibility—by accomplishing the acts that bear its name—of heading toward the unknown of its desire. It could almost be said that following an analysis, the subject gains access not to knowledge but to what is unbeknownst *[l'insu]* to it about its desire: an opening onto the contingent through the necessary, a passage from alienation to free necessity.

Desire is an act at the same time as it is unconscious and determinate thinking. The logic of the unconscious—of fantasy—can modify itself (the unconscious is a process) through the enactment of desire.

Some subjects embark on a psychoanalysis in order to know more, consciously, about their desire: "I don't know if I truly want something or other . . ."; "What is it that I want to do in life?"; "After all these years of analysis, I still don't know what I want . . . I don't know anything about my desire."

The act precedes conscious speech, as the act is, in its contingency, steered by necessity—the real—that is, the unconscious: much to its surprise, the subject gestures, acts, and experiments during analysis, and discovers, retroactively *[dans l'après-coup]*, that it is the effect—the *choice*—of its unconscious desire.

Psychoanalysis is not undertaken to attain conscious knowledge of one's desire, as if unconscious thought could in the end become conscious. Desire is not given as a revelation and cannot be said openly; it remains inarticulable, its meaning is always somewhere else, and it is always *other* in the subject's discourse. It is, rather, a question of exiting from contingency, which is the condition of analytic experience— the real in act *[en acte]* for the subject.

The appearance/disappearance of the subject: the movement of desire. This movement is neither regular nor alternating, as the two forces are concomitant, equally violent and constraining. There is no occasion at which to be a subject and to be simultaneously an object: desire is divided, cut in two, impossible. So then how does one withstand these opposite forces?

Fantasy "accommodates" the division of the subject (the simultaneity between the two contrary vectors that divide the subject in desire), a subject divided between the nonsatisfaction and the alienation of desire. Fantasy orders the temporal problematic of neurosis and permits the subject to exist in the present, while the realization of desire is impelled toward the future. Fantasy sustains neurosis in its impossible desire.

The nonsatisfaction of desire, maintained by fantasy, stabilizes the foundations of a neurosis. A desire that is "possible"—on account of the subject's assumption of castration and its acceptance of the incompleteness and inconsistency of the Other—and that is or is on the way to being realized can overturn fantasy's accommodation and trigger anxiety. Every realization of desire inevitably leaves the subject lacking (which should be distinguished from nonsatisfaction), and the neurotic tolerates this only with difficulty: the subject can neither enjoy nor prevent itself from doing so. The symptom is then what comes to the rescue: anxiety, inhibition, conversion, procrastination, acting out *[passage à l'acte]* ... The subject copes with alienation at the price of the suffering/enjoyment that procures the symptom.

To think suffering/enjoyment of the symptom in relation to fantasy is to regard the obstacle as the form of a screen that has to be pierced. That screen is quite particular, one could say "fundamental," as fantasy also has that function for desire.

The traversal follows an itinerary that leads to a limit point, which is the limit between fantasy and desire. To traverse does not mean to exceed, as there is no beyond of the fantasy, such that the idea of clearing it *[le franchissement]*[12] is a lure—as though there were a promised land, a sort of consolation of knowledge that would be reached of necessity. Everything happens in the movement of the construction and deconstruction of fantasy, during its traversal—all the stakes lie there.

How can one tolerate the passage through an enjoyment that is not castration?[13] Desire is what allows for that. Desire juggles loss and lack, follows its course, unmindful of the subject's weaknesses. Desire is *conatus,* the endeavor to persevere in being, to reference Spinoza once more. Desire is, following Freud, navigation, and navigation is more important than living: *Navigare necesse est, vivere non necesse* ran the motto of the Hanseatic League.[14]

Traversing the fantasy, bypassing the obstacle of desire, is a variant of transgression. Transgression cannot go beyond the limit, for it is realized in the limit. Transgression is an unstable place, provisional territory, at the frontier between the possible and the impossible.

Desire is a very special form of alienation, as it is an alienation that upholds life. Desire is life at the same time as it is the abandonment—the lack—of self: their knot is tied in contradiction, as life and lack enter opposition, flip into each other, and end up becoming confused.

The traversal of fantasy in analysis, which transits all the determinations, overdeterminations, and contradictions of desire, never results—contrary to the many consolations of a certain post-Freudian analysis—in harmony, in some accord between self and Other; it leads, instead, to disequilibrium, division, to lack and unaccomplishment—to the native dimension of desire.

The traversal of the fantasy always remains unfinished: there is always ignorance in the construction/deconstruction of fantasy; something remains unanalyzed that escapes logical thought. As Breton writes, "The greatest weakness in contemporary thought seems to me to reside in the extravagant reverence for what we know compared to what we yet do not know. In order to show how thought is obeying in this way its fundamental hatred of effort, it is more useful than ever to call on Hegel's testimony: 'The spirit is kept wakeful and lively only by its need to develop itself before objects insofar as there remains in them something mysterious to be revealed.'"[15]

As Breton says, a "good solution" can always be found by leaving behind the ordinary logical byways of knowledge. Love follows this alternative route, as it represents, he writes, "the fusion of solutions":[16] solutions that are displaced, unexpected, and disturbing for logical thought. Desire, too, follows this tack: what is unbeknownst steers desire, rendering its cause inexplicable and its *decision* disturbing, fostering of anxiety.

This "disconcerting" union between the necessary and the contingent is intrinsic to the structure of desire. The cause of desire, Lacan's object *a*, is not its hidden origin: the cause only ex-ists retroactively, in the free necessity of the subject's acts, in "objective chance," as Breton would say.

With that concept, Breton proposes that the opposition between the contingent (*contingens*: that which happens by chance) and the necessary (*necessarius*: the inevitable, the ineluctable) be put into question: "It happens that natural necessity," he writes in *Mad Love*, "may agree sometimes with human necessity in such an extraordinary and exciting way that the determinations are indistinguishable [*indiscernables*]."[17] Objective chance is at the origin of encounter—amorous encounter, for instance—but also of the finding (of fragmented, residual objects, and scattered remainders), of artistic works, of every form of the unconscious. And hence, too, of desire.

In the same way as unconscious desire (when it appears in the saying of the subject, for example, such as a dream), objective chance proceeds through the association of elements disconnected from the habitual logical ties of thought. "This finding," Breton declares, "whether it is artistic, scientific, philosophic, or as useless as anything, is enough from my perspective to undo the beauty of everything beside it. In it alone can we recognize the marvelous precipitate of desire."[18]

The formations of the unconscious have the same function as the *trouvaille*. Breton again: "The finding of the object serves here exactly the same purpose as the dream in the sense that it frees the individual from paralyzing affective scruples, comforts him and makes him understand that the obstacle he might have believed insurmountable has been cleared."[19] The obstacle cannot be only language that is petrified

in the univocity of meaning, blocked in the *ritournelle* of prosaic discourse that repeats itself in a vain search for its cause. Language that, in
the fixedness of its signification, only gives itself the possibility—but
does not decide—of opening to the contingent.

The logic of desire, like that of objective chance, follows an "order"
of associations[20] that depends on the encounter—"subjectivity at the
extreme," in Breton's words—between the necessary (the fixed and
determined) and the contingent (the mobile and open): the disparate
elements collide in a signifying manner, granting unanticipated openings to sense and *ex-istence*.

Breton proposes that objective chance be followed. Objective chance
opens to another, sometimes incomprehensible language (like that of
dreams), as the logical and causal links of discourse are interrupted.
This is what psychoanalysis pursues once it has abandoned the search
for the meaning of suffering *[mal-être]* and become a clinical technique
of the real. Language that speaks of desire, which effectuates the conjunction between the necessary and the contingent, the determined
and the open, the finite and the infinite, becomes a different, an "other,"
language: llanguage, la-language of the body, corporeal thinking, corporeal relationship . . . Polyphony, polymorphy, polysemy of a language
that is not limited by causal sense, transparency, and evidence. Poetry
replaces prose! There is no need to translate this other language into
another logic that would provide its meaning; this other language has
nothing to do with language that is intended to understand, to offer
itself an account of, its causes.

The formations of the unconscious are not exclusively structurally
determined, as they do not belong strictly to the contingent: unconscious determination (automaton) is at the origin of every formation,
but the contingent makes them takes another form. The necessary is
repeated otherwise in dreams, witticisms, lapsi, symptoms, and so
forth. The necessary undermines its structure through chance, the unexpected, the unforeseeable *(tuché)* that manifests in the saying of the
subject. Like an analysand who, while recounting a dream during a
session, did not stop with a lapsus: the significance that he attempted
to attribute to his dream was lost in a floridity *[boursouflure]* of sense,
countersense, and neosense that separated it from its—determining
and alienating—signifiers, which were stuck in repetition.

The real changes connotation: it stops being only trauma, unhappy and missed encounter. The *tuché* becomes "objective chance," "magic-circumstantial encounter," an alternative network of associations/dissociations, an astructural and alogical language capable of associating and making *ex-ist* everything that seems unassociable and *inex-istent*.

It has already been recalled that desire in Lacan is shorn of its roots in Freudian *Wunsch*. In "Logical Time and the Assertion of Anticipated Certainty," Lacan examines the subject's progressive shift in analysis from perceiving the structure of unconscious desire (dreams and the other formations) to the enactment *[l'acte]* of its desire, to desire as an act *[une acte]* on its part. The moment of conclusion of an analysis allows the subject of the unconscious to become a subject by act *[un sujet en acte]*: the time of understanding authorizes it to bring things to a conclusion,[21] is an invitation to the subject to assume, *to decide* its desire.[22]

In the decision of desire, thought is associated with the body, since it is through the body—that is, by making itself body[23]—that desiring thought can live. The moment to conclude an analysis is not when unconscious thought becomes, at last, conscious but rather when it is transformed into act, into a corporeal act animated by the desire of the subject, something lived that will thenceforward not be supported by the Other (the subject supposed to know).

In the decision of desire, the dispossession of the self occurs in tandem with empowerment: power to exist, augmentation of the force of existing, highest perfection, in other words *joy*[24] in its Spinozist acceptation. The power of which Spinoza speaks is not being all-powerful but being manifested in the very act of existence: existence—knotted with *ek-sistence* and *ex-sistence*—the realization of which is due to the force of desire. This power in act, however, is not mutually exclusive with the painful lucidity that every subject has of its condition as lacking-being *[manque-à-être]*.

Desire is lack: lack at an ontic level at which the act, the invention of knowledge, creation ex nihilo, and decision become necessary. In other words, ontic lack entails a powerful—ethical—engagement, for it is in emptiness (the emptiness of S($\cancel{A}$), Lacan would say) that decision will create the space of its own inscription.

Desire is lack, which does not mean, it should be recalled, that desire is supposed to alleviate lack (the search for the phallus is not consubstantial with the act of desire). On the contrary, the subject desires on the basis of the power [force] to exist,[25] which is, paradoxically, given by its status as lacking-being [manque-à-être], as that lacking-being is sustained by the ethics of its decision, the decision of its desire. Lacking-being is a dynamic notion, which Lacan wanted to translate into English as "want-to-be," for if the unconscious is not, it nevertheless wants to be something.[26] The unconscious is indeterminate and suspended, but it is also subject to the desire to realize itself. In this sense, the desire of the unconscious for being (the open, the evasive, the fleeting, the contingent, the tuché, objective chance) should be distinguished from unconscious desire (the determined, automaton, Zwangshandlung, compulsive action). The ethics of desire concerns the desire of the unconscious for being—in other words, the decision of desire.

The subject desires through a feeling of joy and power [puissance]. Power is not overpowering [La puissance n'est pas le pouvoir]: it allows the subject to confront lack but without attempting to fulfill it. Power makes lack into a force, an opening: to the unconscious, to the unanticipated, to the other. This power admits—and seeks—the contingent by accepting loss, since the subject no longer has anything to lose.

Spinoza thinks of joy as a transition, as "man's transition from a lesser to a greater perfection."[27] For him, perfection is "the very essence of a thing" and not a state of grace or a moment of ideal accomplishment. "Joy is not perfection itself," explains Spinoza, "for if man were born with the perfection to which he makes a transition, he would possess it without the emotion of pleasure."[28]

Joy is waiting, and unexpected waiting. We enjoy from waiting, in desire: "Independent of what happens and does not happen, the wait itself is magnificent," writes Breton.[29] And Kierkegaard: "I am waiting for a thunderstorm—and for repetition. And yet I would be happy and indescribably blessed."[30]

This is much like the process that leads to the acceptance of castration; the subject wants to be omnipotent and yet realizes that it is castrated and also, much to its surprise, relieved by this. Castration proves to be not a catastrophe but the unsuspected motor of desire. The subject discovers this in the course of analysis.

Joy is a state of incompleteness—of lack—while also being a condition of power. Although it begins as incompleteness, joy can become "contentment," and even satisfaction, such as the satisfaction that the subject finds at the end of analysis, as Lacan says in the preface to the English translation of *Seminar XI*.

To treat the question of satisfaction—a satisfaction that is possible because it has endured the subject's castration and the Other's inconsistency—and joy as the fact of psychoanalysis is still transgressive today, when the tragic spirit of the nineteenth century is still, even if this is not evident, dominant. Freud's genius was not only to discover that it is the subject itself that rejects happiness (so as to be able to seek it infinitely) but also to emphasize, as early as 1895, the banality of neurotic suffering. It is a question of a true ethical revolution apropos nineteenth-century romanticism, which proposed an exaltation of sacrifice and of the man who suffers, as if suffering were synonymous with depth, creativity, and intelligence.

Psychoanalysis neither valorizes nor devalorizes the suffering of the symptom; instead, it attempts to transform it into the motor of creativity, to convert it into acts, desiring acts: subjective potentiality, power to exist, joy, and enjoyment.

The decision of desire is an invitation to enjoyment, a certain enjoyment that plays with its impossibility, which is to say with castration. The subject advances toward the destitution of its phallic being, which leads to the painful collapse of its ideas, including the notion that there might be an end to analysis that could allow it to overcome psychic simultaneity, and offer a stable solution to its own inconsistency as well as that of the Other.

Before the permanent mobility of desire, the only stability is the acceptance of one's own instability. As per Rilke, for whom the sole protection is to have no protection:

> This fashions us, outside of all defense,
> a safebeing, there where the gravity
> of the pure forces takes effect; what saves us at last
> is our defenselessness and that seeing it threaten
> we turned it into the open[31]

To desire is also to defend against desire. "The whole of analytic experience," Lacan offers, "shows us that not to want to desire and to desire are the same thing. To desire involves a defensive phase that makes it identical with not wanting to desire. Not wanting to desire is wanting to desire."[32]

The process of defending from desire is the inverse of that of the Epicureans and the Stoics. For them, it is mastery that protects against the violence of desire (that of the self, of the Other), whereas for the psychoanalyst, it is non-sense and the progressive abandonment of all attempts at resorting to language to keep a grip: castration once again comes to the rescue. Non-sense associates with the plurality of sense by which it is translated into joy (*allegrezza*): joy and enthusiasm[33] for the new,[34] which accompanies the end of every successful analytic itinerary.

Desire is the desire of the Other. There is no possibility of clearing the desire of the Other. Desire stares unremittingly at the infinite, an infinite that more or less bears a likeness to death and/or enjoyment. But the other side of desire, the finite and fixed aspect, which limits at the same time as it consolidates, is always present to make endurable—even attractive—the tension between the being-subject and the being-object of he or she who desires.

Desire: leaving behind the process of returning to the source, the quest to repeat, infinitely, the debut, the traumatic and enjoyful origin point of the collision between the finite and the infinite in desire. The risk is always that a process is turned into a goal. The end of a process is not its infinite continuation but its accomplishment. The finite and the infinite enter into another existential dimension, another *épistémè*. For desire begins with its fulfillment (the object *a* is at once lack and enjoyment).

Like a Moebius strip, the finite and the infinite impinge on, interfere with each other in desire. The caducity of their oppositions is their secret unity: "Spaces reversing. Design / for inner worlds out in the Open."[35] The point of reversal, of the transition from the finite to the infinite, is unlocatable: on both a spot and its obverse, in both the interior and the exterior, at once everywhere and nowhere. There is only the passage from one surface to another, and interior and exterior are abolished in the traversal. In the accomplishment of desire.

The necessary and the contingent cross each other, face off without respite. Castration and potency [*puissance*] together is how desire *ex-ists*, in both wrenching and enthusiasm.

Notes

PREFACE

1. Eros is often translated as "love," in the sense of desirous, passionate love that can turn destructive. In the course of distinguishing love from desire in *Transference,* Jacques Lacan translates *eros* as *desir.* Lacan, *Transference: The Seminar of Jacques Lacan, Book VIII,* trans. Bruce Fink (London: Polity, 2017). He will also write, a few years later, that "the essential, initial moment that is of particular relevance to the question we must ask ourselves about the action of the analyst, is that in which it is said that Socrates never claimed to know anything, except on the subject of *Eros,* that is to say, desire." Lacan, *The Four Fundamental Concepts of Psychoanalysis: The Seminar of Jacques Lacan, Book XI,* trans. Alan Sheridan (New York: Norton, 1978), 232.

2. *Poros* can also be translated as "expedient" and "cunning."

3. "Ruse," "expedient," and "recourse," rather than "wisdom," are, for Kofman, other translations. See Sarah Kofman, *Comment s'en sortir* (Paris: Galilée, 1983), 15.

4. Plato, *The Symposium,* ed. M. C. Howatson and Frisbee C. C. Sheffield, trans. M. C. Howatson (Cambridge: Cambridge University Press, 2008), 40, 203d.

5. Plato, *The Symposium,* 40, 203d.

INTRODUCTION

1. See on this point Mathias Goy's illuminating article, which strongly influenced me in this introductory chapter. Goy, "Désir et ontologie chez Sartre et Levinas," *Alter,* no. 9 (Paris: Alter, 2001), 127–51.

2. Jean-Paul Sartre, *Being and Nothingness: A Phenomenological Essay on Ontology,* trans. Hazel E. Barnes (New York: Washington Square Press, 1993), 575–76, 622–23.

3. Sartre, *Being and Nothingness,* 250.

4. Sartre, *Being and Nothingness,* 419.

5. Sartre, *Being and Nothingness,* 259. For Sartre, the encounter with the other *[autrui]* is effectuated through the gaze: "The Other is on principle the one who looks at me" (257).

6. Sartre, *Being and Nothingness,* 270–71. [Translation modified.—Trans.]

7. In Sartre's work, as in Levinas's (as we are about to see), the term *ego* [*moi*] is employed in a general sense, as a synonym for subject. The ego therefore does not hold for either philosopher the same sense as it does in psychoanalysis. In its psychoanalytic usage, the ego is a surface that corresponds to the unified image that the subject finds of itself in the mirror.

8. Sartre, *Being and Nothingness*, 565.

9. Sartre, *Being and Nothingness*, 566. [Translation modified.—Trans.]

10. "My being for the other is haunted by the indication of an absolute being which would be itself as other and other as itself and which by freely giving to itself its being-itself as other and its being-other as itself, would be the very being of the ontological proof—that is, God." Sartre, *Being and Nothingness*, 365.

11. Emmanuel Levinas, *Totality and Infinity: An Essay on Exteriority*, trans. Alphonso Lingis (The Hague: Martinus Nijhoff, 1979), 33.

12. Levinas, *Totality and Infinity*, 34.

13. In Kant, the *transcendent*, that which is beyond all experience and exceeds all possible knowledge, is distinct from the *transcendental*, which designates conditions of possibility. In phenomenology, the transcendent is that which transcends our consciousness and objective phenomena, in contrast with what is only phenomenon of our consciousness.

14. Levinas, *Time and the Other*, trans. Richard A. Cohen (Pittsburgh: Duquesne University Press, 1987), 87.

15. Levinas, *Time and the Other*, 87.

16. Following the Descartes of *The Meditations*, Levinas writes that "the idea of infinity does not proceed from the 'I.' . . . Infinity *is revealed*, in the strong sense of the term." Levinas, *Totality and Infinity*, 61–62. Like Sartre, Levinas conceives alterity to be not deduced but noticed.

17. Levinas, *Totality and Infinity*, 25.

18. "The idea of infinity . . . is concretely produced in the form of a relation with the face." Levinas, *Totality and Infinity*, 196.

19. Levinas, *Totality and Infinity*, 197.

20. Levinas, *Totality and Infinity*, 27.

21. Levinas, *Totality and Infinity*, 62.

22. Levinas, *Totality and Infinity*, 34.

23. The "not yet" does not designate a possibility but rather the beyond of every possibility.

24. The Other can take different senses in Lacanian theory. The "big Other" should generally be understood to mean the exterior, the foreign, the alterity that influences and determines the subject. If in the course of this work the term is sometimes employed in a different sense, this meaning will be specified. The little other designates, in contrast, the fellow [*le semblable*]. As Bernard Toboul has written, "the distinction between the little other and the big Other in the writings of that moment [1953] signals that tension, so that

the imaginary can give way to the Symbolic." Bernard Toboul, "Le sujet et la différence de la psychanalyse," in *L'anthropologie de Lévi-Strauss et la psychanalyse: D'une structure l'autre*, ed. Marcel Drach and Bernard Toboul (Paris: La Découverte, 2008).

25. According to Lacan, enjoyment is to be distinguished from pleasure. Enjoyment is connected not to agreeable experiences but to the horror and pain of existing (and therefore also to trauma). Enjoyment can be variously understood as *impossible* enjoyment, that enjoyment which is both coveted and feared by the subject (the Other's enjoyment); *sexual* enjoyment; *paradoxical* enjoyment (e.g., the enjoyment of symptoms), and of course the *mortifying* enjoyment of melancholia.

26. Jacques Lacan, *L'insu que sait de l'une-bévue s'aile à mourre* (1976–77), unofficial version (Paris: Association Freudienne Internationale, 2000), seminar of March 8, 1977, p. 102.

27. Jacques Lacan, *Encore—On Feminine Sexuality, the Limits of Love and Knowledge: The Seminar of Jacques Lacan, Book XX*, trans. Bruce Fink (New York: Norton, 1998), 28.

28. "Desire, as in the sense of consciousness, permits in this way the instauration of a passage between phenomenology and ontology that does break with phenomenality, by indicating the type of relation to Being that Man maintains." Goy, "Désir et ontologie chez Sartre et Levinas," 127.

29. See, of course, Sigmund Freud, *The Interpretation of Dreams, Standard Edition*, vols. 4 and 5. Jean Laplanche's rendering of *Wunsch* as "wish" [in his French translation of the text] does not strike me as appropriate, as the term is too weak to signify an unconscious movement. Freud is quite explicit on the subject of the nature of desire in the dream in this text, conceiving it along the lines explored in this book.

30. See, among other texts, Jacques Lacan, *The Psychoses: The Seminar of Jacques Lacan, Book III*, trans. Russell Grigg (New York: Norton, 1993), 197.

31. In linguistics, metonymy is often conceived of as a signifier that has taken the place of another and that designates a part of what the latter signifies. In the Lacanian sense, metonymy is defined as a relation of contiguity between terms. Metaphor, on the other hand, indicates for Lacan a transfer of denomination, the substitution of one term for another on the basis of a relation of analogy between those terms.

32. See Jacques Lacan, *The Sinthome: The Seminar of Jacques Lacan, Book XXIII (1975–1976)*, trans. Adrian R. Price (London: Polity Press, 2016), 124.

33. The imaginary is the dimension that proceeds from the constitution of the image of the body, and is therefore to be understood as essentially involving this image. It is the register of the specular and the lure. The symbolic, on the other hand, is the dimension tied to the function of language and more specifically to that of the signifier. The symbolic is related to the father, and, in Lacan, with the Name-of-the-Father, the dead father that founds the law

and desire. Finally, the real is that which resists, that which is impossible to say and/or imagine. It must be distinguished from reality (the representation of the external world), which is ordered by the symbolic and the imaginary. Trauma is always an experience of the order of the real.

34. There is a tendency, which is incorrect, to read this phrase only in the Hegelian sense of an imaginary reciprocity of desire(s).

35. Alexander Kojève, *Introduction to the Reading of Hegel: Lectures on the Phenomenology of Spirit*, trans. James H. Nichols, ed. Allan Bloom (Ithaca: Cornell University Press, 1980).

36. Let's recall what Kierkegaard said about repetition, in *Repetition*: "The dialectic of repetition is easy, for that which is repeated has been— otherwise it could not be repeated—but the very fact that it has been makes the repetition into something new. . . . [W]hen one says that life is a repetition, one says: actuality, which has been, now comes into existence." Søren Kierkegaard, *Fear and Trembling and Repetition: Kierkegaard's Writings*, vol. 6, trans. Howard V. Hong and Edna H. Hong (Princeton: Princeton University Press, 1983), 190.

37. See Massimo Recalcati, "Le aporie del desiderio." *LETTERa*, no. 1 (2011): 17.

38. This is what Spinoza said about joy. See Baruch Spinoza, *Ethics*, trans. G. H. R. Parkinson (Oxford: Oxford University Press, 2000), Part III, Proposition 37.

39. See Lacan, *The Four Fundamental Concepts of Psychoanalysis: The Seminar of Jacques Lacan, Book XI,* trans. Alan Sheridan (New York: Norton, 1981), 53–64. Lacan borrows these terms from Aristotle in order to define the subject's first, traumatic encounter—*tuché*—and its repetition, or *automaton*. It should be specified that Lacan's usage of them is different from that found in ancient Greek philosophy. In Pierre Pellegrin's translation of Aristotle's *Physics* (Paris: Flammarion, 2000), *tuché* is "chance," and *automaton* is "spontaneity."

40. Lacan treats repetition as necessity, with necessity defined as "not being able to not" *[ne pas pouvoir ne pas]*. He says "'Not being able to not,' that is what properly defines, for us, necessity. Where does it go? From the impossible, 'not able to,' to 'able to not.' Is that the possible or the contingent?" Lacan joins necessity and contingency in the phrase "not being able to not," which is composed of two parts: "not being able" *[ne pas pouvoir]*, necessity, and "able to not" *[pouvoir ne pas]*, contingency. Jacques Lacan, . . . *ou pire* (1971–1972) (unpublished seminar, typed version), seminar of December 8, 1971. [This seminar is currently available in French as Jacques Lacan, *Le séminaire, livre XIX: . . . ou pire* (Paris: Seuil, 2011).—Trans.]

41. "If enjoyment is unusual, and if it is ratified by having the sanction of the unary trait and repetition, which henceforth institutes it as a mark—if this

happens, it can only originate in a very minor variation in the sense of enjoyment." Jacques Lacan, *The Other Side of Psychoanalysis: The Seminar of Jacques Lacan, Book XVII*, trans. Russell Grigg (New York: Norton, 2007), 50.

42. Prior to Lacan, Spinoza and Hume had already shown that it is often impossible to grasp the link between an event and its cause.

43. Sigmund Freud, "Instincts and Their Vicissitudes," *Standard Edition*, 14:118.

44. Jacques Lacan, "On a Question Preliminary to Any Possible Treatment of Psychosis," in *Écrits*, trans. Bruce Fink (New York: Norton, 2006), 459.

45. Jacques Lacan, *Television: A Challenge to the Psychoanalytic Establishment*, trans. Dennis Hollier, Rosalind Krauss, and Annette Michelson, ed. Joan Copjec (New York: Norton, 1990), 5.

46. Jacques Lacan, "L'étourdit," in *Autres écrits* (Paris: Seuil, 2001), 454.

47. Psychoanalysis, too, occupies a position, according to Lacan, "in outside" *[en dehors]*, of ex-centricity. As a clinical technique of the real *[clinique du réel]*, it has to do with the unconscious: "It should be noted that psychoanalysis has, since it *ex-ists*, changed. Invented by a solitary, an incontestable theoretician of the unconscious (which is not one imagines it to be—the unconscious, I would say, is real)." Lacan, *The Four Fundamental Concepts of Psychoanalysis*, vii. [Translation slightly modified.—Trans.]

48. "I can nonetheless mark something, which is that if *ex-istence* is defined in relation to a certain consistency, if *ex-istence* is only in the last analysis this outside which is not a non-inside, if this eksistence is in some way this around-which a substance is elaborated, if *ex-istence,* as Kierkegaard advances to us, is essentially pathetic, it remains nonetheless the notion of a fault, the notion of a hole, even in something as extenuated as existence that keeps its sense. Now if I told you that there is a repressed in the Symbolic, there is also in the Real something that makes a hole, and there it is as well in the Imaginary; Freud indeed perceived it, and this is why the finishing touches he put on all he had to say about the drives in the body were centered on their passage from one orifice to the other." Lacan, *RSI (1974–1975)* (unpublished seminar, typed version), seminar of January 14, 1975.

49. [Citation missing in original—Trans.]

50. [Citation missing in original—Trans.]

51. Lacan, "Position of the Unconscious," *Écrits*, 708.

52. Spinoza, *Ethics,* Part I, Definition 7.

53. Freud, "Repression," *Standard Edition,* 14:148. [The English translation is "trains of thought."—Trans.]

54. Lacan, "Science and Truth," *Écrits,* 737.

55. "The unconscious is not without reference to the body." Lacan, *The Sinthome,* 116.

56. Lacan, *Television,* 6.

57. Lacan, *RSI,* seminar of April 8, 1975.

58. Sigmund Freud, "Project for a Scientific Psychology," *Standard Edition,* 1:283–397.

59. See Gilles Deleuze, *Spinoza: Practical Philosophy,* trans. Robert Hurley (San Francisco: City Lights Books, 1988), 17–18.

60. Spinoza, *Ethics,* Part III, Proposition 2, Scholium. The Latin term Spinoza uses is *decretum,* which is translated here, following Guérinot, as "decision." [Translation slightly altered.—Trans.]

61. Spinoza, *Ethics,* Part III, Proposition 2, Demonstration.

62. See again Deleuze, *Spinoza,* 18.

63. The precise definition of *conatus* is "each thing, insofar as it is in itself, endeavors to persevere in its being." Spinoza, *Ethics,* Part III, Proposition 6.

64. Spinoza does not make a distinction between appetite and desire: "there is no difference between appetite and desire, except that . . . 'Desire is appetite together with a consciousness of the appetite.'" Spinoza, *Ethics,* Part III, Proposition 9, Scholium.

65. Spinoza, *Ethics,* Part III, Proposition 9, Scholium.

66. Jacques Lacan, "Kant with Sade," *Écrits,* 663.

67. In the celebrated Proposition 6 of Part III, Spinoza utilizes *contaur,* the third-person singular of the active present. See the bilingual edition of the *Ethics,* trans. B. Pautrat (Paris: Seuil, 1988), 216.

68. Alfred Ernout and Antoine Meillet, *Dictionnaire étymologique de la langue latine: Histoire des mots* (Paris: Klincksieck, 2001), 138.

69. This act is not any generic action, and it always proceeds from a saying. By "act" we understand every action that involves the desire of the subject and his assumption, an assumption that commits its name—the act of the subject necessarily bears its signature. This act is distinguished from the "analytic act," which Lacan understands as that by which one undergoes the passage from analysand to analyst. See Jacques Lacan, *L'acte psychanalytique* (1967–68), unpublished seminar, typed version. More generally, "the analytic act" indicates the effect that the analyst triggers in the analysand through transference: through words *[parole],* silences, scansions, breaks, etc. The analyst directs not the analysand but the cure, a cure that can modify—subvert—the subjective coordinates of the analysand.

70. [*Trancher,* the verb translated here as "cut," is most familiar to English speakers for its culinary usage (e.g., *trancher la pain*: to cut or to slice bread), but it also means to settle a question or decide a matter *(trancher la question).—*Trans.]

71. "The endeavor by which each thing endeavors to persevere in its being involves, not a finite time, but an indefinite time." Spinoza, *Ethics,* Part III, Proposition 8.

1. DESIRE, SQUEEZED BETWEEN SIGNIFIERS

1. Plato, *Gorgias,* in *Complete Works,* ed. John M. Cooper (Indianapolis: Hackett, 1997), 836 (493b-c).

2. Brad Inwood and L. P. Gerson, eds., *The Epicurus Reader: Selected Writings and Testimonia* (Indianapolis: Hackett, 1994), 29–30.

3. Jacques Lacan, *Formations of the Unconscious: The Seminar of Jacques Lacan, Book V,* trans. Russell Grigg (London: Polity Press, 2017), 202.

4. Jacques Lacan, *The Ethics of Psychoanalysis: The Seminar of Jacques Lacan, Book VII,* trans. Dennis Porter (New York: Norton, 1997), 71. The desire of the mother too is determined by its "Other": she desires on the basis of the constellation of desires that are transmitted in her line. It is in this sense that Lacan speaks of a primordial and prehistoric Other.

5. Jacques Lacan, "The Direction of the Treatment and the Principles of Its Power," *Écrits,* 524.

6. Jacques Lacan, "The Instance of the Letter in the Unconscious, or Reason since Freud," *Écrits,* 436.

7. In *Anxiety,* Lacan specifies that "the desire of the Other" in his sense differs from that of Hegel. The latter conceives of two consciousnesses as having a relation of violence, while in Lacan, the relation between the subject and the Other is open to a sort of mediation. See Lacan, *Anxiety: The Seminar of Jacques Lacan, Book X,* trans. A. R. Price (London: Polity Press, 2016), chapter 2.

8. The schema appears both in Jacques Lacan, *The Ego in Freud's Theory and the Technique of Psychoanalysis: The Seminar of Jacques Lacan, Book II,* trans. Sylvana Tomaselli, with notes by John Forrester (New York: Norton, 1988), 243; and in "On a Question Preliminary to Any Possible Treatment of Psychosis," *Écrits,* 458.

9. This applies even to the most primary needs, like hunger. That most people eat at set times confirms that hunger and eating are caught in symbolic conventions.

10. Lacan, *The Ego in Freud's Theory and the Technique of Psychoanalysis,* 234.

11. Demand "succeeds in handing all of one's self and all of one's needs over to an Other from whom the signifying material for every demand is borrowed, and it thereby assumes a different tone." Lacan, *Formations of the Unconscious,* 84.

12. "S/s" is Lacan's inversion of the Saussurean algorithm "s/S" in *Course in General Linguistics.*

13. Lacan, *Encore,* 77.

14. Lacan, "The Signification of the Phallus," *Écrits,* 579.

15. "Perhaps it is not even necessary for the child to yet speak for this mark, this imprint made on need by demand, to be exercised at the level of alternating

cries." Jacques Lacan, *Le désir et son interprétation* (1958–59) (Paris: Association Lacanienne Internationale, 2000), seminar of November 12, 1958, p. 22.

16. "So I say to you, ask and it will be given you; search, and you will find; knock and the door will be opened to you. For everyone who asks receives, and everyone searches finds, and for everyone who knocks, the door will be opened." Luke 11:10–11, *The New Oxford Annotated Bible: New Revised Standard Version,* ed. Michael D. Coogan (Oxford: Oxford University Press, 2010).

17. This recognition is often confused with love. Every amorous subject loves to be recognized as being loved. However the disymmetry of feelings between lovers and the dependence of the other is destabilizing: love is then revealed to be an injury to narcissism—the ego is fragile, and nothing is more unstable then love—rather than the source of its reassurance.

18. Jacques Lacan, *Freud's Papers on Technique, 1953–1954: The Seminar of Jacques Lacan, Book I,* edited by Jacques-Alain Miller (New York: Norton, 1991), 180.

19. Lacan, *Formations of the Unconscious,* 81. [Translation slightly modified. —Trans.]

20. See Freud, "Repression," *Standard Edition,* 14:148.

21. Lacan, "Can Psychoanalysis Constitute the Kind of Ethics Necessitated by Our Times?" in *The Triumph of Religion,* trans. Bruce Fink (London: Polity, 2013), 14–15.

22. "An entire aspect of desire continues to circulate in the form of scraps of signifiers in the unconscious." Lacan, *Formations of the Unconscious,* 86.

23. Rainer Maria Rilke, "The Eighth Elegy," in *The Poetry of Rilke,* trans. Edward Snow (New York: North Point Press, 2011). [This phrase translated from the French edition cited by Lippi: Rainer Maria Rilke, *Les Élégies de Duino, suivi de Les Sonnets a Orphée* (Paris: Seuil, 1972), 71.—Trans.]

24. Rilke, "The Eighth Elegy," 71.

25. Martin Heidegger, *Off the Beaten Track,* trans. Julian Young and Kenneth Haynes (Cambridge: Cambridge University Press, 2002), 213.

26. "There is not, contrary to what they say, anxiety about death, since each man believes himself immortal. This has often been seen to be on display in every kind of belief: he cannot think about death. He has the best of reasons for it. Every anxiety is an anxiety about life, it is the only thing that is anxious: that we should continue to live tomorrow, that is what causes anxiety *[c'est ça qui est angoissant]*." Jacques Lacan, "Conférences donnée au Centre Culturel Français le 30 mars 1974," in *Lacan in Italia, 1953–1978/ En Italie Lacan* (Milan: Le Salamandra, 1978). If it can be said, to paraphrase Socrates, that philosophy teaches one how to accept death, psychoanalysis reveals a technique that can lead the subject to accept life—and, per Freud's wishes, to enjoy it.

27. Heidegger, *Off the Beaten Track*, 211.

28. Heidegger, *Off the Beaten Track*, 211. Heidegger is speaking here not of desire but of being, which he defines as "risk." (I am the one risking the comparison with desire.) For Heidegger, desire is a reduction to "an ontic, inauthentic, and already fallen modality of *Dasein*," while Lacan recognizes in desire "the very truth of *Dasein* as being-open-to-and-with-the-other." See Bernard Bass, *De la chose à l'objet: Jacques Lacan et la traverée de la phénemé-nologie* (Louvain: Peeters Vrin, 1998), 131.

29. Heidegger, *Off the Beaten Track*, 211.

30. Heidegger, *Off the Beaten Track*, 215. The poem is Rilke's "Poem of July 4, 1924, written in Mouzot, for Helmuth, Baron Lucius von Stoedten."

31. Heidegger, *Off the Beaten Track*, 215.

32. The symbolic Other is also lacking: "the Other, locus of speech, is also the locus of lack." Lacan, "The Direction of the Treatment and the Principles of Its Power," *Écrits*, 524.

33. Freud, *The Interpretation of Dreams*, 5:565.

34. The first or original satisfaction is for Lacan mythical, and he thinks it differently than Freud, Otto Rank, Sandor Ferenczi, and Melanie Klein.

35. See Sigmund Freud, *Project for a Scientific Psychology, Standard Edition*, vol. 1, and *The Interpretation of Dreams*, 4:233.

36. "The removal of the stimulus is only made possible here by an intervention which for the time being gets rid of the release of $Q\eta'$ in the interior of the body; and this intervention calls for an alteration in the external world (supply of nourishment, proximity of the sexual object). . . . At first, the human organism is incapable of bringing about the specific action. It takes place by extraneous help, when the attention of an experienced person is drawn to the child's state." Freud, *Project for a Scientific Psychology*, 361.

37. "If a perception arrives which is identical with the idea or similar to it, it finds its neurones precathected by the wish—that is, either all of them already cathected or a part of them—so far, in fact, as the agreement goes. The difference between the idea and the approaching perception then gives occasion for the process of thought, which reaches its end when the superfluous perceptual cathexes have been conveyed, along some pathway that has been found, into ideational cathexes. With this, identity is achieved." Freud, *Project for a Scientific Psychology*, 361. This idea of an identity of perception is upheld in *The Interpretation of Dreams*, 5:566: "the aim of this first psychical activity was to produce a 'perceptual identity'—a repetition of the perception which was linked with the satisfaction of a need."

38. Freud, *The Interpretation of Dreams*, 5:566.

39. Sigmund Freud, "A Metapsychological Supplement to the Theory of Dreams," *Standard Edition*, 14:217–35.

40. Freud, *The Interpretation of Dreams*, 5:566.

41. Freud, *The Interpretation of Dreams*, 5:565.

42. Freud, *The Interpretation of Dreams*, 5:565.

43. This is what leads Lacan to say that the psychotic carries the *objet a* in his pocket. Lacan, "Petit discours aux psychiatres de Saint-Anne," unpublished 1967 lecture. Lacan also later says that the subject himself becomes "object a." See "L'étourdit," *Autres écrits*, 30. In English, see Cormac Gallagher's partial translation in *The Letter* 41 (2009): 31–80.

44. Freud, *The Interpretation of Dreams*, 5:566.

45. This nonsatisfaction corresponds to the—structural—lack for the subject of the object. In this sense, Freud's theory of desire is not so far from Lacan's.

46. Lacan, *The Ego in Freud's Theory and in the Technique of Psychoanalysis*, 212–13.

47. Freud employs several German terms to indicate different degrees of satisfaction: *Geniess* (jouissance), *Lustbefriedigung* (satisfaction), *Erfüllung* (achievement), *Realisierung* (realization). The "strong" terms, *Geniess* and *Lustbefriedigung*, are not used in the passages from *The Interpretation of Dreams* that I have discussed: the "realization" of desire in unconscious formations does not amount, as Lacan explains, to its effective satisfaction.

48. Gérard Pommier, "(Anti-Éros): Le cercle brisé de l'amour," in his *Le nouveau recueil: Encore l'amour* (Seyssel: Champ Vallon, 2003), 88.

49. Lacan, *Formations of the Unconscious*, 74. For an extensive discussion of the unique use Lacan makes of the concept of metonymy, see "The Insistence of the Letter in the Unconscious, or Reason since Freud" and "The Direction of the Treatment and the Principles of Its Power," both in *Écrits*. See also "Radiophonie," trans. Stuart Schneiderman, in *On Signs*, ed. M. Blonsky (Baltimore: Johns Hopkins University Press, 2001).

50. Lacan, *Le désir et son interprétation*, 121.

51. This provides a good illustration of a psychoanalytic cure. It is by means of the reactualization of a subject's successive demands in transference that desire surfaces.

52. Lacan, *Anxiety*, seminar of March 13, 1963.

53. See Roberto Harari, "Le sinthome turbulent et dissipatif," *La clinique Lacanienne*, 1 (Toulouse: érès, 2000), 44.

54. "Only love allows enjoyment to condescend to desire." Lacan, *Anxiety*, 179.

55. Heidegger's concept of *ek-sistence* should be recalled here: "*Ek-sistence* can be said only of the essence of the human being, that is, only of the human way 'to be.' For as far as our experience shows, only the human being is admitted to the destiny of *ek-sistence*." For Heidegger, to *ek-sist* means "to stand in the clearing of being," a being that is "the nearest to man" and nevertheless also "the farthest." Martin Heidegger, "Letter on Humanism," in *Pathmarks*, ed. William McNeill (Cambridge: Cambridge University Press, 1998), 247, 252.

2. PERVERSE AND PERVERTED DESIRE

1. Lacan, *Formations of the Unconscious,* 293. Emphasis mine.

2. Diogenes Laertius, *Lives of Eminent Philosopher,* ed. Tiziano Dorandi (Cambridge: Cambridge University Press, 2013).

3. Seneca, *Letter on Ethics to Lucilius,* trans. Margaret Graver and A. A. Long (Chicago: University of Chicago Press, 2015), 224.

4. Epicurus, *Letter to Menoecus,* in *Classics of Moral and Political Theory,* ed. Michael L. Morgan (Cambridge: Hackett, 1992), 418.

5. Lucretius, *On the Nature of Things,* trans. Ronald Melville (Oxford: Oxford University Press, 1999), 36 (Book Two, 16–23).

6. Epicurus, *Letter to Menoecus,* 418.

7. Sigmund Freud, *Beyond the Pleasure Principle, Standard Edition,* 18:9.

8. Lacan, *The Other Side of Psychoanalysis,* 18.

9. William Faulkner, *If I Forget Thee, Jerusalem,* in *Novels, 1936–1940* (New York: Library of America, 1990), 526.

10. Dino Buzzati, *A Love Affair,* trans. Joseph Green (London: Carcanet Press, 1987).

11. "Desire . . . would no doubt be willing to call itself 'will to enjoyment.'" Lacan, "Kant with Sade," *Écrits,* 652.

12. In *The Ethics of Psychoanalysis,* Lacan insists on the difference between pleasure and enjoyment: "Even before the formulations of Beyond the Pleasure Principle, it is evident that the first formulations of the pleasure principle as an unpleasure principle, or least-suffering principle, naturally involves a beyond, but that it is, in effect, calculated to keep us on this side of it rather than beyond it. Freud's use of the good can be summed up in the notion that it keeps us a long way from our enjoyment" (185).

13. Does not this state of zero-degree tension, to speak in Freudian terms, of man when he is not affected by passions, resemble organic death? Although Freud clearly distinguishes between the pleasure principle and the nirvana principle, which designates the extinction of human desire, they seem in this case to coincide. For that distinction, see "The Economic Problem of Masochism," *Standard Edition,* 19:155–70.

14. Lacan, *Formations of the Unconscious,* 293.

15. For Lacan, a "structure" is the organization of the ensemble of the effects that language produces in the subject. It is neither a category nor a classification. In structural analysis, one accounts not for the singularity of a given element but for the relations that exist between the different elements of several ensembles. See Lacan, *The Psychoses,* 183. Such ensembles always involve reciprocal reference, in the same way that a signifier is always accompanied by another (structure and the signifier are inseparable notions for Lacan). Lacan's structural clinical technique reformulates the nosographic entities of neurosis, psychosis, and perversion and thereby allows the different factors that orient their cure to be illumined.

16. Lacan, "Kant with Sade," *Écrits,* 648.

17. Immanuel Kant, *Critique of Practical Reason,* trans. Mary Gregor (Cambridge: Cambridge University Press, 2015), 28.

18. Kant distinguishes the categorical imperative, which is unconditioned, from hypothetical imperatives. There are two species of hypothetical imperatives. The "problematic imperative" represents an action as necessary if one of an innumerable number of possible ends is to be achieved: when an end is possible for us, an imperative states how we can attain this end. The "assertoric imperative" represents an action as necessary for arriving at happiness. For example, a proposition that indicates the way to be happy is hypothetical rather than categorical because it concerns the choice of means with respect to happiness.

19. Lacan, "Kant with Sade," *Écrits,* 650. [Translation slightly modified. —Trans.]

20. Max Horkheimer and Theodor Adorno, *Dialectic of Enlightenment,* trans. John Cumming (New York: Continuum, 1989).

21. Lacan, *Formations of the Unconscious,* 318.

22. "The eccentricity of desire in relation to every satisfaction . . . makes it possible for us to understand what, in general, its profound affinity with pain is. At the limit, this is what desire borders on—not in its developed, masked forms, but in its pure and simple form, it the pain of existing." Lacan, *Formations of the Unconscious,* 318.

23. See Freud, "Instincts and Their Vicissitudes," *Standard Edition,* 14:119–20.

24. "Perversion is an experience which allows one to enter more deeply into what one can call, in the full sense, [the] human passion, to use the Spinozan term, that is to say what there is in man which is open to this division from himself." Lacan, *Freud's Papers on Technique,* 221.

25. In Spinoza's famous formula, "desire is nothing other than the essence of man." *Ethics,* Part III, Proposition 9, Scholium.

26. "The homoestasis of the living being is always too quickly reestablished at the lowest threshold of tension at which he scrapes by." Lacan, "Kant with Sade," *Écrits,* 773.

27. For what I mean by this, see chapter 9, "Enjoyment: All and Not-All."

28. Lacan, *Formations of the Unconscious,* 301. [Translation altered.—Trans.]

29. Lacan, "Kant with Sade," *Écrits,* 773.

30. A certain conception of love is that it is plenitude. We might think of the myth of Aristophanes in Plato's *Symposium,* where it is Eros that allows men to reattain their unity: the two halves into which Zeus divided them become reunited, each of them fulfilling the other, and realizing their original fullness.

31. As Catherine Millot puts it, "Fantasy starts with loss and attempts to deflect it." Millot, *Abîmes ordinaires* (Paris: Gallimard, 2001), 149.

32. "We do not know how other animals enjoy, but we know that for us, enjoyment is castration." Jacques Lacan, "Propos sur l'hysterie" (a talk given in Brussels on February 26, 1977), *Quarto* 2 (1981).

33. "The breast is created by infant over and over again out of the infant's capacity to love or (one can say) out of need. A subjective phenomenon develops in the baby, which we call the mother's breast. The mother places the actual breast just there where the infant is ready to create." Donald W. Winnicott, *Playing and Reality* (New York: Routledge, 2005), 15.

34. Roland Barthes, *A Lover's Discourse: Fragments,* trans. Richard Howard (New York: Penguin Books, 1977), 40.

35. Lacan, "Subversion of the Subject and the Dialectic of Desire," *Écrits,* 699.

36. Renaud Barabas, *Le désir et la distance: Introduction à une phénoménologie de la perception* (Paris: Vrin, 1999), 146.

37. Lacan, *The Ethics of Psychoanalysis,* 18.

38. Giacomo Leopardi, *Canti,* trans. Jonathan Galassi (New York: Farrar, Straus, and Giroux, 2011), 177.

3. GAP, DISTANCE, AND LACK IN DESIRE

1. Lacan's interrogation of being had already begun in 1953, at the time of *Freud's Papers on Technique,* when he maintained that Being reveals and realizes itself in speech. For a fuller perspective on ontology in Lacan, see François Balmès, *Ce que Lacan dit de l'Être* (Paris: Presses Universitaires de France, 1999).

2. *Le désir et son interprétation,* 31. In "The Direction of the Treatment and the Principles of Its Power," Lacan casts desire as "the metonymy of the want-to-be *[manque-à-être]." Écrits,* 622. The first version of the text was published before the 1958 seminar on desire, but the version found in *Écrits* is subsequent to it. In the next chapter I will analyze the formula of "The Direction of the Treatment and the Principles of Its Power."

3. See Lacan, "Radiophonie," *Autres écrits,* 426, and *Encore,* 11.

4. Lacan, *The Four Fundamental Concepts of Psychoanalysis,* 29.

5. This fragment from *The Will to Power* is cited in Heidegger, "Why Poets?" in *Off the Beaten Track,* 208.

6. André Lalande, *Vocabulaire technique et critique de la philosophie* (Paris: Presses Universitaires de France, 1972), 308. There are two words in German for "being": *Wesen,* being in the sense of essence, and *Sein,* being properly speaking, i.e., the conjugable verb. Note that Heidegger used the term *Sein* and not *Wesen* when speaking of being.

7. "The 'essence' *[Wesen]* of this being lines in its being. The whatness *(essentia)* of this being must be understood in terms of its being *(existentia)* insofar as one can speak of it at all." *Existentia* has here the sense of *Dasein* and not of present-at-hand, existence in the common sense of the term. "We

can avoid confusion by always using the interpretive expression objective presence *[Vorhandenheit]* for the term *existentia,* and by attributing existence *(Existenz)* as a determination of being only to Dasein."

8. On the relation between *Dasein* and the subject in Lacan, see "On a Question Preliminary to Any Possible Treatment of Psychosis," *Écrits,* 551. See also Bernard Toboul, "Le sujet et la différence de psychanalyse," in *L'anthropologie de Lévi-Strauss et la psychanalyse: D'une structure à l'autre,* ed. Marcel Drach and Bernard Toboul (Paris: La Découverte, 2008), 284.

9. *Parlêtre* designates, in Lacan's words, "the carnal being ravaged by the word." Lacan, *Le triomphe de la religion* (Paris: Seuil, 2005), 90. Lacan will also say of the *parlêtre* that "it speaks this thing . . . namely, being." Lacan, "La troisième," *Lettres de l'École Freudienne* 16 (1975): 177–203. The neologism reintroduces the dimension of the drive into speech while sending the subject of the unconscious into exile. [Following a common practice and for clarity, *parlêtre* will be translated as "speaking being" here, although the reader should note that the force of the contraction of the two words in the neologism is thereby lost.—Trans.]

10. Heidegger, *Being and Time,* §4, 11: "If we reserve the term ontology for the explicit, theoretical question of the being of beings, the ontological character of Dasein referred to here is to be designated as preontological. This does signify simply being *[seiend]* ontical, but rather being *[seiend]* in the manner of an understanding of being."

11. Heidegger distinguishes the existentiel, which concerns the existence of an ontic point of view, from the existential, existence in rapport with being.

12. Note that Freud speaks of a subject that seeks to account for "the demand made upon the psychical apparatus for work in consequence of its connection with the body." Freud, "Instincts and Their Vicissitudes," *Standard Edition,* 14:122.

13. Ego psychology caved before the difficulty presented by that division by treating the unconscious as though it were composed of elements as much intellectual (verbal representations) as affective (nonverbal). The psychoanalytic question of the Freudian unconscious, defined as a "lacuna in psychism," is obscured in a psychology aimed at reinforcing an "ego" supposedly able to respond to an adaptive orthopedics.

14. The question of being and language is explicitly raised by Foucault in *The Order of Things* (London: Routledge, 1995), 333–34: "What relation is there between language and being, and is it really to being that language is always addressed—that which, at least, speaks truly?" Foucault then asks himself whether "thought—that thought that has been speaking for thousands of years without knowing what speaking is or even that it is speaking—is about to apprehend itself again in its entirety, and to illumine itself once more in the lightning flash of being?"

15. Lacan, *Le désir et son interprétation*, 374. Lacan refers to the imaginary object.

16. Lacan, *Formations of the Unconscious*, 318.

17. Lacan, "Response to Jean Hippolyte's Commentary on Freud's *Verneinung*," *Écrits*, 318–24.

18. [I have followed convention by translating *béance* as "gap." The reader should be advised that "cleft" is closer to the word's immediate sense and will sometimes be used to translate it, with an appropriate indication.—Trans.]

19. Barabas, *Le désir et la distance*, 20.

20. Edmund Husserl, *Logical Investigations*, trans. J. N. Findlay (London: Routledge, 2001).

21. Edmund Husserl, *Ideas Pertaining to a Pure Phenomenology and to a Phenomenological Philosophy, First Book: General Introduction to a Pure Phenomenology*, trans. F. Kersten (The Hague: Martin Nijhoff, 1983), §42, 92.

22. James Joyce, *Giacomo Joyce*, (London: Faber and Faber, 1968), 9.

23. Joyce, *Giacomo Joyce*, 1.

24. Joyce, *Giacomo Joyce*, 16.

25. Heraclitus, *The Art and Thought of Heraclitus: An Edition of the Fragments with Translation and Commentary*, ed. Charles H. Kahn (Cambridge: Cambridge University Press, 1979),

26. Lacan, *Le désir et son interprétation*, 25.

27. Lacan, "Direction of the Treatment and the Principles of Its Power," *Écrits*, passim.

28. "I wasn't making a strict use of the letter when I said that the locus of the Other was symbolized by the letter A. On the contrary, I marked it by redoubling it with the S that means signifier here, signifier of A insofar as the latter is barred: S($\cancel{A}$). I thereby added a dimension to A's locus, showing that qua locus it does not hold up, that there is a fault, hole, or loss therein. Object a comes to function with respect to that loss. That is something that is quite essential to the function of language." Lacan, *Encore*, 28.

29. It appears in *Formations of the Unconscious*, 485, and "The Subversion of the Subject and Dialectic of Desire," *Écrits*, 817.

30. Rainier Maria Rilke, "On Shawls and Lemons," in *Inner Sky: Poems, Notes, Dreams*, trans. Damion Searls (Boston: David R. Godine, 2010), 93.

31. Heidegger, *Being and Time*, §6.

32. Lacan, *Le désir et son interprétation*, 241.

33. Lacan, "The Direction of the Treatment and the Principles of Its Power," *Écrits*, 520.

34. Jean Clavreul, *Le désir et la loi: Approches psychanalytiques* (Paris: Denoël, 1987), 224.

35. For Heidegger, the Nothing is not nonbeing but an original dimension of Being as such. See *Being and Time*, §58, and "What Is Metaphysics?" in *Pathmarks*, 82–96.

36. Lacan, *Anxiety*, 132.

37. Lacan, *Formations of the Unconscious*, 152.

38. Lacan's saying "La réel—c'est ce qui resiste" was inspired by Alexandre Kojève. At the same time, Lacan's real differs from Kojève's, which resists action but not thought. For Lacan, the opposite is almost the case.

39. To conceive the real as an autonomous, almost transcendent instance is to risk falling into metaphysics.

40. "The definition of the Borromean knot starts with 3. Namely, that if, you break one of the rings, they are all three freed; that is to say, the two other rings are freed." *RSI*, hand-typed seminar, December 10, 1974. In both that seminar and that of the next year, *The Sinthome*, Lacan also proposes the model of the four-ring Borromean knot, which is unfortunately not reproduced here, since it strays too far from my purposes.

41. Lacan, *The Ego in Freud's Theory and in the Technique of Psychoanalysis*, 313.

42. "There was first the primary expulsion, that is, the real as exterior to the subject." Lacan, "Response to Jean Hyppolite's Commentary on Freud's 'Verneinung,'" *Écrits*, 324. [Translation modified.—Trans.]

43. "The nothing that names beyond what 'I' understand come to the place of repression, is substituted as the symbol of lack, and its sublime Kantian emptiness is thus invested with the highest value." Gérard Pommier, *La névrose infantile de psychanalyse* (Toulouse: érès, 1989), 252. It should once again be stressed that the real is not itself lack, and only is so for we who never manage to symbolize it.

44. Freud, "Hysterical Phantasies and Their Relation to Bisexuality," *Standard Edition*, 9:155–66. It should be stressed that the fantasy of bisexedness occurs with both sexes. Men are in search of the phallus as much as women, for as Freud showed, the phallus is not an organ but a symbol.

45. Lacan, *Formations of the Unconscious*, 290.

46. Lacan, *Formations of the Unconscious*, 291.

47. As Lacan shows in *Anxiety*, two forms of lack must be distinguished—that is, two forms of castration: one that belongs to the order of the real and another that is linked to the Oedipus complex and situated between the symbolic and the imaginary. Lacan, *Anxiety*, 89–95.

48. Lacan, *Formations of the Unconscious*, 290. [Translation slightly altered. —Trans.]

49. That is, symbolic castration.

50. A mark on the body "chosen" by the subject itself, like a tattoo or piercing, cannot hold the same ritual and symbolic value as a mark "imposed" by the community, the aim of which is commemorative and initiatic.

51. See Freud, "Fragment of an Analysis of a Case of Hysteria," *Standard Edition*, 7:1–122.

52. Lacan, *The Four Fundamental Concepts of Psychoanalysis*, 141.

53. "There was one factor in the state of affairs produced by the elimination of the father which was bound in the course of time to cause an enormous increase in the longing felt for him. Each single one of the brothers who had banded together for the purpose of killing their father was inspired by a wish to become like him and had given expression to it by incorporating parts of their father's surrogate in the totemic meal." Sigmund Freud, *Totem and Taboo, Standard Edition,*13:148.

54. This is S1.

55. Lacan, *D'un autre à l'Autre: Le seminaire, livre XVI* (Paris: Seuil, 2006), 356.

56. It should be recalled that the subject begins early on to include himself when counting others. The child, Lacan specifies, is implicated in an unconscious activity of counting. See, in particular, his example of the child who counts himself when numbering his brothers: *"I have three brothers: Paul, Ernest, and me." The Four Fundamental Concepts of Psychoanalysis,* 20. It is only at another moment that the child recognizes himself to be counting and can then subtract himself.

57. Lacan, *D'un autre à l'Autre,* 356.

58. "A signifier represents a subject for another signifier." Lacan, "Position of the Unconscious," *Écrits,* 712–13.

59. The phallus—the erect penis—represents, simultaneously, the growth of life and castration. "It seems, then, that things are such that this extreme point of the manifestation of desire in its vital appearance can only enter the field of the signifier by unleashing the bar." Lacan, *Formations of the Unconscious,* 327.

60. Lacan, *La relation d'objet: Le seminaire, livre IV* (Paris: Seuil, 1994), 374.

61. Lacan, *Encore,* 58.

62. Lacan, "L'étourdit," *Autres écrits,* 458.

63. Jean-Luc Nancy, "The 'There Is' of Sexual Relation," in *Corpus II: Writings on Sexuality,* trans. Anne O'Byrne (New York: Fordham University Press, 2013), 11.

64. Lacan, *Freud's Papers on Technique,* 147. The very first articulation of the theory of the mirror stage, however, takes us back to 1949, to a communication Lacan gave in Zurich, at the Sixteenth International Congress of Psychoanalysis. See "The Mirror Stage as Formative of the Function of the 'I,'" in *Écrits.*

65. Lacan, *Freud's Papers on Technique,* 147

66. Freud, *Beyond the Pleasure Principle,* 36.

67. Freud, "On the Universal Tendency to Debasement in the Sphere of Love," *Standard Edition,* 11:188–89.

68. Lacan, *Le désir et son interprétation,* 11.

69. Lacan, *Anxiety,* 53.

70. Lacan, *Anxiety*, 331. [Translation modified to accord with the quoted French.—Trans.]

71. Lacan, "On Freud's *Trieb* and the Desire of the Psychoanalyst," *Écrits*, 723.

72. "Both sexes ultimately dread exactly the same thing, *aphanisis.*" Ernest Jones, "Early Female Sexuality," in *Papers on Psychoanalysis* (London: Karnac Books, 1948), 440.

73. Lacan, *Le désir et son interprétation*, 217.

74. The ego ideal, which belongs to the imaginary matrix, is formed from the mother's amorous and idealizing recognition of its child, while the ideal ego is constructed from a paternal trait. For Freud, the ideal ego is a substitute for the ego ideal and formed through the agency of the superego. For Lacan, it holds a symbolic function, ruling the problematic of the subject's identifications and conflicts with its fellows. See chapter 5.

75. Lacan, *The Four Fundamental Concepts of Psychoanalysis*, 273.

76. Jacques Lacan, "Proposition du 9 Octobre 1967 sur Le Psychanalyste de l'École," *Autres écrits*, 254. [I was greatly helped by Russell Grigg's unpublished translation of this passage.—Trans.]

77. Jacques Lacan, "Discours à l'École Freudienne de Paris," *Autres écrits*, 273.

78. Lacan, "La méprise du sujet supposé savoir," *Autres écrits*, 335.

79. "Disbeing . . . is the question of knowing how the pass can contend with decking someone out with an ideal that disbeing had laid bare, precisely that the analyst no longer supports the transfer of knowledge to himself." Lacan, "Discours à l'École Freudienne de Paris," *Autres écrits*, 274.

4. THE OBJECT SLIPS OFF, A SIGNIFIER TAKES ITS PLACE

1. It should be recalled that when Lacan was delivering *Encore*, he had broken "with anything whatsoever that is enunciated as philosophy. . . . As for being, a being that would be posited as absolute, it is never anything but the fracture, break, or interruption of the formulation 'sexed being,' insofar as sexed being is involved in *jouissance.*" Lacan, *Encore*, 11.

2. I am distinguishing, following Lacan, the real of the drives *[le réel pulsionnel]* from primary repression, Freud's *Urverdrängt*. The real of the drives corresponds to a hole in the body, an orifice—a cleft or opening—while *Urverdrängt* is a plugged orifice. The real of the drives is not this *Urverdrängt* but is related to it: the drive aims to transform the body into a phallus for the mother. *Urverdrängt* is the point where body and language are pitted in an impossible encounter. The spatial metaphor of the umbilicus, of a knot closed in on itself, illustrates the point of tension between the body as real— the body as phallus for the Other—and its *Darstellbarkeit* (the symbol supposed to become speech), whence the fog of undecipherability. See Jacques

Lacan, "Réponse de Jacques Lacan à une question de Marcel Ritter," *Lettres de l'École Freudienne* 18 (1976).

    3. Gérard Pommier, *Qu'est ce que le "réel"?* (Toulouse: érès, 2004), 126.

    4. Freud, "Repression," *Standard Edition,* 14:146–47

    5. Lacan, "The Signification of the Phallus," *Écrits,* 579.

    6. Freud, "Infantile Genital Organization," *Standard Edition,* 19:142.

    7. As Catherine Millot stresses several times in her *Horsexe,* the penis would merely be a small piece of insignificant flesh if it were not articulated to maternal desire. See Millot, *Horsexe: Essay on Transsexuality* (New York: Semiotext(e), 1989).

    8. Lacan, *La relation d'objet,* 153.

    9. Lacan, "The Signification of the Phallus," *Écrits,* 581.

    10. "It is only on the basis of clinical facts that the discussion can be fruitful. These facts reveal a relation between the subject and the phallus that forms without regard to the anatomical distinction between the sexes. . . . The phallus is a signifier, a signifier whose function, in the intrasubjective economy of analysis, may lift the veil from the function it served in the mysteries. For it is the signifier that is destined to designate meaning effects as a whole, insofar as the signifier conditions them by its presence as signifier." Lacan, "The Signification of the Phallus," *Écrits,* 576, 579.

    11. Lacan, *Encore,* 79.

    12. Lacan even says that "there is no castration because, in the locus at which it occurs, there is no object to castrate. The phallus would have to have been there for that. Now, it is only there so that there won't be any anxiety. The phallus, where it is expected as something sexual, only ever appears as a lack. And all that means that the phallus is only called upon to function as an instrument of potency." Lacan, *Anxiety,* 269.

    13. Jacques Lacan, "Symbolic, Imaginary, and Real," in *Des Noms-du-Pères* (Paris: Seuil, 2005), 38.

    14. It is initially the Other's castration that is difficult to accept: "the subject does not want to deny the phallus to the mother. The subject has always been teaching this doctrine, wants to maintain the mother's phallus—the subject refuses the castration of the Other." Lacan, *Le désir et son interprétation,* 255.

    15. Lacan, *La relation d'objet,* 77.

    16. "The pressure of the drives turns the body toward a nightmarish emptiness, which is [thus] ejected to the outside." Pommier, *Qu'est ce que le "réel"?* 13.

    17. In Lacan, "La troisième." In his sketch of the Borromean knot, Lacan made the ring of the imaginary correspond to the body: he accidentally replaced "imaginary" with "body."

    18. Lacan, *The Sinthome,* 129.

    19. "What is it that we fear? Our body." Lacan, "La troisième."

20. Pommier, *Qu'est ce que le "réel"?* 126.

21. "Freud designates the prohibition of incest as the underlying principle of the primordial law, . . . and at the same time he identifies incest as the fundamental desire." Lacan, *The Ethics of Psychoanalysis*, 67.

22. Lacan, *The Ethics of Psychoanalysis*, 313–14.

23. Lacan, "Signification of the Phallus," *Écrits*, 579–80.

24. Remember that desire—of the Other, of the subject—is always beyond demand.

25. Moustapha Safouan, *La sexualité féminine dans la théorie freudienne* (Paris: Seuil, 1976), 84.

26. "The subject has a certain relationship with omnipotence, to potency quite simply, to power. Its power, on this occasion the phallus, which it is suitable to preserve at all cost, to keep out of the game because the phallus can be lost when in play." Lacan, *Le désir et son interprétation*, 226. See also Mustapha Safouan, *Études sur l'OEdipe* (Paris: Seuil, 1974), 45.

27. Lacan, *Le désir et son interprétation*, 342.

28. Lacan, *Le désir et son interprétation*, 533.

29. "The imaginary object is found in some way in the position of condensing into itself what could be called the virtues or dimensions of being, such that it can become this veritable lure of being that is the object of human desire: . . . [this] is the relation of man with the object of his desire, the relation of the miser with his coffer, which seems to fulfill for us in the most evident way the character of the fetish, which is that of the object of human desire." Lacan, *Le désir et son interprétation*, 342.

30. Freud, "Fetishism," *Standard Edition*, 21:152–53.

31. Lacan, *La relation d'objet*, 151–95.

32. Freud, "Fetishism," 156–57.

33. Lacan, *Le désir et son interprétation*, 237.

34. Lacan, *Le désir et son interprétation*, 237.

35. The next chapter deals with Lacan's development of the notion of the object *a*.

36. Lacan, "The Direction of the Treatment and the Principles of Its Power," *Écrits*, 537. [Translation modified.—Trans.]

37. "It's in proportion to a certain renouncement of his relation to the phallus that the subject enters into possession of a sort of infinity, plurality, and omnitude of the world of objects that characterizes [is characteristic of] the world of man." Lacan, *La désir et son interprétation*, 337.

5. THAT SINGULAR CAUSE OF DESIRE

1. Martin Heidegger, *What Is a Thing?* trans. W. B. Barton and Vera Deutsch (Chicago: Henry Regnery, 1968).

2. Martin Heidegger, "The Thing," in *Poetry, Language, Thought*, trans. Albert Hofstader (New York: Harper & Row, 1971), 168.

3. Maurice Merleau-Ponty, "Cézanne's Doubt," in *Sense and Nonsense,* trans. Hubert L. and Patricia Allen Dreyfus (Evanston: Northwestern University Press, 1964).

4. Merleau-Ponty, "Cézanne's Doubt."

5. Lacan, *The Ethics of Psychoanalysis,* 141.

6. Lacan, *The Ethics of Psychoanalysis,* 141.

7. Lacan, *The Ethics of Psychoanalysis,* 141.

8. Immanuel Kant, *Anthropology from a Pragmatic Point of View* (Cambridge: Cambridge University Press, 2006), 140

9. See Rudolf Eisler, *Kant-Lexicon* (Hildesheim: Verlag, 1984), 505.

10. Freud, "Psychopathic Characters on the Stage," *Standard Edition,* 7:303–10.

11. In the *Critique of Practical Reason,* Kant equally contends, of course, with the problem of synthesis—how can an empirical action issue from an autonomous will?—and resolves it by arguing that to be moral, empirical action should be able to pass the test of the form of a universal law. Pursuing its relation to the subjects at hand would take us too far away from them.

12. Bernard Baas, *Le désir pur: Parcours philosophiques dans les parages de J. Lacan* (Louvain: Peeters, 1992), 68.

13. Lacan, *The Ethics of Psychoanalysis,* 118.

14. "To a certain extent *a* is assimilable to a signifier; but more precisely, it is that which resists this assimilation to the function of the signifier." Jacques Lacan, *Angoisse* (Paris: Association Lacanienne Internationale, 2001), 227. [See also Lacan *Anxiety,* 174, which differs markedly from the quoted version. —Trans.]

15. Lacan, *D'un autre à l'Autre,* 224.

16. "The most striking manifestation of this objet *a,* the signal that it is intervening, is anxiety." Lacan, *Anxiety,* 86.

17. "Original" is to be taken here in its Heideggerian sense: what is most essential: "What we mean, here, by the word 'origin' is thought out of the essence of truth." Heidegger, "The Origin of the Work of Art," in *Off the Beaten Track,* 51.

18. Lacan, "Remarks on Daniel Lagache's Presentation," *Écrits,* 549–50. [Translation modified.—Trans.]

19. Lacan, *Le désir et son interprétation,* 405.

20. Lacan, *Le désir et son interprétation,* 311.

21. Lacan, *Anxiety,* 33. [Translation slightly altered.—Trans.]

22. Lacan, *The Four Fundamental Concepts of Psychoanalysis,* 30–31.

23. "The *a,* desire's support in the fantasy, isn't visible in what constitutes for man the image of his desire." Lacan, *Anxiety,* 41.

24. Lacan, "Introduction to the Names-of-the-Father Seminar," in *Television: A Challenge to the Psychoanalytic Establishment* (New York: Norton, 1990), 87. [Translation modified.—Trans.]

25. Lacan, *Le désir et son interprétation*, 381.

26. Lacan, *Anxiety*, 231. [Translation modified.—Trans.] The "partial object" is one of the acceptations of the object *a*, as we will later see.

27. "There is only desire insofar as the objects of maternal enjoyment are forbidden. Milk, for example, dissolves the drinker in its kindness, and the enjoyment of it always borders on disgust, on the disappearance into satisfied maternal demand. . . . To drink [is the] drive to drink infinitely, a desire that resides infinitely, unsatisfied. The object-cause is in this way its own *remainder,* which it reproduces boundlessly *[sans borne],* always exceeding itself." Gérard Pommier, *Le dénouement d'une analyse* (Paris: Point Hors Ligne, 1987), 267. Note that encountering the object can trigger psychosis.

28. "That act by which the little one, in some sense astonished, throws his head back while removing himself from the breast, shows that it is only apparently that the breast belongs to the mother. To him, fundamentally it belongs to him." Lacan, "Introduction to the Names-of-the-Father Seminar," *Television*, 85. [Translation modified.—Trans.]

29. Lacan, *Le désir et son interprétation*, 534.

30. In 1972, Lacan spoke of the object *a* in these terms: "We know what produces language: it produces what? What I called surplus enjoyment, because it is the term that is applied at this level and that we know well, which is called desire. More exactly, it produces the cause of desire. And it is that which is called the petit objet *a*. The petit objet *a* is the true support of everything that we saw functioning and that functions in a way that becomes more and more pure in order to specify each in his desire." "Discours de Jacques Lacan à l'Université de Milan le 12 Mai 1972," in *Lacan in Italia, 1953–1978/ En Italie Lacan* (Milan: Salamandra, 1978), 23–55.

31. Karl Marx, *Manuscrits de 1844* (Paris: Flammarion, 1996), 65.

32. "I have already shown you that in the master's discourse, the *a* is precisely identifiable with what the thought of a worker, Marx's, produced, namely, what was, symbolically and really, the function of surplus value." Lacan, *The Other Side of Psychoanalysis*, 44.

33. Lacan, "D'une reforme dans son trou" (1969, unpublished manuscript). This article was intended for *Le Monde* but never published.

34. "And let magnitudes having the same ratio be called proportional [analogous]," Euclid, *Elements* Book V, definition 6, cited by François Regnault, "Le Marx de Lacan," Lettre Mensuelle de l'ECF n 242, 2005. (This is a summary report of his seminar at l'École de la Cause Freudienne.)

35. "Marx denounces this process as spoliation," Lacan says of the process of making surplus value. Lacan, *The Other Side of Psychoanalysis*, 80.

36. Louis Althusser, "Comment lire 'le Capital,'" in *Positions* (Paris: Éditions Sociales, 1976), 52.

37. Lacan, *The Other Side of Psychoanalysis*, 107–8. [Translation modified. —Trans.]

38. Lacan, *D'un autre à l'Autre*, 178.

39. "Only, all of this holds only if the stake is assessed as worth nothing. . . . The object *a* has no use value. It no more has exchange value either, as I already stated." Lacan, *D'un autre à l'Autre*, 178.

40. Lacan, "The Freudian Thing, or the Meaning of the Return to Freud in Psychoanalysis," *Écrits*, 334–63. The assonance between *res* and French *rien* should be noted.

41. In his commentary on the dream of the burning son in *The Four Fundamental Concepts of Psychoanalysis*, Lacan explains that the real returns, as a "missed encounter" (as *tuché*), in the dream: "Thus the encounter, forever missed, has occurred between dream and awakening." He adds a bit later that "the real has to be sought beyond the dream—in what the dream has enveloped, hidden from us, behind the lack of representation of which there is only one representative *[un tenant-lieu]*," i.e., the signifier (59–60).

42. Lacan, "The Freudian Thing," *Écrits*, 349.

43. Lacan, *The Four Fundamental Concepts of Psychoanalysis*, 22.

44. Freud, "Repression," *Standard Edition*, 14:141–58. In this text, Freud speaks of "chains of thoughts," while "The Unconscious," written in 1915, sees him speaking of "mnemic residues" and even "mnemic images." See "The Unconscious," *Standard Edition*, 14:159–215.

45. Freud, "The Ego and the Id," *Standard Edition*, 19:1–66.

46. Lacan, "Le troisième." [This neologism is, as Bruce Fink indicates in a note to his translation of *Encore*, "a term Lacan creates by putting together the feminine article *la* with the noun *langue* (language, but also spoken language, as in tongue)." What Lacan means by the term, Fink continues, is "very roughly speaking . . . the acoustic level of language, the level at which polysemy is possible due to the existence of homonyms. . . . It is the level at which an infant (or songwriter) may endlessly repeat one syllable of a word (for example, 'la la la'), the level at which language may 'stutter'—hence the translation provided here, borrowed from Russell Grigg, 'llanguage.'" Lacan, *Encore*, 44n15.—Trans.]

47. Lacan, *Encore*, 139.

48. "The product of unconscious knowledge is the cause of desire." Gérard Pommier, *La névrose infantile de la psychanalyse* (Paris: Seuil, 1975), 145. Unconscious knowledge does not, though, correspond to a lifting of repression: "What is forever unconscious is knowledge itself" (140).

49. "The product of unconscious knowledge is the cause of desire." Pommier, *La névrose infantile*, 145. Unconscious knowledge does not amount to lifted repression: "What is for unconscious is knowledge itself" (140).

50. Lacan, *The Four Fundamental Concepts of Psychoanalysis*, 105.

51. "The most striking manifestation of this objet *a*, the signal that it is intervening, is anxiety." Lacan, *Anxiety*, 86.

52. "In the end, what meaning does the term 'defense apropos neuropsychosis' have, if it's not a defense against what? Against something that is not something other than desire." Lacan, *Le désir et son interprétation* (November 12, 1958), 11.

53. Pommier, *Le dénouement d'une analyse*, 246.

54. "The object of desire is the cause of desire, and this object-cause of desire is the object of the drive—that is to say, the object around which the drive turns." Lacan, *The Four Fundamental Concepts of Psychoanalysis*, 243.

55. "For isn't it plain to see that the—partial—characteristic, rightly emphasized in objects, is applicable not because these objects are part of a total object, which the body is assumed to be, but because they only partially represent the function that produces them?" *Écrits*, 693.

56. The fragmented body of the schizophrenic opens this problematic to other questions, which will not be entered into so as not to distract us from the present topic.

57. Lacan, *Écrits*, 692.

58. Lacan, *Formations of the Unconscious*, 148.

59. Freud, "Instincts and Their Vicissitudes," *Standard Edition*, 14:109–40, 123.

60. $\$\Diamond D$, "barred subject losange demand," is the algorithm of the drive.

61. Baruch Spinoza, "Letter 58 (OP): To the Very Learned and Able Mr. G. H. Schuller, From Benedict de Spinoza," in *The Collected Works of Spinoza*, ed. and trans. Edwin Curley (Princeton: Princeton University Press, 2016), 428.

6. "ONESELF" AS OBJECT OF DESIRE AND LOVE

1. "The term narcissism," Freud states, "denotes the attitude of a person who treats his own body in the same way in which the body of a sexual object is ordinarily treated—who looks at it, that is to say, strokes and fondles it till he obtains complete satisfaction from these activities." Freud, "On Narcissism: An Introduction," *Standard Edition*, 14:73.

2. *Psyché* is distinct from *nous*, "intellect," "intelligence," "intuition." *Nous* is a form of perception of the mind and not of meaning/sense.

3. Aristotle, *On the Soul*, in *The Complete Works of Aristotle: The Revised Oxford Translation* ed. Jonathon Barnes (Princeton: Princeton University Press, 1984), 1437 (412b5–10).

4. This is not, though, an image of the body *(eidos)*.

5. Spinoza, *Ethics*, Part II, Proposition 7, Scholia, and Part III, Proposition 2, Scholia.

6. "Instinct *[Trieb]* appears to us a concept on the frontier between the mental and the somatic, as the psychical representative of the stimuli originating from within the organism and reaching the mind, as a measure of the demand made upon the mind for work in consequence of its connection

with the body." Freud, "Instincts and Their Vicissitudes," *Standard Edition,* 14:120–21.

7. "It suffices," says Lacan, "to understand the mirror stage in this context *as an identification,* in the full sense analysis gives to the term: namely, the transformation that takes place in the subject when he assumes an image—an image that is seemingly predestined to have an effect at this phase, as witnessed by the use in analytic theory of antiquity's term, *'imago.'*" Lacan, "The Mirror Stage as Formative of the Function of the *I* Function," *Écrits,* 93.

8. Lacan, *Freud's Papers on Technique,* 173. [Translation slightly modified. —Trans.]

9. In the sense of the social bond.

10. Lacan, "The Mirror Stage," *Écrits,* 78.

11. "If we put our confidence in the idea . . . that the ego is not only a surface, but the projection of a surface, then the problem has to be posed in the topological terms of pure surface." Lacan, *Anxiety,* 96. Lacan had already perceived by 1949 the danger of the infant's identification with a surface, the specular body. See "The Mirror Stage," *Écrits,* 80–81.

12. Lacan, *Formations of the Unconscious,* 209. See also "A Question Preliminary to Any Possible Treatment of Psychosis," *Écrits,* 462.

13. Lacan, *Freud's Papers on Technique,* 177.

14. Lacan, *Anxiety,* 88.

15. Lacan, *The Four Fundamental Concepts of Psychoanalysis,* 182–83.

16. Gérard Wacjman, *Fenêtre: Chronique du regard et de l'intime* (Paris: Verdier, 2004), 319.

17. "Oh, how I wish that I and my body could now be parted. . . . In wild distress, he ripped the top of his tunic aside / and bared his breast to the blows he rained with his milk-white hand. / His first brought up a crimson weal on his naked torso, / like apples tinted both red and white, or a multicoloured / cluster of grapes just ripening into a blushing purple." Ovid, *Metamorphoses,* trans. David Raburn (New York: Penguin Books, 2004), 115–16.

18. "If we grant the ego a primary cathexis of libido, why is there any necessity for further distinguishing a sexual libido from a nonsexual energy of the ego-drives?" Freud, "On Narcissism: An Introduction," 76.

19. "A differentiation of libido into a kind which is proper to the ego and one which is attached to objects is an unavoidable corollary to an original hypothesis which distinguished between sexual instincts and ego-instincts." Freud, "On Narcissism: An Introduction," 77.

20. Freud, *The Ego and the Id, Standard Edition,* 19:25.

21. Freud, *The Ego and the Id,* 30n1.

22. Freud, *Beyond the Pleasure Principle,* 45–46.

23. Freud, *The Ego and the Id,* 20. Freud adds in a note on page 26 that "the ego is ultimately derived from bodily sensations, chiefly from those springing from the surface of the body. It may thus be regarded as a mental projection

of the surface of the body, besides, as we have seen above, representing the superficies of the mental apparatus."

24. Freud, "On Narcissism: An Introduction," 76–77.

25. "The instinct is not directed toward other people, but obtains satisfaction from the subject's own body." Freud, *Three Essays on the Theory of Sexuality, Standard Edition,* 7:181. Freud adds in "On Narcissism: An Introduction" that "The first autoerotic sexual satisfactions are experienced in connection with vital functions which serve the purpose of self-preservation" (87).

26. "This leads us to look upon the narcissism which arises through the drawing in of object-cathexes as a secondary one, superimposed upon a primary narcissism that is obscured by a number of different influences." Freud, "On Narcissism: An Introduction," 75.

27. Freud, "On Narcissism: An Introduction," 94.

28. See on this point Gérard Pommier, *Les corps angéliques de la postmodernité* (Paris: Calmann-Lévy, 2000), 31.

29. Freud, *The Ego and the Id,* 30.

30. In "identification with the father, the boy wants to be in his father's place because he admires him and wants to be like him, and also because he wants to put him out of the way." Freud, "Dostoyevsky and Parricide," *Standard Edition,* 21:183.

31. "The subject kills itself because it is so much at a distance from itself that it does not recognize itself: you aim for a phantom, a puppet, a caricature whose promiscuity embarrasses or dishonors ." Marcel Jouhandeau, in his portrait of Don Juan, cited by Christine Toutin-Thelier, "Soi-même dans le narcissisme et la mélancholie," *Littoral,* nos. 27–28, Exercises de Désir (Toulouse: érès, 1989), 95.

32. Freud, "Mourning and Melancholia," *Standard Edition,* 14:249.

33. "Thus the shadow of the object fell upon the ego, and the latter could henceforth be judged by a special agency, as though it were an object, the forsaken object." Freud, "Mourning and Melancholia," 249.

34. Lacan, *Transference: The Seminar of Jacques Lacan, Book VIII,* trans. Bruce Fink (New York, Polity: 2017), 396.

35. Lacan, *Transference,* 396. This thesis of Lacan's would appear to contradict Freud, who designates melancholia "narcissistic neurosis," an expression that can lead to some confusion. Freud uses the term in "Mourning and Melancholia" to draw a contrast between melancholia and "transference neurosis." Narcissistic neurosis thus belongs to psychosis in general. Freud will return to the question of melancholia in 1924, when he proposes calling it "narcissistic psychoneurosis" in order to distinguish it as much from neurosis as psychosis. See Freud, "Neurosis and Psychosis," *Standard Edition,* 19:149–56. In both cases, the term "narcissistic" should not be understood to mean "egoic" *[moïque],* "egocentric," and "specular," as the term indicates a withdrawal of the subject into itself (which is found in psychosis, particularly

in schizophrenia and autism) and its impossibility of investing in external objects, as is the case in pathological mourning.

36. The subject heavily identifies with the lost, introjected object—it *has* and at the same time *is* the object—and without any imaginary mediation to keep a screen between subject and object (as follows from the foreclosure of the Name-of-the-Father).

37. "The self-tormenting in melancholia, which is without doubt enjoyable, signifies, just like the corresponding phenomenon in obsessional neurosis, a satisfaction of trends of sadism and hate, which relate to an object, and which have been turned round upon the subject's own self." Freud, "Mourning and Melancholia," 251.

38. "The melancholic is he who does not know the experience of loss and of a first, subjectivating mourning; not that he was engulfed by the sort of maternal desire specific to the psychotic rendering; on the contrary, he was desperately fulfilled: desperately, which is to say miserably." Jacques Hassoun, *La cruauté mélancholique* (Paris: Aubier, 1995), 98.

39. "Erotogenic masochism proper . . . on the one hand has become a component of the libido and, on the other, still has the self as its object." Freud, "The Economic Problem of Masochism," *Standard Edition,* 19:163.

40. "The transformation from sadism to masochism betokens a return to the narcissistic object." Freud, "Instincts and Their Vicissitudes," 132.

41. Étienne Balibar, "Scène tragique et structure psychanalytique," in *La pulsion de mort entre psychanalyse et philosophie,* ed. Michel Plon and Henri Rey-Flaud (Toulouse: érès, 2004), 113.

7. *CONATUS* AND/OR THE DEATH DRIVE

1. Spinoza, *Ethics,* Part III, Proposition 6.

2. Spinoza, *Ethics,* Part III, Proposition 4.

3. Freud, *Beyond the Pleasure Principle,* 27.

4. Freud, *Beyond the Pleasure Principle,* 44–45. Freud also speaks just afterward of a conflict between the two kinds of drives: "psychoneuroses are based on a conflict between ego-drives and sexual drives" (46).

5. "Our argument had as its point of departure a sharp distinction between ego-drives, which we equated with death drives, and sexual drives, which we equated with life drives." Freud, *Beyond the Pleasure Principle,* 47.

6. Freud, *Beyond the Pleasure Principle,* 33.

7. Freud, *Beyond the Pleasure Principle,* 34–35.

8. Freud, *Beyond the Pleasure Principle,* 34–35.

9. "The dominating tendency of mental life, and perhaps of nervous life in general, is the effort to reduce, to keep constant, or to remove internal tension due to stimuli (the 'Nirvana principle,' to borrow a term from Barbara Low)—a tendency which finds expression in the pleasure principle; and our recognition of that fact is one of our strongest reasons for believing in the

existence of death instincts." Freud, *Beyond the Pleasure Principle*, 49–50. It can be recalled that in 1924, Freud distinguished the nirvana principle from the pleasure principle on account of the tensions that can accompany pleasure, especially sexual excitation, and the unpleasantness of their subsequent relaxation. The pleasure principle thus comes to represent "the demands of the libido." See Freud, "The Economic Problem of Masochism," 155–70.

10. Gilles Deleuze, *Spinoza: Practical Philosophy*, trans. Robert Hurley (San Francisco: City Lights, 1988), 18.

11. Hofmannsthal writes "I mean life" when speaking of *nature morte.* See Hugo von Hofmannsthal, *Briefe 1890–1901*, vol. 1 (Berlin: S. Fischer, 1935), 89.

12. Lacan, *The Ethics of Psychoanalysis*, 216–17.

13. Lacan, *The Ethics of Psychoanalysis*, 216–17.

14. Freud, *Beyond the Pleasure Principle*, 49–50.

15. Freud, *Beyond the Pleasure Principle*, 34.

16. Freud, *Beyond the Pleasure Principle*, 35.

17. At the same time, Freud hesitates over this idea, qualifying it as "mystical." *Beyond the Pleasure Principle*, 114.

18. Arthur Schopenhauer, *The World as Will and Representation*, trans. E. F. J. Payne (Mineola, N.Y.: Dover, 1969), 514. [Translation adjusted to match the French translation cited by Lippi.—Trans.]

19. Lacan, *The Four Fundamentals of Psychoanalysis*, 205.

20. Brigitte Lemérer, "La pulsion de mort: Une speculation psychanalytique," in *La pulsion de mort entre psychanalye et philosophie*, ed. M. Plon and H. Rey-Flaud (Toulouse: érès, 2004), 19.

21. Lacan, *The Ethics of Psychoanalysis*, 211. [Translation modified.—Trans.]

22. Lacan, *The Ego in Freud's Theory and the Technique of Psychoanalysis*, 232.

23. Lacan, *The Ego in Freud's Theory and the Technique of Psychoanalysis*, 90. [Translation modified.—Trans.]

24. Deleuze, *Spinoza*, 21.

25. Lacan's concept of object *a* perfectly incarnates this paradox: the object *a* is at once the object cause of desire and the object of the drives. Desire and drive should of course be distinguished, even if they join at some point. If desire is instituted with castration, it is castration that the drive encounters at the end of its travels.

26. Lacan, *The Ethics of Psychoanalysis*, 211. "Don't put," he adds on the next page, "the emphasis on the term 'will' here. Whatever interest may have been aroused in Freud by an echo in Schopenhauer, it has nothing to do with the idea of a fundamental *Wille*. And it is only to make you sense the difference of register relative to the tendency to return to equilibrium that I am using the word in this way here."

27. This is the term Freud proposed for indicating forms of existence marked by the repetition of unfortunate scenarios.

28. Lacan, *The Four Fundamental Concepts of Psychoanalysis*, 59. [Translation modified.—Trans.]

29. "The somewhat grandiloquent nomination of the 'death drive' loses its air of romantic mystery once its enjoyful *[jouissive]* origin has been considered, which is the identification of oneself with the phallus that the mother lacks; the rejoining of the nothing equal to the death drive, the first *rendez-vous* given by love." Gérard Pommier, *Louis du néant: La mélancholie d'Althusser* (Paris: Aubier, 1998), 223.

30. It remains to be seen if the subject's fixation on and thus repetition of objective traumas might always manifest something of the order of a subjective trauma. Pommier, again: "If for example a war trauma takes the place of a sexual seduction, that nightmare will take hold so much less easily once it contains an enjoyment." Gérard Pommier, "Respiration du symptôme," in *La clinique lacanienne no 6: Du symbole au symptom* (Tolouse: érès, 2002), 106.

31. In "Repression," Freud speaks of "chains of thoughts," while in "The Unconscious," which he wrote in the same year (1915), he employs the terms "acoustic traces," "memory-traces," and "memory-images."

32. "The child cannot possible have felt his mother's departure as something agreeable or even indifferent. How then does his repetition of this distressing experience as a game fit in with the pleasure principle? It may perhaps be said in reply that the her departure had to be enacted as a necessary preliminary to her joyful return, and that it was in the latter that lay the true purpose of the game. But against this must be counted the observed fact that the first act, that of departure, was staged as a game in itself and far more frequently than the episode in its entirety, with its pleasurable ending." Freud, *Beyond the Pleasure Principle*, 8–9.

33. "What the child asks *[demande]* of his mother with his demand is designed to structure the presence/absence relation for him, as is demonstrated by the originative *Fort/Da* game, which is a first exercise of mastery." Lacan, *Anxiety*, 64–65. [Translation slightly altered to accord with the quoted French text.—Trans.]

34. The same distinction could be employed to distinguish between kinds of art.

35. An actor is directed and is in that sense passive.

36. Lacan, *The Four Fundamentals of Psychoanalysis*, 61.

37. Lacan, *The Ethics of Psychoanalysis*, 212 [translation slightly altered. —Trans.]. Lacan was doubtlessly inspired, like Freud before him, by Sabina Spielrein, who maintained that only the clash between destructive forces can create anything new. See Spielrein, *Entre Freud et Jung* (Paris: Aubier, 2004).

38. We should remind the reader here that enjoyment and prohibition act in tandem in the symptom.

39. Note that in thermodynamics, entropy can be interpreted as the measure

of the degree of disorder within a given system. The higher its entropy, the less its elements are organized and bound.

40. Freud, "The Economic Problem of Masochism," 377–80.

41. Lacan, "Position of the Unconscious," *Écrits,* 719.

42. Lacan, *The Sinthome,* 63.

43. Freud, "'A Child Is Being Beaten': A Contribution to the Origin of Sexual Perversions," *Standard Edition,* 17:175–204.

8. THE LAWS OF DESIRE

1. George Bataille, *Erotism: Death and Sensuality,* trans. Mary Dalwood (San Francisco: City Lights Book, 1986), 64. [Translation slightly modified. —Trans.]

2. For more regarding this sort of silencing, see Michel Foucault, "A Preface to Transgression," in *Aesthetics, Method, and Epistemology,* ed. James Faubion (New York: The New Press, 1999), 69–88.

3. Transgressing sex is not the same as its sublimation. See Roland Barthes, "Metaphor of the Eye," in *Critical Essays,* trans. Richard Howard (Evanston: Northwestern University Press, 1972), 246.

4. George Bataille, *Story of the Eye,* trans. Joachim Neugroschel (San Francisco: City Lights Book, 1987), 49.

5. When she has already changed her object from being the mother to being the father.

6. "The father must . . . represent in all its fullness the symbolic value crystallized in his function." Jacques Lacan, *Le mythe individuel du névrosé* (Paris: Seuil, 2007). [In English, Jacques Lacan, "The Neurotic's Individual Myth," ed. Jacques Alain-Miller, trans. Martha Noel Evans, *Psychoanalytic Quarterly* 48 (1979): 405–25.—Trans.]

7. Bataille, *Story of the Eye,* 8.

8. Lacan, "La troisième."

9. "There is a rapport between language and sex. . . . As I said earlier, we can only reach odds and ends *[des bouts]* of the real. This real, the real at issue in what is called my thought, is always an odd or end, a core *[un trognon].*" Lacan, *The Sinthome,* 102, 104.

10. Lacan, *The Sinthome,* 58. [I have included the English translation's retention of Lacan's French phrase, as there is no way to reproduce in English Lacan's play on the homonymy between *jouissance* and *j'ouis sens.*—Trans.]

11. See Lacan, *The Sinthome,* chapter 5, "Was Joyce Mad?"

12. Oedipus, like the neurotic, acts unconsciously: he is unaware that he has killed his father and married his mother, and discovers it only at the end of Sophocles's tragedy.

13. The law and the murder of the father are tightly linked: "If there is anything that makes it the case that the law is founded on the father, it is neces-

sary that the father be murdered. . . . The father, insofar as he promulgates the law, is the dead father, that is, the symbol of the father. The dead father is the Name-of-the-Father, which is there, constructed over the content." Lacan, *Formations of the Unconscious*, 132.

14. Lacan, *The Other Side of Psychoanalysis*, 123.

15. As St. Paul said, "What then should we say? That the law is sin? By no means! Yet, if it had not been for the law, I would not have known sin. I would not have not known what it is to covet if the law had not said, 'You shall not covet.' Yet sin, seizing an opportunity in the commandment, produced in me all kinds of covetousness. Apart from the law, sin lies dead." Romans 7:7–8. *The New Oxford Annotated Bible: New Revised Standard Version*, ed. Michael D. Coogan (Oxford: Oxford University Press, 2010).

16. "Resulting from the introjection of paternal authority [the prohibition on enjoying the mother] and consisting of the repression of incestuous movements of the drives [desire for the mother, the wish for the father's death], the superego is charged with the powers of the Id. So far as it is a prohibiting agency, the superego is the representative of lost enjoyment." Catherine Millot, *Nobodaddy* (Paris: Point Hors Ligne, 1988), 74.

17. Lacan, "Subversion of the Subject and the Dialectic of Desire," *Écrits*, 695.

18. Freud, "The Economic Problem of Masochism," 167. In "The Ego and the Id," Freud also speaks of the categorical imperative apropos the cruelty of the superego that manifests in the feeling of guilt.

19. Immanuel Kant, *Critique of Practical Reason*, trans. Mary Gregor (Cambridge: Cambridge University Press, 2015), 54.

20. "Desire *(appetitio)* is the self-determination of a subject's power through the representation of something in the future as an effect of this representation." Immanuel Kant, *Anthropology from a Pragmatic Point of View*, trans. Robert B. Louden (Cambridge: Cambridge University Press, 2006), 149.

21. Lacan, "Kant with Sade," *Écrits*, 749.

22. Immanuel Kant, *The Metaphysics of Morals*, trans. Mary Gregor (Cambridge: Cambridge University Press, 1991), 209.

23. "The law in effect would command, "Enjoy!" Lacan, "Subversion of the Subject and the Dialectic of Desire," *Écrits*, 696 [translation altered—Trans.]. Lacan had already written in 1960 that "it is enough for enjoyment to be a form of evil for the whole thing to change its character completely, and for the meaning of the moral law itself to be completely changed. Anyone can see that if the moral law is, in effect, capable of playing some role here, it is precisely as a support for the enjoyment involved; it is so that the sin becomes what Saint Paul calls inordinately sinful. That's what Kant on this occasion simply ignores." Lacan, *The Ethics of Psychoanalysis*, 189.

24. Jean Clavreul, *Le désir et la loi* (Paris: Denoël, 1987), 148.

25. Clavreul, *Le désir et la loi,* 204.

26. In the seminar "Symbolique, imaginaire, et réel," Lacan states that the father is just the superego, that is, law without speech (typed version, 57).

27. Lacan, "The Subversion of the Subject and the Dialectic of Desire," *Écrits,* 696.

28. In Spanish, *goce* covers the acceptation of the substantive (enjoyment) and of the imperative of the verb *gozar,* i.e., "Enjoy!"

29. Note that in Lacan's "Kant with Sade" the word *law* appears alternately uncapitalized and capitalized in order to indicate the two senses of law that I discuss below. See, e.g., Lacan, "Kant with Sade," *Écrits,* 659. I therefore maintain Lacan's convention here.

30. Lacan, "Kant with Sade," *Écrits,* 663.

31. Lacan, "Kant with Sade," *Écrits,* 660.

32. Lacan, "Kant with Sade," *Écrits,* 665.

33. Lacan, "Kant with Sade," *Écrits,* 664.

34. Lacan, "Kant with Sade," *Écrits,* 658.

35. Lacan, *The Four Fundamentals Concepts of Psychoanalysis,* 274–75.

36. "Antigone pushes to the limit the realization of something that might be called pure desire, the pure and simple desire of death as such. She incarnates that desire." Lacan, *The Ethics of Psychoanalysis,* 217

37. Lacan, *The Other Side of Psychoanalysis,* 18.

38. Lacan, *The Ethics of Psychoanalysis,* 282–83. [Translation slightly altered—Trans.]

39. George Bataille, *Ma mère* (Paris: Pauvert, 1966), 75.

40. Homosexuality can of course occur in each of the clinical structures [neurosis, psychosis, perversion—Trans.], and homosexuality as an object-choice for the same sex and homosexuality as perversion are to be distinguished. (It should also be noted that perversion's structure is too often confused with that of criminality, which further muddles things.)

41. Lacan, *The Ethics of Psychoanalysis,* 319.

42. Lacan, *The Ethics of Psychoanalysis,* 315.

43. Lacan, *The Ethics of Psychoanalysis,* 298.

44. Lacan, *The Other Side of Psychoanalysis,* 19. Just before he says, "What analysis shows, if it shows anything at all . . . is very precisely the fact that we never transgress. Sneaking around is not transgressing."

45. In *The Four Fundamental Concepts of Psychoanalysis,* Lacan comments on the dream of the burning dead son that Freud recounts in the *Traumdeutung.* For Lacan, this dream does not fulfill a wish, which is what Freud claims, but a point in the father's enjoyment, a place where "desire is made present in the dream by the loss imaged at the most cruel point of the object" (59).

46. "Freud was the first to articulate boldly and powerfully the idea that the only moment of enjoyment that man knows occurs at the site where fan-

tasies are produced, fantasies that represent for us the same barrier as far as access to enjoyment is concerned, the barrier where everything is forgotten." Lacan, *The Ethics of Psychoanalysis*, 298.

9. ENJOYMENT: ALL AND NOT-ALL

1. Phallic enjoyment passes, according to Lacan, through the phallic symbol, i.e., through castration (hence through language): "What man would be if the sexual relationship could be written in a sustainable way, a way that is sustainable in a discourse—man is but a signifier because where he comes into play as a signifier, he comes in only *quoad castrationem,* in other words, insofar as he has a relation to phallic enjoyment." Lacan, *Encore*, 35. Lacan conjectures that phallic enjoyment is limited to the pleasure of an organ: "Phallic enjoyment is the obstacle owing to which man does not come *[n'arrive pas],* I would say, to enjoy woman's body, precisely because what he enjoys is the enjoyment of the organ" (13).

2. Lacan, *Encore*, 73. On the next page, Lacan explains that "It's not because she is not-wholly *[pas-toute]* in the phallic function that she is not there at all. She is *not* not at all there. She is there in full *[à plein].* But there is something more *[en plus].*"

3. This supplementarity is to be read as the possible opening in every structure, despite structure being a closed ensemble. See Lacan, *The Psychoses,* 183. In the present case it is phallic enjoyment that constitutes the closed, limited ensemble. But it is through the limit of a structure that there can be an opening.

4. "Mysticism . . . is something serious, about which several people inform us—most often women, or bright people like Saint John of the Cross, because one is not obliged, when one is male, to situate oneself on the side of ∀xFx [i.e., every speaking being is subject to castration]. One can situate oneself on the side of the not-whole. There are men who are just as good as women. It happens. And who also feel just fine about it. Despite—I won't say their phallus—despite what encumbers them that goes by that name, they get the idea or sense that there must be an enjoyment that is beyond. Those are the ones we call mystics." Lacan, *Encore*, 76.

5. Lacan, *Encore*, 74. It should be noted that the Other enjoyment will always remain a supposition for Lacan.

6. Michel Bousseyroux, *Au risque de la topologie et de la poésie: Élargir de la psychanalyse* (Toulouse: érès, 2011), 20.

7. Hadewijch, *The Complete Works,* trans. Mother Columbia Hart (New York: Paulist Press, 1980) 279.

8. André Breton, *Nadja,* trans. Richard Howard (New York: Grove Press, 1960), 160.

9. Charles Baudelaire, "Hymn to Beauty," in *The Flowers of Evil,* trans. James McGowan (Oxford: Oxford University Press, 1998), 45.

10. St. John of the Cross, *Dark Night of the Soul*, trans. E. Allison Peers (New York: Image Books, 1959), 16.

11. Lacan emphasizes this point in the following passage: "I have already spoken about other people who were not too bad in terms of mysticism, but who were situated instead on the side of the phallic function, Angelus Silesius, for example. Confusing his contemplative eye with the eye with which God looks at him, must, if kept up, partake of perverse enjoyment." Lacan, *Encore*, 76.

12. Bousseyroux, *Au risque de la topologie et de la poésie*, 31. "What Hadewijch, Theresa of Avila, and John of the Cross learn is that to know God is to enjoy his absence. This is the reason that they are veritable *atheologians*" (33). As we will see shortly, certain mystical texts, including John of the Cross's and Angelus Silesius's, contradict Bousseyroux on this point.

13. Recall here Lacan's "We know that for us [speaking beings], enjoyment is castration." Lacan, "Propos sur l'hystérie," *Quatro* no. 2 (1977).

14. Bousseyroux, *Au risque de la topologie et de la poésie*, 35.

15. Bousseyroux, *Au risque de la topologie et de la poésie*, 36. Bousseyroux is referring to Hadewijch, whom Lacan speaks of in *Encore* (71).

16. Bousseyroux, *Au risque de la topologie et de la poésie*, 33.

17. In the mystic's Other enjoyment, what is at issue is the assumption of the absence of God.

18. Hadewijch, *The Complete Works*, 80. [*Jouissance* appears in the indicated places in the French translation quoted by Lippi.—Trans.]

19. Bousseyroux, *Au risque de la topologie et de la poésie*, 35.

20. Bousseyroux, *Au risque de la topologie et de la poésie*, 34.

21. I will not say, with Hume and Bousseyroux, that mystics are true atheists.

22. And not J(Ⱥ).

23. This is not what John of the Cross thinks in the sixteenth century, as he states in the preamble to *Dark Night of the Soul* that "exposition of the stanzas describing the method followed by the soul in its journey upon the spiritual road to the attainment of the perfect union of love with God, to the extent that is possible in this life" (16).

24. John of the Cross writes in *Dark Night of the Soul* that "the soul learns to commune with God with more respect and more courtesy, such as a soul must ever observe in converse with the Most High" (38).

25. Lacan, *Encore*, 70.

26. Bernini is a baroque artist, and the art of the seventeenth century tends to develop a system of intense expression, involving an overabundance of (sometimes inauthentic) passion. See Giulio Carlo Agran, *Storia dell'arte italiana*, vol. 3 (Florence: Sansoni, 1968), 318.

27. Orgasm indicates, according to my hypothesis, a conjuncture of physi-

cal enjoyment and psychic enjoyment. The term "enjoyment" *[jouissance]* itself will often be employed here without either of those two modifiers to convey its more general sense of "coming." [Slight modification to original. —Trans.]

28. If each and every man has no need for every single woman, this is because "they are not (all) consonant with his unconscious." Jacques Lacan, "Conférence à Genève sur 'Le symptom,'" *Le bloc-notes de la psychanalyse,* no. 5 (1985).

29. "Far from the body, there is the possibility of what last time I called resonance, or consonance." Lacan, *The Sinthome,* 29.

30. For a woman, it is in her entire body that she loses her erection.

31. "Detumescence in copulation deserves to hold our attention as a way of highlighting one of the dimensions of castration. The fact that the phallus is more significant in human experience through its possibility of being a fallen object than through its presence is what distinguishes the possibility of the place of castration in the history of desire." Lacan, *Anxiety,* 168.

32. Autoeroticism is the appropriate term and not masturbation, and in the sense of "self-eroticism." In the autoerotic phase of the infant, incestuous fantasy still predominates, and the subject has still not separated itself from mother, not detached itself from its position as the object of desire of the Other. Masturbation, in contrast, involves true separation from the mother in that it permits the child self-satisfaction. It is only partially satisfied, of course, as it has the experience of enjoyment and satisfaction at the same time. See Silvia Lippi, *Transgressions: Bataille, Lacan* (Toulouse: érès, 2008), 154.

33. Despite having had sexual experiences with women, this woman was neither homosexual nor bisexual.

34. Lacan states apropos of men that "the sex [organ] of woman is of no interest to them *[ne leur dit rien].*" *Encore,* 7. He then explains that the physical enjoyment of men necessarily passes through the intermediary of the body, and more specifically, through the phallic organ, although that does not entail that it is universally the case that coitus is equivalent to masturbation for men. (The image of the "macho" man who thinks only of his own enjoyment to the neglect of his partner's does not correspond to reality. Clinical work shows that for so many men, their partner's body and enjoyment matter enormously, and become sources of excitement for them.)

35. When Lacan spoke of the Other enjoyment (that of woman), he did not succumb to that mistake. Nevertheless, the relation between the Other enjoyment and the enjoyment of the Other remains problematic in Lacanian theory and it is best that they are kept separate.

36. This insight comes from Orsola Barberis. See Pascal Quignard, *Le sexe et l'effroi* (Paris: Gallimard, 1994).

37. Frigidity is not exclusively feminine, as men also suffer from it.

38. Sigmund Freud, "Psychoanalytic Notes on an Autobiographical Account of a Case of Paranoia (Dementia Paranoides)," *Standard Edition*, 12:69.

39. "The homologue of the . . . anxiety-point is orgasm itself as a subjective experience." Lacan, *Anxiety,* 239. Lacan assimilates orgasm to physiological discharge. He shows that the subject can have an orgasm—he means by this that the subject can ejaculate—by entering into an anxiety-producing situation that is independent of the sexual scene and of the physical presence (physical or imaginary) of the partner.

40. Piera Aulagnier-Spairani, "Remarques sur la femininité et ses avatars," in *Le désir et la perversion,* ed. Piera Aulagnier-Spairini, Jean Clavreul, François Perrier, Guy Rosolato, and Jean-Paul Valabrega (Paris: Seuil, 1967), 59–65.

41. The point is not to be taken as being universally the case.

42. Beyond Nietzsche himself, see also Gilles Deleuze, *The Logic of Sense,* trans. Mark Lester with Charles Stivale (New York: Columbia University Press, 1990), appendices I and II (253–79).

43. Jacques Lacan, *D'un discours qui ne serait pas du semblant* (1970–71), unpublished seminar (Association Lacanienne Internationale, n.d.), January 20, 1971.

44. Lacan, *Encore,* 10. [Translation modified.—Trans.]

45. Lacan, *Encore,* 10.

46. [This is an allusion to Lacan's seminar of the same name.—Trans.]

47. In sexual love, man is not necessarily the father, just as the woman is not the mother: the partner can become a means of evasion and liquidation, albeit partial, of parental love. David Lynch's *Wild at Heart* (1990) beautifully illustrates the ambiguous conflict between Lula's mother and Lula's lover.

48. In Lacanian theory, *a* designates at once the specular other and the object-cause of desire. The little other that brings enjoyment in fantasy is both at once.

49. [Lippi is playing here on the title of Lacan's seminar *Encore,* which itself plays on the homonymous relation between French *encore*—"still," "again," "once more"—and *en corps,* "in the body." The sense conveyed here by her *encorps* is that amorous ecstasy makes the body exist once more, in a (different) body that is beyond fantasy.—Trans.]

50. Lacan, *The Other Side of Psychoanalysis,* 66.

51. For Lacan, materialists are the only true believers: "Their god is matter," he declares (*The Other Side of Psychoanalysis,* 66) Lacan does not account for the fact that for materialists, *everything* is matter (body, spirit, God, etc.), and matter that does not possess any transcendent character. In materialist thought, there is neither alterity nor the big Other. Materialism can for that reason be regarded as a doctrine that lacks alterity and is thus

without an ethics. There are derivations of materialist theory, such as Stalinism or Maoism, that can and have become ideological beliefs, but they are not the theory itself.

52. Loss, rather the unification that is often believed to ensue with love.

CONCLUSION

1. Lacan's initial theory of alienation should not be forgotten, of course: imaginary alienation, conceived in terms of a specular apparatus constituted by the narcissistic relation of the subject to its image.

2. Lacan, *The Four Fundamental Concepts of Psychoanalysis*, 212.

3. "My definition of the signifier (there is no other) is that the signifier is what represents the subject to another signifier." Lacan, "Subversion of the Subject and the Dialectic of Desire," *Écrits*, 693–94.

4. Lacan, *The Four Fundamental Concepts of Psychoanalysis*, 207.

5. Lacan, *Les non-dupes errent*, seminar of February 19, 1974.

6. "What the child asks of his mother is designed to structure the presence/absence relation for him, as is demonstrated by the originative Fort-Da game, which is a first exercise of mastery." Lacan, *Anxiety*, 64–65.

7. Lacan, *The Four Fundamental Concepts of Psychoanalysis*, 239.

8. The idea of an alienation from the Other *tout court* is revealed to be a dead end: there is neither faith nor empty revolt for Lacan! There is a dissymmetry of structure that prevents all reciprocity between subject and Other. This goes against the English school, which conceives of a reciprocity between the subject and its environment, by which an accord between the terms is possible. It is possible at an empirical level, perhaps, but not at a structural one: the Other will remain "Other" for the subject.

9. Bernard Toboul, "Le sujet et la différence de la psychanalyse," in *L'anthropologie de Lévi-Strauss et psychanalyse: D'une structure l'autre*, ed. Marcel Drach and Bernard Toboul (Paris: La Découverte, 2008), 292. See also Freud's "The Neuropsychoses of Defense," *Standard Edition*, 3:43–61.

10. The unreconcilable of the fantasy is clinically reparable, when the symptom of the subject is displaced (e.g., a neurotic subject can pass from a panic attack to agoraphobia to nosophobia, and then to somatization, anorexia, etc.). The symptom finds a reconciliation, albeit momentarily, in the unreconcilable of fantasy, and will remain so during the "symptomatic" traversal of the subject, and even during the "analytic" traversal, as we will see. Yet once the analytic traversal has taken place, the unreconcilable takes another form for the subject; in the best of cases, it is less invalidating than the symptom.

11. Lacan, *The Four Fundamental Concepts of Psychoanalysis*, 210.

12. Note that in *The Four Fundamental Concepts of Psychoanalysis*, Lacan speaks of "crossing [*franchir*] the plane of identification" (287), not that of fantasy.

13. Jacques Lacan, "Propos sur l'hystérie," *Quarto* no. 2 (1981).

14. Sigmund Freud, "Thoughts for the Times on War and Death," *Standard Edition*, 14:291.

15. Breton, *Mad Love*, 41.

16. Breton, *Mad Love*, 42.

17. Breton, *Mad Love*, 21. He states, a couple of pages later (23) that *"chance is the form making manifest the exterior necessity which traces its path in the human unconscious* (boldly trying to interpret and reconcile Engels and Freud on this point)."

18. Breton, *Mad Love*, 13.

19. Breton, *Mad Love*, 36.

20. This order can appear to be disorder. As clinical experience shows, an analysand undergoing a moment of openings will often say things like "I'm lost, I don't know where I'm going . . . ," "Everything is jumbled together," "I'm saying just about anything . . . ," "I'm losing the thread . . . ," "What is it I'm saying right now?"

21. I would like to thank Bernard Toboul for bringing my attention to this observation.

22. Lacan says about the moment to conclude that "the logical value of [this] third evidential moment, which is formulated in the assertion by which the subject concludes his logical movement . . . reveals, in effect, a form proper to an *assertive logic*. . . . This form is undoubtedly related to the logical originality of the subject of the assertion; that is why I characterize it as *subjective assertion,* the logical subject here being but the *personal* form of the knowing subject who can only be expressed by '*I*.' Otherwise stated, the judgment which concludes the sophism can only be borne by a subject who has formulated the assertion about himself, and cannot be imputed to him unreservedly by anyone else." Lacan, "Logical Time and the Assertion of Anticipated Certainty: A New Sophism," *Écrits,* 169–70.

23. "The mind does not know itself, except in so far as it perceives the affections of the body." Spinoza, *Ethics,* Part II, Proposition 23. He also writes, in Part III, Proposition 27, Demonstration, that "the images of things are the affections of the human body whose ideas represent external bodies as if they were present to us . . . that is, . . . whose ideas involve the nature of our body and at the same time the present nature of the external body."

24. "When it happens that the mind can think of itself, by the very fact that it is supposed to make a transition to a greater perfection, that is, . . . to be affected by joy, and the more so, the more distinctly it can imagine itself and its power of acting." Spinoza, *Ethics,* Part III, Proposition 53, Demonstration. ["Joy" has been substituted for the "pleasure" that appears in the English translation.—Trans.]

25. "When I say 'a greater or lesser force of existing than before,' I do not understand that the mind compares the present constitution of the body with a past one, but that the idea that constitutes the form of an emotion affirms

something of the body, which genuinely involves more or less reality than before." Spinoza, *Ethics*, Part III, "General Definition of the Emotions."

26. Jacques-Alain Miller, "La nouvelle alliance conceptuelle de l'inconscient et du temps chez Lacan," *Le temps de savoir: Revue de la cause freudienne* (Paris: Seuil, 2000), 11.

27. Spinoza, *Ethics*, Part III, "Definition of the Emotions," 2.

28. Spinoza, *Ethics*, Part III, "Definition of the Emotions," 2, Explanation.

29. Breton, *Mad Love*, 25.

30. Kierkegaard, *Repetition*, 214.

31. Rainier Maria Rilke, untitled poem to Baron Lucius von Stoedten, quoted in Heidegger, *Off the Beaten Track*, 206–7.

32. Lacan, *The Four Fundamental Concepts of Psychoanalysis*, 235.

33. "If an analyst does not bring enthusiasm, there will not be an analysis." Jacques Lacan, "Lettre addressé en Avril 1974 à trois psychanalystes Italiens: Verdiglione, Contri, et Drazien," *Spirales* 9 (1981): 60.

34. Lacan speaks in "L'étourdit" of the manic-depressive state of the subject who has reached the end of the cure. "Then mourning is finished," he says. This manic-depressive state occurs at the same time as the subject encounters its desire. Lacan, "L'étourdit," *Autres écrits*, 487. This desire without object, bearing the new, is parallel to Spinozist joy.

35. Rilke, "Gong (II)," *The Poetry of Rilke*, trans. Edward Snow (San Francisco: North Point Press 2009), 607 [886 in ebook]. This space is for Rilke the "open," "angelic space," or "the inner space of the world" *(der Weltinnenraum)*. I follow Catherine Millot's commentary in her *La vocation de l'écrivain* (Paris: Gallimard, 1991), 210.

SILVIA LIPPI is a practicing psychoanalyst in Paris, where she is affiliated with the Espace Analytique clinical association and the Centre de Recherche Psychanalyse, Médecine, et Societé at the Université de Paris VII.

PETER SKAFISH directs the Institute of Speculative and Critical Inquiry and is the editor of *The Otherwise*. He has held research and teaching positions at the Collège de France; University of California, Berkeley; and McGill University. He is the editor and translator of *Cannibal Metaphysics* by Eduardo Viveiros de Castro (Univocal/Minnesota, 2014).